Language and Computers

EDINBURGH TEXTBOOKS IN EMPIRICAL LINGUISTICS

CORPUS LINGUISTICS
by Tony McEnery and Andrew Wilson

LANGUAGE AND COMPUTERS
A PRACTICAL INTRODUCTION TO THE COMPUTER ANALYSIS OF LANGUAGE
by Geoff Barnbrook

If you would like information on forthcoming titles in this series, please contact
Edinburgh University Press, 22 George Square, Edinburgh EH8 9LF

EDINBURGH TEXTBOOKS IN EMPIRICAL LINGUISTICS

Series Editors: Tony McEnery and Andrew Wilson

Language and Computers

A Practical Introduction to the Computer Analysis of Language

Geoff Barnbrook

EDINBURGH UNIVERSITY PRESS

EDINBURGH UNIVERSITY PRESS

© Geoff Barnbrook, 1996

Reprinted 1998, 2004

Edinburgh University Press
22 George Square, Edinburgh EH8 9LF

Typeset in 11/13pt Bembo by
Koinonia, Manchester
and printed and bound in Great Britain by
CPI Bath

A CIP record for this book is available from the British Library

ISBN 0 7486 0848 6 (cased)
ISBN 0 7486 0785 4 (paperback)

For Angela and Gioia, who had begun to wonder who I was

Contents

Introduction

This book is intended to make you aware of the computer's potential for analysing language. It describes the simple, accessible tools which you can use to discover the properties of corpora you have selected or assembled, and the range of information that you can get from them.

Chapter 1 explores the reasons for wanting to use a computer, and shows you how you can tell whether you ought to be using it or not, and if so, for which parts of your project.

Chapter 2 explains the basic principles underlying the selection, design and construction of the corpus, the collection of computer-readable texts that you want to analyse.

Chapter 3 explains the first basic analysis tool, the word frequency list, examining both its operation and the output that it can produce.

Chapter 4 shows how concordance programs can put the words selected from the frequency list back into their original context, allowing you to focus on their textual environment in as much detail as you need.

Chapter 5 describes collocation analysis, the combination of frequency list and concordance data which allows automatic quantitative analysis and identification of text patterns around words of interest.

Chapter 6 explores the methods and benefits of tagging and parsing texts to provide more information for your analysis, and describes the sub-language approach and the basis of Natural Language Processing.

Chapter 7 outlines the main applications of natural language processing in commercial and academic work.

Chapter 8 provides detailed examples of research using the language analysis tools through case studies.

Chapters 1 to 4 also include exercises which allow you to test your understanding of the main concepts and explore their practical application.

The appendices are mainly for the benefit of anyone interested in developing their own analysis tools. Appendix 1 considers the main programming languages and their suitability for language analysis, Appendix 2 outlines the operation of awk, particularly useful for the development of language analysis tools, and Appendix 3 contains program examples with detailed commentaries, expanding on the outlines given in the chapters.

Regardless of your level of computer expertise or experience, this book should enable you to appreciate the benefits and potential of the use of the computer for language analysis and to carry out your own research as efficiently and effectively as possible.

Acknowledgements

Many people have contributed to this book, directly and indirectly. My first and greatest debt is to those who taught me how to explore language with computers, my second to those that I have taught over the last six years. Of the former, John Sinclair and Tim Johns, both of Birmingham University, and Jeremy Clear of Cobuild must share the greatest responsibility for my initial interest in the subject. Of the latter, I must extend particular thanks to Abda, Daniel, Julie, Rachel and Teresa, who not only raised no objections when their course was turned into a glorified think-tank and proof-reading session, but also contributed some of the ideas behind the examples and exercises. Special thanks must also go to Louise Ravelli, who tried to bully me into writing it five years ago.

The difficult task of actually writing the book has been made much easier by the encouragement and guidance provided by Edinburgh University Press, in particular by Jonathan Price, Jackie Jones and Marguerite Nesling, and by the series editors Tony McEnery and Andrew Wilson.

Abbreviations

ANSI	American National Standards Institute
ASCII	American Standard Code for Information Interchange
CLAWS	Constituent-Likelihood Automatic Word-tagging System
FS	field separator
KDEM	Kurzweil Data Entry Machine
KWIC	Keyword in Context
LOB	Lancaster-Oslo/Bergen Corpus
NF	number of fields
NLP	natural language processing
OCR	optical character recognition
PC	personal computer
SGML	Standard Generalised Mark-up Language

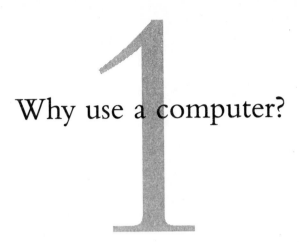

Why use a computer?

1. A SPECIFIC EXAMPLE

A few years ago I decided to investigate spelling variation in Chaucer's writing. For those unacquainted with the peculiarities of fourteenth-century Middle English, spelling systems of the time were rather less than standardised, and there is fairly wide variation in the spelling of words even within the same manuscript. For example, *brought, broughte, broghte* and *broght* all represent the same word with the same meaning in one manuscript of *Canterbury Tales*. The investigation that I wanted to carry out demanded, as a first stage, the identification of word forms which constituted spelling variations of each other, so that they could be used as a basis for determining what rules of substitution, if any, could be constructed for the spelling system used in the manuscripts. I decided to carry out the investigation using a computer.

The single most important reason for the involvement of the computer was the scale of the exercise. It would have been theoretically possible to carry out the analysis manually. This would probably have involved reading through the selected texts, listing all word forms found in them, comparing the word forms with each other to assess their suitability for inclusion as spelling variations, and then summarising the types of variations found to extract some form of rule and an estimation of its likely consistency of application within the text examined. In practice, the amount of time that would have been needed to analyse a sufficiently large piece of Chaucer's writing in this way would have made the whole task impossible, and this option was never seriously considered. The speed and accuracy of computer processing was seen from the outset as an essential requirement for the research.

This does not mean that the computer was capable of performing the task in exactly the same way as I would have done it manually. In fact, significant alterations and limitations arose from the use of the computer, and the problems encountered and the compromises that they demanded provide some useful examples of the main advantages and disadvantages of computerised language analysis. The general implications of the use of the computer are discussed in this chapter, while the details of the project itself are examined as a case study in Chapter 8.

1.1. Selection of texts to be examined

If I had been approaching the project as a manual exercise I could have selected text from one or more of several authoritative modern editions of Chaucer's complete works, or even from several original manuscripts, though access to these would have been more difficult to arrange. I could even, given the time, have compared results from several different sources to establish the dominant patterns and the extent of any variations from them. The involvement of the computer meant that I needed the text in computer-readable form, and a version of Robinson's edition of *Canterbury Tales* of 1957 was readily available from Oxford Computer Services. This was not necessarily an ideal choice, whether considered in terms of the quantity of data, the text itself or the edition. On the other hand, creating a computer-readable version from individually selected editions of specific texts was not a viable option because of the time and expense that would have been involved.

This is obviously a potentially serious problem. As it happened, in the context of this particular project it did not represent a major limitation, and reasonable results were produced from the text that was used, but the availability of texts is a serious consideration in assessing the suitability of a specific research project for treatment by computer. Developments in electronic text availability through major world text archives should reduce this problem significantly in the future. Text availability is considered in more detail in Chapter 2.

1.2. Text preparation

Although the text that I selected for the project was already in computer-readable form, some preparation was needed before it could be used on my computer system. It was supplied on a magnetic tape capable of being read only by a mainframe computer, and had to be transferred in appropriately sized chunks to a format compatible with the set-up that I was using, a small IBM-compatible PC. This process took several days and needed substantial expert help. All of the extra work involved was caused directly by the use of the computer, and would not have been needed if a manual analysis had been performed. However, the days used up in the process of preparation must be set against the very different time scales of computerised and manual analysis. Once data has been prepared the analysis process can be very much quicker using a computer, especially when large quantities of data are involved. In the context of the project the extra time was not at all significant.

Even when the text had been loaded on to the computer which was being used for the project it still needed further treatment before it could be dealt with efficiently. The fact that the text was all in upper case was no real problem, since processing eliminated case differences between words. Its other main characteristic was that each line of the text contained other information apart from the text of *Canterbury Tales*, and this needed to be made separately identifiable to prevent it from interfering with processing. The general problems which can be encountered in preparing text for use in computer-based research are dealt with in Chapter 2, and the specific methods devised to deal with the problems inherent in the Chaucer text are described in Chapter 8. It is important to be aware of the extra expenditure of time and effort that can be caused by such factors when considering the use of the computer.

1.3. Nature of processing

If the process of word identification and comparison had been carried out manually it would have been a relatively straightforward, if tedious, task. Each word of the text would have been listed, probably on cards, kept in alphabetical order for ease of future reference. As each new word form was encountered, a check could be carried out against the existing word forms already registered on the cards, to assess the likelihood that the new form might represent a spelling variations of existing forms. Comparisons between the word forms would need to take into account the contexts in which they were used, and some information detailing the position in the text, such as line numbers, could be recorded on each card as each further occurrence of a word form was encountered. Obviously, the process of comparison between word forms would become increasingly cumbersome as the number of cards increased.

The actual approach was rather different. The computer was first used to produce a list of all the word forms encountered together with their frequency of occurrence. The general nature of this very useful language analysis tool is described in Chapter 3. In this case it replaced the card index suggested in the last paragraph, and was constructed so that it automatically recorded the line number of each occurrence of each word form for future reference. At first sight this seems to be a pure gain in efficiency with no drawbacks. The computer reads the text, and produces exactly the same list of word forms as the researcher would produce manually, but much more quickly and accurately.

In practice, things were not quite so simple. To the human reader, the question of what constitutes a word rarely arises. Hyphens and other textual conventions may occasionally present minor difficulties, but it is likely that the researcher would deal with these intuitively and produce fairly consistent and accurate results. To the computer, word boundaries are likely to produce a more significant problem, and will almost always need to be specified in detail when processing instructions are being written. This requires a detailed and complete analysis of the nature of word boundaries before the list can be produced. Any failure to deal with a significant feature of the text contents is likely to reduce the accuracy of the list and therefore its value as a source of word form information. The types of problem typically encountered in this area are described in Chapter 3, and the special problems of the Chaucer text are dealt with in Chapter 8.

The construction of the list of words followed roughly the same path as the theoretical manual approach. The identification of potential spelling variations was a rather more complex process, and the approach adopted in the computer analysis illustrates the profound and crucial difference between the computer and the human researcher. Consider how the researcher would go about comparing a new word form to those already found to assess its chance of representing a spelling variation of one or more of them. Assuming that they were reading and understanding the text while extracting and checking word forms against the card index, they would have at least a rough idea of the meaning of the word form in front of them. Even before checking the card index they might have a general grasp of other forms already extracted that could represent the same word being used in the same way.

The human memory, though erratic, is also extremely powerful, especially where patterns and variations from patterns are involved. This could make the checking process slightly easier, since attention could be concentrated where it would be most likely to be relevant. Certainly, without any such focusing the manual checking process would soon become so cumbersome as to be almost impossible. Every word form would need to be checked against every other word form, since the researcher could not know in advance the nature or extent of possible differences between two spelling variants of the same word.

However, human researchers have another important advantage over computers. Because they understand the text they are reading they can make a decision about potential variant word forms while they are checking them, and this decision is likely to be based on complex factors involving the contexts of the word forms being compared and a detailed knowledge of the language of the text. The computer can only have this knowledge if it is programmed into it, and a full specification of all the factors used by the human researcher in making the decision would be extremely difficult, if not impossible, to produce. This is the central problem of almost all computer-based language analysis, and it is also arguably one of the main advantages of using a computer for this kind of work.

This paradox arises because certain risks are involved whenever human intuition plays a part in language analysis. The main danger is that researchers will tend to find what they expect to find, because their 'knowledge' of the area under investigation affects their assessment of results. This can be a partic-ular problem where the work hinges on the identification of potentially significant items for analysis, as in this case. The focusing effect of memory, already mentioned as an almost essential short cut in the comparison of word forms, is likely to be influenced by existing views of likely forms of spelling variation. The potential blurring of the identification process that this entails is often avoided by computerisation simply because the computer cannot be programmed with the researcher's intuitive knowledge. There is, of course, a corresponding disadvantage in computer analysis. In this project, for example, the rules for identifying potential spelling variants needed to be simplified to a considerable extent, so that only pairs of words which varied in one character were selected and listed for further analysis. This was by no means the only possible solution, but it had some significant advantages, described in Chapter 8. It meant that many potential spelling variations were omitted from the further analysis, but it also meant that the sample finally produced was entirely unaffected by human bias.

1.4. Program development and testing

In practice, it often happens that the features of the text under analysis are not completely established until several attempts have been made at constructing the software, so that a cyclic process of program specification, output checking and program amendment is needed before a completely usable result is produced. This need to repeat some of the processing can erode some of the speed advantage of the computer, but this is unlikely to be a significant problem in any project involving large amounts of data. More important is the degree of complexity involved in the development of the program, which will depend on the nature of the project, the extent to which existing software can be reused and the programming language selected.

It is never quite as easy to develop a language analysis program as it would be to design a means of processing the data manually. Most computer analysis involves some element of this extra stage of program specification. Even where existing computer software can be used, the format of the data may need to be changed to make it suitable for the software, and the results may need further analysis. In the Chaucer research, all of the software used in the final version of the project was specially developed for it, and this took up a significant amount of time. Existing software could have been used at some stages, for example in the creation of the original word list, but the special demands of the research meant that it would not have been the most efficient solution.

1.5. Speed and consistency of processing

Once the approach to the computer-based analysis had been established the processing itself was, of course, automatic. It was also reasonably fast. The final comparison of all word forms in the list with each other took over 30 hours, but this involved an enormous number of character by character checks. It also involved no direct human intervention, so that the time taken for the processing was available for other work. This represents, however, only the processing time needed for the final successful run. Many hours of testing and modification were needed to produce the final version of the program, but even this development time was still much less than the time that would have been needed for manual analysis. The main reason for this enormous advantage is the scale of the exercise. If the analysis had been aimed at a much smaller text, manual analysis may have been faster.

There is another aspect of computer processing which needs to be considered alongside its speed. It will generally be completely consistent in a way which is unlikely to be the case with manual processing. This is not an unmixed blessing, since any errors in the program will also be carried out completely consistently, while a human researcher carrying out manual analysis would probably notice errors in the approach and be able to correct them before too much time and effort had been wasted. Successful program development demands that the cycle of rigorous testing, evaluation and amendment is fully completed before the results of analysis can be relied upon, and even if this is done as well as possible some problems are likely to emerge only when full scale output is examined in detail. Errors will of course occur in manual processing, but they are more likely to be isolated problems caused by human misunderstanding, carelessness, tiredness, boredom and so on. They may therefore have less overall effect on the final output, but they are also much more difficult to eliminate. Certainly, the repetition of the complete analysis process after errors in the approach have been identified and eliminated is only realistically possible if you are using a computer.

1.6. Analysis of results

The processing described so far formed only the first stage of the Chaucer spelling investigation. A great deal of further analysis was needed to convert the list of word forms into a summary of general spelling variation features. As explained in detail in Chapter 8, this involved the production of a complete summary of the types of differences found between word forms so that the implications of each of them could be assessed. This form of analysis, simple, straightforward and very fast using a computer, would have been extremely difficult and time-consuming to perform manually.

Consider how it would be carried out without a computer. Assuming that a list of words has already been produced using the card index approach described, then for each word or set of words on the list the type of difference found between potential spelling variations would need to be identified and classified so that general principles could be extracted. As an example, consider the different forms of the word *brought* already listed at the start of this chapter: *brought, broughte, broghte* and *broght*. A manual analysis of the differences between these would have to take account of the final *e* difference between *brought* and *broughte*, and between *broghte* and *broght*, as well as the *u* difference between *broght* and *brought*, and between *broghte* and *broughte*. The easiest way of doing this might well be to consider the differences separately. In that case, all the words which differed only in the presence or absence of final *e*, like *brought* and *broughte*, could be gathered together, as could all the ones differing in the insertion of a *u*, like *broghte* and *broughte*. Once the basis of classification had been established, all the examples of each type of difference could be counted to find which were the most frequent, and the importance of each for further investigation could be assessed.

The computer analysis of the spelling variations proceeded in much the same way, but with almost no manual intervention. The word pair list described in section 1.3 was very easily analysed into groups corresponding to the type of variation encountered. Because the word pair list was produced by the computer it could be fed into later analysis programs for automatic summarisation. This not only saved a great deal of time, it also produced far more accurate results than would have been likely with a manual approach.

1.7. Output formats

Once data is available to the computer it can be selected and arranged in any output format that is needed. This could include both human-readable output, on screen or paper, and computer-readable output, in files, for use in further processing. The word pair list generated from the first stages of analysis in the Chaucer project was produced as a computer file so that the types of variation could be summarised for further processing, as described in section 1.6. Other output from the project was produced in a printed form so that I could assess it and make sensible decisions on the basis of the results. At any stage it was possible to select the data that would be included, the output medium and the detailed format of the information produced. In a manual system any rearrangement of the data to produce output in another sequence or form would be tedious and time-consuming. Even the process of sorting a card index into another sequence is difficult and long-winded, whereas computers can sort files into different orders, based on different pieces of data, very quickly and easily.

2. THE GENERAL DECISION

It should be apparent from this description of the Chaucer spelling investigation that the effect of using a computer in language analysis projects is not always straightforwardly beneficial. Because of this, you need to consider all the potential benefits and drawbacks in detail before deciding on the approach to be adopted. It might help to begin by summarising the main positive and negative factors that are likely to affect the decision, many of which have been illustrated by the spelling variation work. The main advantages of the use of a computer for this research were:

- the speed, accuracy and consistency of processing
- the ability to perform further processing on the results
- the ease with which data could be manipulated, selected, sorted and formatted

- the lack of any human bias.

The main disadvantages were:

- the restricted availability of computer-readable data and the extra work involved in preparing it for processing

- modifications to the analysis process demanded by the nature of the computer's operations

- the extra work involved in program development and testing

- the computer's lack of normal human background knowledge.

These factors will not apply to all projects under consideration, and their relevance to the research and their possible implications need to be explored fully before deciding whether the use of a computer is likely to be the best option. In some cases, as in the Chaucer research, the scale of the exercise may be an overriding consideration, and the use of a computer, whatever the associated drawbacks, may be the only viable strategy. If the decision is not so clear cut, you will need to carry out a detailed analysis to decide the best approach.

3. DETAILED ANALYSIS OF THE PROJECT

Before we consider the main items to be included in a detailed project analysis, it may be helpful to consider the general characteristics of the forms of linguistic research which are likely to be best and worst served by the use of a computer. The ideal computer project would demand the relatively simple analysis of large quantities of data, already available in a usable form. This analysis would be at least partially achievable by the use of existing software, so that program development would be minimal. Conversely, a project that involves complex analysis of a small amount of data, especially where extensive data preparation and program development are both needed, is unlikely to be dealt with more efficiently by the use of a computer. Even in these cases, however, other benefits may still make the use of the computer worthwhile.

It is also important to remember that different aspects of a specific research project may have different needs, so that while it could be worth using the computer for some of the more routine parts of the work, the more complex and intractable parts may still need to be dealt with using manual analysis. In the case of the Chaucer project, the selection of the word pairs and the summarisation and analysis of the types of variation were capable of being performed automatically, but the assessment of the effect of the variation had to be performed manually and recorded for further analysis by the computer.

For each of the areas dealt with in the detailed descriptions below, the full cost implications of the answers to the questions need to be identified, quantified and assessed in making the final decision.

3.1. The availability of data

The initial problem created by the use of the computer is the need for the data to be in an appropriate form for access by the computer hardware and software that you intend to use. The considerations arising from this are dealt with in detail in Chapter 2, but in the initial analysis of the project the following questions need to be considered, at least in outline.

3.1.1. Is the data needed for the project already available in computer-readable form?

Among other things, this may depend on the extent to which one specific collection of data is needed for the project, rather than a generally representative sample of the type of language under investigation. As an example, consider a project to explore the characteristics of the language used by George Gissing, the nineteenth-century English novelist. Gissing's works are less likely to be available from general text archive sources than the writings of other, more popular authors of the same period. Hardy, Dickens and Trollope, for example, are all much more frequently encountered in archives, on literary CD-ROMS and so on. On the other hand, if the project simply demands a sample of nineteenth-century novels, a reasonably large body of data could be collected fairly easily from existing electronic texts. One result of this review may be that the scope of the project is adjusted to concentrate on data which is more readily available, and care should be taken to ensure that this will not impair the quality of the research being carried out. Any effects that it will have on your work must obviously be considered when making the decision, as must the cost of obtaining the data if you need to buy it, for example on a CD-ROM.

3.1.2. If so, will it need extensive preparation before it can be used?

Even when data is available from existing sources, it may not be in exactly the right form for use in the research. The technical details of the likely problems and solutions in this area are discussed in Chapter 2. The Chaucer project described in section 1 illustrates a common problem: the text obtained from the Oxford Text Archive was on a physical medium and in a format which were both unreadable by the machine which was going to be used for the research. Converting from one format to another is usually relatively straightforward, although you will need access to hardware and software which is compatible with both the original data and the equipment you intend to use for the work. Some examples of methods of achieving data conversion are described in Chapter 2.

A more complex problem arises when the data is available but contains elements which will cause processing problems. As an example, the text may contain special annotations which will not be needed in the research and which could distort the results of analysis, like the mark-up codes described in Chapter 2. If these are consistently entered and easily detected they will only cause a small amount of extra work. More difficulties are created by the need to insert your own mark-up codes, an area also discussed in detail in Chapter 2, and this could involve significant extra work. More problematic is the need to correct errors in texts which have not been entered to a sufficiently high standard. In extreme cases this may involve detailed manual proof-reading. You need to calculate the full costs, in time, money or both, of any preparation work that will be involved, and take this into account in making the overall decision.

3.1.3. If not, how is it going to be entered?

The main methods of data entry are described in Chapter 2, and you will need to consider the type of data you are dealing with very carefully before selecting the method that would be best for your project. Once you have decided on the method you would use, you will need to estimate the time and costs that would be involved in the same way as for data preparation work and use it in your decision.

3.2. The Nature of the Investigation

3.2.1. Can it be carried out using existing software?

Before this question can be answered you will need to make sure that you understand exactly what you want from your research project. Fairly detailed analysis of language can be performed using only the most basic language analysis tools, such as the frequency list and concordance described in detail in Chapters 3 and 4. Because proprietary versions of these tools can often be used without any need to develop your own programs this can save an enormous amount of time at relatively low cost. In some cases the software may even be available free of charge through your own academic institution or through the public domain. At the very least, software like this is likely to enable you to select the areas of work on which you need to concentrate, and may even be able to generate files of selected data for use in the programs that you develop specifically to carry out further analysis. Developing your own software when it is already freely available is usually a very costly way of reinventing the wheel, and is not recommended. If existing software can be used directly, adapted, or used as a preliminary stage towards fulfilling your processing needs, you should always take advantage of it. Obviously, not all existing software is available free of charge within the public domain, and the use of some software may have implications for hardware costs.

3.2.2. If not, what software will need to be developed?

This is often the most difficult stage of project analysis. If a piece of research is being carried out manually the details of the work performed may well develop as the investigation proceeds and as more details of the project's needs become apparent. To some extent this will also be true even when a computer is used, but any attempt to develop specific software will be significantly improved if a detailed analysis of requirements is carried out first, and in more complex cases it may be impossible to achieve effective program development without this stage. The main difficulty is often a lack of clear understanding of the capabilities and basic operations of computers. If you have access to a programmer or to someone else who has this basic understanding this problem will be reduced, but there may still be problems of communication where the person who understands computers does not understand language analysis, and vice versa. Because of this, it is important to understand at least the main steps involved in processing text. Generally, when you are developing software of your own you will need to specify even the most basic aspects of the text handling that you need to implement your research objectives successfully.

As an example, consider a simple exercise to calculate the average sentence length, expressed as a number of words, within a piece of text. This would present few problems for a manual investigation: the number of words in each sentence could be counted, and the average number calculated in the usual way. For a computer, the notions of a word and a sentence would be meaningless unless they were defined within the software, and the calculation of the average would usually need to be fully specified. The following piece of text, from the beginning of an electronic text version of Hardy's *Far from the Madding Crowd*, obtained from the Gutenberg Project, should illustrate the main problems involved. The line numbers have been added purely to make reference easier, and are not present in the original text.

```
When Farmer Oak smiled, the corners of his mouth¶
spread till they were within an unimportant distance of ¶
his ears, his eyes were reduced to chinks, and diverging¶
wrinkles appeared round them, extending upon his¶
countenance like the rays in a rudimentary sketch of ¶     5
the rising sun.¶
His Christian name was Gabriel, and on working¶
days he was a young man of sound judgment, easy¶
motions, proper dress, and general good character. On¶
Sundays he was a man of misty views, rather given to¶       10
postponing, and hampered by his best clothes and¶
umbrella : upon the whole, one who felt himself to¶
occupy morally that vast middle space of Laodicean¶
neutrality which lay between the Communion people¶
of the parish and the drunken section, – that is, he went¶    15
to church, but yawned privately by the time the con-¶
gegation reached the Nicene creed, – and thought of ¶
what there would be for dinner when he meant to be¶
listening to the sermon. Or, to state his character as¶
it stood in the scale of public opinion, when his friends¶    20
```

and critics were in tantrums, he was considered rather a¶
bad man ; when they were pleased, he was rather a good¶
man ; when they were neither, he was a man whose¶
moral colour was a kind of pepper-and-salt mixture.¶

This text is arranged in lines, the ends of which are marked above by the printed symbol ¶. The lines do not necessarily correspond to sentences, although the end of a paragraph is also the end of a line, as in line 6. Because of the method of entry of the original text, in one case (line 16) the end of a line splits a word. This word is then hyphenated in accordance with normal printed text conventions. The difficulties in handling the text arise from the fact that most programming languages access the file either character by character or line by line, rather than following any of the normal textual boundaries recognised by the human user. Part of the software would need to convert the existing data units into the units needed by the research, and this would have no direct counterpart in a manual approach to the same problem.

Dividing the text into usable sentences, the first stage of this analysis, would depend on the detection of sentence boundaries. This does not seem to be too problematic in this small extract, since the only sentence boundary used is the full stop. Other boundary markers are likely to be used in larger text samples, but they should be reasonably easy to identify. They may not, however, invariably mark the ends of sentences, since full stops are also typically used within abbreviations, and a means of distinguishing between these uses would need to be developed. Reconnecting words broken by a hyphen may also cause problems, but these will probably be reasonably easy to deal with.

The main general point to bear in mind is the need to understand the implications of the research requirements for the use of the computer, and the implications of the computer's limitations for the research approach. Once the relationship between needs and possibilities has been properly established, the correct mix of computer and manual analysis can be determined. To make sure that all the significant factors of this relationship have been considered, you need to adopt a fairly formal approach which specifies the overall requirements and then gradually breaks them down into increasingly detailed processing stages until the exact method of applying the computer emerges. For the example used above this might begin with the general statement of research needs:

Count the words in each sentence and calculate the average number.

This could then be broken down into three main elements:

1. Reorganise the text into sentences and count them.

2. Count the words in the text.

3. Calculate the average number of words in a sentence as the total of the number of words divided by the number of sentences.

The first stage can then be broken down further, along the lines already discussed, and this specification could then form the basis for detailed software development:

a)   Specify the sentence boundary markers.

b)   Count the number of sentence boundaries, including the end of the text

In the small text sample shown above the sentence boundaries are very simple: only the full stop is used, and this is not used for anything else. Texts which contain a fuller range of possibilities such as question marks, exclamation marks, full stops used within abbreviations, and so on, would need a more complex specification. A similar process could be adopted to specify word boundaries, probably based on a combination of spaces and sentence boundaries.

This form of analysis enables you to construct a detailed computational approach without using a specific programming language. The choice of a programming language for the development of the software may have a significant effect on some of the details of processing, but because there is much common ground between them this type of analysis can provide a useful basis for selecting a language and for deciding the development strategy. An outline of the main features of some of the most popular programming languages is given in Appendix 1.

4. MANUAL OR COMPUTERISED? A WORKED EXAMPLE

Allocating research tasks between the manual and the computerised approach can sometimes be difficult. Remember that you are only using the computer because you are convinced that it will save time or money or both, improve the quality of the research, or provide some other overall advantage. In many cases you can achieve both cost savings and improvements in quality, but only if you make the most efficient use of the computer. To illustrate some of the considerations involved this section describes the design of an investigation into rhyming schemes.

4.1. The research tasks

An undergraduate who was interested in child language acquisition wanted to investigate the role of nursery rhymes, and the rhyming schemes used in them. In particular, she wanted to establish whether there were any favoured rhyming schemes and, if so, try to determine why they were more frequent. The basic source of data was the standard reference work on the subject, the *Oxford Dictionary of Nursery Rhymes* (Opie and Opie 1951). This book contains the text and bibliographical details of around 550 nursery rhymes of various lengths. The following tasks needed to be carried out:

●   identify the rhyming scheme for every nursery rhyme

●   count the number of times each rhyming scheme is used and produce a list.

For both tasks a decision needed to be made: should it be performed manually, or using the computer?

4.2. Identifying rhyming schemes

The manual identification of rhyming schemes is reasonably straightforward. For each item in the collection the researcher would simply need to examine enough of the verse to establish the rhyming pattern and record the result. Before the computer could carry out the same task it would be necessary to convert the entire collection of rhymes to computer-readable form and develop software capable of analysing the rhyming schemes. Neither of these is a trivial task. The main methods used for data entry are described in Chapter 2, and whichever of these was chosen, applying it to 550 nursery rhymes would take a substantial amount of time and effort. The development of the software would be more problematic. To say that spelling in English is not rigorously phonetic is a major understatement, and the program would need either substantial operator intervention, probably taking as much of the researcher's time as the manual identification of the rhyming scheme, or a complex set of rules and exception lists detailing the vagaries of English spelling. Under the circumstances, this part of the project is not a promising subject for computerisation.

4.3. Constructing the frequency list

Once the rhyming schemes have been established they could be counted manually. However, little or no extra effort would be involved in typing the rhyming schemes into a computer-readable text file. Once the details had been entered, the file could easily be sorted so that all instances of the same rhyming scheme were brought together, and a simple program was written to count them and produce a summary. The details of the program are given in Appendix 3. An added advantage of this approach is that similarities between rhyming schemes, which might not be obvious to the researcher, could be revealed by the sorted list. Obviously, once the data is in a computer file, it is very easy to carry out other investigations on it. On balance, it seems worthwhile to computerise this element of the work.

4.4. How it worked in practice

The identification of the rhyming schemes was carried out manually, and took the researcher about 8 hours altogether. Some problems were encountered in trying to deal with nursery rhymes which had very long or complex patterns (sometimes involving an alternative structure to the standard rhyming scheme), but these would have created insoluble difficulties for any analysis software, and would have had to be dealt with manually in the end. Entering the details of schemes on to the computer took little more than an hour, and developing the counting program, running it against the data and printing out the results took about ten minutes more altogether.

It is difficult to estimate how long it would have taken to enter the complete texts of the nursery rhymes and to develop suitable software, but it would have been significantly longer. It would, of course, have provided a useful set of computer-readable texts and would probably have revealed a great deal of information about the nature of English spelling, but these benefits would not necessarily have assisted in the achievement of the specific research objectives.

4.5. Implications for other projects

Every research project has its own special problems, but the basic considerations underlying the choice of research method are reasonably constant. The main point that emerges from this example is the fact that data preparation and the development of complex software can both be very time-consuming. You should consider all the alternative approaches very carefully before you commit yourself to an approach that demands either of them. Some research tasks are so complex that the development of appropriate software, even if it is successful, may take longer than doing the work manually. The project described was, of course, relatively small. A very large-scale investigation is likely to leave you little or no choice of research method, but it is important to quantify the time and cost implications of the alternative approaches as accurately as possible. The next section contains a checklist that should help you to do this.

5. IS IT WORTH USING A COMPUTER? A CHECK LIST

Once a detailed analysis of the projected use of the computer has been made, this checklist can be used to ensure that a complete statement of costs is prepared. Circumstances will dictate whether the cost measurement is carried out in terms of time, money or a combination of both. In some cases, elements of the project may not lend themselves to alternative treatments. The use of the checklist should make it easier to identify the correct basis for carrying out comparisons and the areas where comparison becomes irrelevant. Notes are given in italics after each of the questions suggesting possible ways of finding the answers.

A) THE SCALE OF THE INVESTIGATION
How much data needs to be processed?

This may need to be estimated by counting a sample and scaling up the results.

How long would manual analysis take?

Again an estimate could be made by taking a small sample, finding the time needed for full manual analysis and scaling up the result.

B) AVAILABILITY OF COMPUTER-READABLE DATA

Is the data already available in computer-readable form?

This is not necessarily as straightforward as it sounds: it may be possible to substitute available computer-readable texts for the ones originally selected without reducing the quality of the research, although this should be the prime consideration.

If not, how will it be made readable, and what costs will be involved?

Data entry methods are considered in Chapter 2. Once you have identified the most likely approaches, you could experiment with a sample, as before, and scale up the results to estimate the time and costs involved in the whole set of data.

If it is, how much preparation will be needed before processing can take place?

You may need to consult local computer experts once you have established the medium and format in which the data is available. Chapter 2 deals with the main considerations. Once again, scaling up the results from a small sample is probably the most effective way to find out.

C) SUITABILITY OF EXISTING SOFTWARE

Can existing software be used for all or part of the processing?

Existing software includes standard operating system utilities (such as sort routines, text search facilities, etc., often also found in word processing packages on a smaller scale) as well as general language analysis tools such as frequency list and concordance packages (dealt with in Chapters 3 and 4). Be prepared to consult plenty of experts and to be flexible and imaginative.

How much adaptation of the software or the data will be needed to make them compatible?

This is probably another area where you will need expert advice. Factors which can affect it include existing data format and the input format expected by the software, options available within the software and the need for pre- or post-processing to get what you need.

D) SOFTWARE DEVELOPMENT NEEDS

What new software will need to be developed?

This obviously only arises after exploring the options in (c) above. The identification of processing needs and the specification of the necessary software both involve a rigorous analysis of the tasks involved in achieving your research objectives and the way in which they can be performed most efficiently.

What programming language will be used, and how much time and other costs will be involved in acquiring the necessary expertise?

Costs may include the need to acquire the compiler or program development environment for the programming language selected. Some general guidance on languages is given in Appendix 1. Learning to use the chosen language can be a long and frustrating business, and again you may need to get expert advice. Estimating the time involved is likely to be quite difficult, but it almost always takes longer than expected.

What other costs will be involved?

Programming by professionals is expensive, but it may be worth considering if time is more important than money. Otherwise, this will include any extra costs involved in the time taken for you to develop the software. Remember to allow for the time needed to test it fully and to amend it.

E) OTHER FACTORS

What other factors need to be taken into account in making the decision (including any differences in the nature of processing which depend on the selection of the method)?

There may be overriding considerations of scale or the nature of the investigation that make the use of the computer almost unavoidable. The rest of the checklist is still important, to give you an idea of the implications of carrying out the research.

6. SUMMARY

This chapter has described the main advantages and disadvantages of using a computer for language research. Before deciding whether its use will be beneficial for a specific research project, you should carry out a full analysis of any extra costs and cost savings which will be involved, and consider them, together with any special demands of the project, in assessing the overall implications of the possible alternative solutions.

7. EXERCISES

1. Complete the questionnaire in section 5 for the Chaucer spelling variation project. The text file of *Canterbury Tales* contains about 20,000 lines, around 180,000 words altogether.

2. You want to investigate the use of the passive in a text. Describe how it could be done:
   a) manually;
   b) using a computer.

3. Suggest an approach to the identification of rhyming schemes using a computer, and describe any problems you might encounter.

FURTHER READING

Barnbrook, G. (1992) 'Computer analysis of spelling variants in Chaucer's *Canterbury Tales*', in G. Leitner (ed.), *New Directions in English Language Corpora*, Berlin: Mouton de Gruyter, pp. 277–87.

Svartvik, J. (ed.) (1992) *Directions in Corpus Linguistics: Proceedings of Nobel Symposium 82*, Berlin: Mouton de Gruyter. (The sections on pp. 17–125 are especially relevant.)

First capture your data

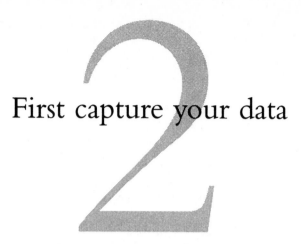

1. THE BASIC PROBLEM: WHAT'S ALREADY AVAILABLE?

When you consider using a computer to carry out language research, you are likely to become aware very quickly that the availability of data for manual research is very different from the availability of data for computer-based research. This problem was mentioned in section 3.1.1 of Chapter 1, and because it can have a fundamental effect on project viability it is worth considering it now in some detail.

With some important exceptions, most types of language are available in much greater quantity and variety in manually readable forms than in computer-readable forms. The main exceptions, rapidly becoming more significant, are the texts which have been generated by computer, such as e-mail and its analogues and word-processed documents. This second group includes most recent printed publications, although access to them may still be problematic for the general researcher because of copyright and confidentiality problems, which are discussed in more detail in section 3.3 below. Manually readable data of the same type may suffer from corresponding restrictions, but determined researchers can generally get satisfactory access to the contents of even the rarest of books and the most precious of manuscripts. Computer-readable versions of these and other older documents may simply not exist and would therefore need to be created before the project can begin.

As has already been pointed out in Chapter 1, the availability of data can affect the scope of the research, and the extra problems involved in obtaining computer-readable data may restrict your choices to an unacceptable extent. This problem needs to be considered in the initial analysis of the project as part of the benefits and drawbacks of the use of the computer in the research. This chapter describes the points to be considered in selecting data for examination and the main methods of acquiring it and making it suitable for use in the research work.

The collection of computer-readable language that you assemble for your project, selected on the basis of your research criteria, is usually referred to as a **corpus** to distinguish it from the more random collections of texts held in text archives. The next section describes the main factors that you will need to consider in designing your own research corpus.

2. WHAT DO YOU WANT TO LOOK AT? THE PROBLEMS OF CORPUS DESIGN

Whatever your research objectives are you need to ensure that your corpus will be capable of fulfilling them. You may decide to use an existing corpus, in which case some of the points raised in this section may be less relevant, but they will still be worth considering to ensure that you select your data properly.

2.1. Contents: the corpus as a sample

Before you can consider the availability of data for your research project you will need to decide exactly what you need to examine. This is not as simple or straightforward a question as it may seem to be. In most cases, if not all, the corpus is a sample of a larger collection of language, and is intended to allow conclusions to be drawn about this larger body rather than about itself. This is often true even in cases where the corpus contains everything that is available from within a specific manifestation of language.

As a typical example, consider the Chaucer project described in Chapter 1. The corpus consisted of the entire text of Chaucer's *Canterbury Tales*, but this fact does not prevent it from being merely a sample. Even if the point of the research had been only to identify characteristics of spelling variation within this work, the existence of many other manuscript versions of part or all of the text prevents it from being an exhaustive collection of the entire body of language under review. A set of conclusions based only on the Ellesmere manuscript would naturally provide some evidence of the variations found within that manuscript, but the *Canterbury Tales* manuscript presumably forms only a part of the output of the scribe or scribes responsible, and so again could only be considered as a sample of the language being examined. The fact that other manuscripts produced by the same scribe or scribes may not be identifiable with the necessary degree of accuracy, or may not even have survived, does not affect the conceptual basis of the research: it simply makes the accumulation of a properly representative sample more difficult.

The question of representativeness underlies the whole question of corpus design. If useful conclusions are to be drawn from a sample, the sample must have similar characteristics to the population from which it is drawn. In many cases, these characteristics are themselves the subject of the investigation, and cannot be known in advance, so that some other basis for selection needs to be found. The results of the investigation may be the only opportunity for testing the selection method which has been adopted, and it may be that you will need to carry out a pilot study of an exploratory corpus to refine the basis of selection for the final corpus which will be used in the project itself. The details of this process will vary enormously from one project to another, and will need to be considered thoroughly before work begins.

2.2. Size: how much is enough?
Once the contents of your ideal corpus have been specified, you will need to decide how much of it you need. The representativeness of the corpus as a sample of the area of language under investigation also depends on its size in relation to the needs of the research project. The most common features of the language will be well represented even in relatively small quantities of text, and if these are the main subject of the work you may only need a relatively small corpus. Unfortunately, it is generally difficult, if not actually impossible, to know in advance what size of corpus will meet the requirements of any given research project. The most effective way of fulfilling the investigative needs of a particular project may well be, again, to carry out a pilot survey based on a relatively small corpus and to extend it if necessary.

3. WHERE DID YOU GET THOSE TEXTS?
There are several ways of acquiring computer-readable texts. In some cases the text may already be available in computer-readable form, and can be bought from commercial or academic organisations, or may even be available free of charge. Some extra work may be involved in preparing the data to make it compatible with the computer hardware and software being used, and this is considered in more detail in section 4 below. In other cases, the text may only be available in printed or manuscript form, and will need to be converted to make it computer-readable before it can be used.

3.1. Texts already available elsewhere
Three main developments have greatly increased the availability of computer-readable text over the last few years:

- the expansion of the large institutional text archive sites
- the expansion of the world-wide computer network system, often called the **internet**
- the increasing importance of the domestic CD-ROM market
- the use of word processing for the origination of new published material.

The detailed implications of these developments for computer-based language research are dealt with below.

3.1.1. Text archives
Collections of computer-readable texts have been accumulated at large academic sites for a number of years. Both the number of text archive sites and

the range of texts held are increasing at a significant rate. The major sites from which English language texts are currently available include the Oxford Text Archive and Project Gutenberg, both of which have large numbers of texts freely available over the internet. It is fairly easy, using the internet directory and search facilities, to find the full range of sites currently available and the texts held at them.

Obviously, if you decide to build your corpus entirely from the holdings of text archives, its composition will be restricted to the range of texts held at them, and this could prove to be a very serious limitation. There seems to be a preponderance of literary texts in the major archives, often skewed towards particular periods. In the English language section of the Oxford Text Archive, for example, there is a relatively large number of Old English and Medieval texts, and a similar abundance of nineteenth-century literature. This could be very useful for the historical researcher engaged with these periods, but rather less so for general modern language work.

3.1.2. The internet

A system of connection between major international academic and commercial computer sites has existed for many years and has allowed the exchange of information through e-mail and other forms of file transfer. This international networking system is now generally known as the internet (though other, more romantic metaphors are also used, 'information superhighway' seeming particularly attractive to politicians and journalists). During the last few years this system has expanded enormously and has become both more generally available and much easier to use. Access to the internet is available from almost any computer. The only additional hardware required is a communications accessory known as a **modem**, which allows connection to telephone lines, together with appropriate communications software.

If you have access to an academic computer system there will almost certainly be an internet connection already available, and you should get local advice on the best way of using it. If not, you will need to explore the hardware and software options to find the best possible way of getting access, and then take account of the costs of the chosen solution in appraising the project.

One of the main advantages of access to the internet is the fact that many of the text archives described above are connected to it, and at least some of the texts held in them may be available through it. In some cases they can be transferred directly over the internet without the need for prior arrangement or payment of fees, and this can provide a very useful basis for the construction of corpora from the wide selection of texts held in the archives, often with minimal effort and at little or no initial cost. There are usually some conditions affecting the use of texts obtained in this way, but these tend to relate to commercial exploitation and would rarely affect their use for normal academic research purposes.

Facilities for file transfer form an integral part of the internet connection system, and once an appropriate site has been located, the required texts can usually be copied to your own machine using standard file transfer software. The exact nature of the software in use varies greatly from one installation to another, but the international computer-using community is eagerly pursuing the twin goals of standardisation and simplification, so that at most academic sites' files can be transferred using a program which may actually be easier to use than your normal word processor.

The text of *Canterbury Tales* which was used for the project described in Chapter 1 was obtained from the Oxford Text Archive before file transfer through the internet became available. It was supplied on a tape which was readable only by a large mainframe computer. The data on the tape required the extensive involvement of specialist computer operating staff, and significant manipulation using text editors on the mainframe, before it could be transferred to a storage medium which was accessible to the machine used for the project. The tape, of course, could only be sent physically through the postal system, so that the text took some days to reach me and then needed several more days work before it was usable. Texts obtained recently from the same site have been transferred over the internet in a matter of minutes, using a few very simple instructions which also allowed interactive browsing through the site catalogue.

In some cases the texts held at a particular site may not be available for transfer to other machines, but may be directly accessible for research purposes from other sites. In these cases, generally involving public access to established large scale corpora, only the software available at the host site can be used to access and analyse the texts, and restrictions may be placed on the nature of the work that can be carried out. The disadvantages inherent in these restrictions may well be outweighed by the advantages of access to such large scale reference corpora. COBUILD's Bank of English is currently available on this basis. In some cases corpora may also be available on CD-ROM, as described in the next section, and you may be able to analyse them using your own software.

In addition to texts, a wide range of software is available from some internet sites, which act as national or international software archives. The material available relates to the whole range of computing needs, and some of it is potentially useful for language analysis purposes. The conditions attached to the use of the software varies significantly from one item to another. In many cases it is freely available as public domain software and can be used without payment. In other cases the software is deposited in the archive as **shareware**, freely available for you to test to check whether it is appropriate for your needs, but subject to a registration fee if you wish to use it in your work. The conditions of use will be made clear in the documentation accompanying the software.

The standard of both the software available at these sites and its documentation vary enormously, and you should take great care in assessing its suitability for use in your research before relying on its operation. It is also important to ensure that it is free of **viruses** or other malignant interference before installing it on your system, and you may need to obtain expert local help. Despite the potential problems, the software available at these sites can provide a very useful source of analysis tools, which may be capable of fulfilling at least part of your research requirements. You can use the usual internet directory facilities to find details of the archives and their currently available range of software.

3.1.3. CD-ROM

The availability of the CD-ROM as an extremely inexpensive mass-storage medium has led to its adoption for storage-hungry multimedia applications, such as complex computer games or editions of encyclopaedias and other reference works. These typically include visual images, short video clips and sound, often alongside large quantities of text. When the storage capacity of the CD-ROM, usually around 650 megabytes, is used exclusively for text, it can accommodate enormous quantities of it. The increased market penetration of the CD-ROM drive in the domestic market, initially driven by the desire for more complex computer games, has accelerated the development of electronic publishing, and this has led to the release of many text collections on CD-ROM. Some of them could be useful for your language research project.

The range of text available in this form suffers from problems similar to those described in section 3.1.1 in relation to the text archives. Many of the texts found in the archives turn up in these collections, often in the same editions, simply because they have been compiled from the same original public domain sources. This is changing, however, and publishers are becoming more aware of the potential of electronic publishing and of the market for computer-readable texts. In particular, publishers of periodicals have begun to release their text on CD-ROM at regular intervals, so that the complete texts of newspapers and magazines can be easily purchased and used for analysis. Major literary collections like the Chadwyck-Healey English Poetry database are also being developed, and are often available through academic libraries.

At the more specialised end of the market, several complete or part corpora are also available in this form. These include:

- the ICAME Collection of English Language Corpora, including the Brown, Lancaster-Oslo/Bergen (LOB), Kolhapur and London-Lund corpora and the diachronic part of the Helsinki corpus, in versions for the Apple Macintosh, MS-DOS and Unix

- the COBUILD word-bank

- the British National Corpus.

The main disadvantage of texts made available on CD-ROM is likely to be the physical format in which they are stored. Despite the relatively large storage capacity of the individual CD-ROM, many text collections are so enormous that they still need significant data compression to allow them to be fitted into the available space. The software provided with the CD-ROM allows the text to be decompressed, but it may not be possible to transfer readable text files to another storage medium to allow analysis using other, more standard software. Even where it is physically possible to do this, the licensing agreement may prohibit it to protect intellectual property rights. Any such restrictions will need to be considered very carefully when assessing the project.

3.1.4. Word-processed texts

Because most publications are now prepared using word processing or desk-top publishing software a computer-readable version of the text automatically exists. In some cases you may be able to get access to it, although publishers will almost certainly wish to impose restrictions on your use of the text and may well charge for it. The best approach is probably direct application to the publisher explaining the nature of the research, and emphasising the safeguards that would be applied to protect copyright. From then on the negotiations will probably depend on the nature of the research, any benefit (such as good publicity) which would accrue to the publishers, and any potential for commercial exploitation of the data which will be obtained form the text.

In some cases the copyright owner will not be a commercial publisher. If, for example, an investigation is to be carried out into academic writing, large quantities of suitable word-processed example texts are likely to be available from within academic institutions, and a simple request for donations of copies of these text is likely to be reasonably productive. Even in these circum-stances the originators of the texts are likely to seek reassurance on the protec-tion of their rights over the contents and the uses to which the data will be put.

The sources of word-processed texts are becoming more varied as the use of the computer for text initiation increases. Business communications, e-mail messages and the writing of children from the earliest stages of education are all likely to be available in fairly large quantities. They each present slightly different problems for the researcher in terms of methods of collection and the formal safeguards that will be demanded, but as with commercial publishers a direct approach to the individuals or organisations involved, explaining the basis of the research, will usually be the best way of dealing with them.

3.2. Making texts computer-readable

If, after searching the sources described in section 3.1, it becomes apparent that the texts needed for your research are not already available, it will be necessary to consider how they are to be converted into a form suitable for use by the computer. The main methods available are described in the following sections, but before deciding which you will use you must consider the position of the copyright holder of the text, if there is one. The law of intellectual property is complex and varies significantly from one country to another, but the basic consideration is that the permission of the copyright holder will almost certainly be needed before texts can be converted to computer-readable form. Some of the considerations surrounding the legal implications of the use of texts in research projects are dealt with in section 3.3 below.

3.2.1. Scanning

Before you can analyse a text it needs to be in a format in which the computer can recognise it, usually in the form of a standard text file on a storage medium such as a floppy disk or a hard disk. If the text is only currently available in printed or written form this file must be created, since it is not normally convenient, or indeed possible, for the computer to read the data directly from the paper copy. This is not to say that computers are completely incapable of recognising printed text, but the process of scanning printed text, storing it as a visual image and then recognising the visual patterns as a collection of characters is extremely complex, relatively slow and rather prone to error. Because of this text scanning is normally carried out as a separate process of data input, and the results are stored in a file and checked for correctness before any analysis is performed.

The process of scanning and recognising text needs specialised hardware, some form of scanning device, and text recognition software which is compatible with it.

3.2.1(a) Scanning hardware An enormous range of hardware is available, including small hand-held devices, desktop A4-size flatbed scanners and large free-standing units. Hand-held scanners are relatively inexpensive, but can usually only handle relatively narrow blocks of text, often needing two or three passes over the page to scan in a single A4 sheet, and are generally too slow and inaccurate for language research work. At the other end of the market, free-standing units such as the KDEM (Kurzweil Data Entry Machine) are capable of handling large amounts of text rapidly and fairly accurately, but their price and size restricts them to large institutions or major research projects which have significant continuing text scanning requirements. They are often used, for example, in public libraries as part of the automatic reading systems installed for the benefit of visually impaired people. Some large academic institutions may have access to this type of equipment and may provide a scanning service. The middle ground of scanning hardware is occupied by the desktop flatbed scanner, which is relatively easy to use and can handle reasonable amounts of text fairly quickly and accurately.

3.2.1(b) Character recognition software The software needed to convert the scanned image into meaningful text, often referred to as **OCR (optical character recognition)** software, also varies greatly in complexity and ability to deal with different types of text, and one of the more expensive packages will be needed to achieve an acceptable level of accuracy from any text other than perfect quality laser-printed originals, in association with a good quality flatbed scanner.

For a small research project the expenditure that would be involved in obtaining a good quality scanner and adequate recognition software would probably be excessive, especially if there is no likelihood of a continuing need for its use once the project has finished. Luckily, several companies offer a range of scanning services and printed texts can be converted into computer-readable files in a range of formats at relatively low cost.

3.2.1(c) Problems of scanning The main problem associated with the use of scanners is their tendency to error. The following extract shows the uncorrected result of scanning a document. Line numbers have been inserted for ease of reference, and are not present in the scanned text. The original text was a photocopy of a Victorian printed book, and the scanning was carried out on a KDEM:

> That, however, we had some foes, I shall have occasion
> presently to show; but I must rcturn to the scene I was
> describing. I may be pardoned for first giving a slight
> sketch of myself. I hope that I may escape being accused
> of vanity, as I shall not dwell on my personal appearance. 5
> I believe that I inherited some of my parents' good looks;
> but the hardships I have endured have eradicated all traces
> of them. I was well grown for my age (I was barely fifteen),
> but, dressed in my loose shooting costume, my countenance
> ruddy with fresh air and exercise, I looked much 10
> older.
> "What do you suppose would be the lot of a poor man's
> son, if he were to lie discovered acting as you are constantly
> doing in spite of my warnings and commands?" continued
> my father, his voice growing more serious and his look 15
> more grave. "I teil you, boy, that the consequences may
> and will be lamentable; and do not believe, that because
> you are the son of a gentleman, you can escape the punish-
> ment due to the guilty.

Despite the age of the original printed text, and the fact that a photocopy was used to prevent damage to the original, the computer-readable version is fairly accurate. The obvious errors are in lines 2 ('rcturn' instead of 'return') and 16 ('teil' instead of 'tell'), but there is also a less obvious error in line 13. Here the word 'lie' should actually have been 'be', but this is not absolutely obvious even from the surrounding text, and would be much more difficult to detect and correct than the other two errors. However good the scanning process is, some errors will remain, and scanned texts are likely to need significant proof-reading and manual editing to make them suitable for use in research. Some guidance on automatic and semi-automatic methods of text correction is given in section 4.2 below.

3.2.2. Keyboard entry

Scanning is a useful and fairly efficient method of text conversion where the original text is clearly printed in a form recognisable by the software. Where the format or condition of the text makes it unsuitable for scanning it may need to be keyed directly into the computer. This effectively replaces the scanner and its recognition software with the human keyboard operator. Assuming that the operator has an adequate knowledge of the type of text involved, combined with adequate keyboard skills, the result should be significantly more accurate than input by scanning. On the other hand, the process also tends to be significantly more time-consuming, and unless you have the time to carry out the data entry yourself the costs of keyboarding by commercial operators can be very high indeed.

In some cases, however, there will be no other options. OCR software can cope reasonably well with good quality straightforward printed originals, but if there is any significant degree of complexity in the text format, or if the original is handwritten rather than printed, it is unlikely that scanning will work adequately, or in some cases at all. As an example, a researcher needed to convert the entire text of Johnson's *Dictionary* to computer-readable form to enable the preparation of an electronic edition. The *Dictionary* exists in facsimile editions which photographically reproduce the original eighteenth-century printing. Because of the high cost of direct keyboard entry scanning was attempted, using a sophisticated KDEM unit which is capable of being trained to recognise a wide range of different typefaces. The accuracy rate of the scanning process was rather less than 50 per cent, and the results were completely unacceptable. In the end, despite the high cost, the entire text of the first and fourth editions of the *Dictionary* was entered by keyboard operators employed by a commercial data entry firm.

Part of the reason for the high cost of keyboarding lies in the method normally adopted to increase accuracy. To detect and correct typographic errors caused by miskeying the entire set of data is verified by a complete second keying process. During the second data entry stage the computer compares the second set of keystrokes with the data entered during the first run through, and requests clarification of any discrepancies.

Apart from greatly increased accuracy, the main advantage of direct keyboard entry is the facility that it provides for adding other information during the input process. This is discussed in section 4.3 below.

3.2.3. Spoken language

The discussion of text scanning and keyboard entry above have assumed that the original form of the language involved in your research is printed or written. Spoken language raises an extra set of complications in the shape of the steps needed to convert information which exists only as sound into written form before it can be entered into the computer. Obviously, if your starting point is a transcription of spoken language it is already in written form and can be dealt with as described above. Otherwise, you will need to adopt and apply a transcription convention of some sort to produce the written form which the computer will ultimately analyse.

It would, of course, be much more convenient if the computer could be fed the sound of the spoken language and either analyse it directly or automatically convert it to its written equivalent. This would involve the development of software which would be the audio equivalent of OCR, perhaps 'audio character recognition'. Although some progress has been made in the area of speech recognition (as outlined in Chapter 7) there is not, as yet, an effective method of interpretation which would allow sound to be processed as language.

3.3. Which texts can you use?

All of the methods described above for converting text to computer-readable form assume that you are legally entitled to use the texts you have chosen for your research. With manual research this is rarely a significant problem, since the examination of a text and reasonable quotations from it in an academic publication are covered by well-established and generally recognised conventions. The main problem introduced by the use of the computer is the need to store the text in electronic form. This is often specifically precluded in publishers' copyright notices within publications, and the need to do it may bring you up against the complex laws, varying between different countries, which regulate the concept of intellectual property. There is, however, a basic approach which may help you to avoid most of this complexity.

The first point that you need to establish relates to the precise details of the ownership of any copyright which exists in the text. If the particular edition of a text that you wish to use was published a sufficiently long time ago copyright may well have lapsed. The exact length of time involved varies from one country to another and will need to be checked. It is important to remember that a new edition, even of an old work, may reinstate some form of copyright, and that this also applies to the production of an electronic edition.

Once the copyright owner has been identified, you should write and ask for their formal permission to use the text for your research. You should give them full details of the nature of your research, the medium on which their text will be stored and any form of publication that will be produced from it, and of the acknowledgement that you intend to make if they give you permission. In the case of texts obtained from text archives, the question of copyright and permitted uses will normally have been established when the text was deposited, and there will generally be a set of standard conditions which you agree to when getting access to the text.

4. WHAT ELSE NEEDS TO BE DONE?

Even when the texts that you need are available or have been specially entered using the most appropriate method, they may still need some adjustment. The physical or logical format of the data may be incompatible with the hardware or software that you intend to use, or there may be an unacceptable level of errors in the text. It is also possible that you may want to add other information to an otherwise perfectly suitable set of texts. This section describes the most likely problem areas and the most useful ways of overcoming them.

4.1. File formats

Computer-readable texts available by transfer from other internet sites, on CD-ROM or in other forms, may still not be usable on the hardware and with the software that you have available. The reasons for this normally relate to the physical format of the text, in other words the medium on which it is stored, or its logical format. Unless both are compatible with your own set-up you will not be able to use the data without carrying out appropriate conversion processes. There are too many possible combinations of formats to deal with the individual conversion methods, but the general principles described in the following sections should cover most eventualities.

4.1.1. Physical formats

Since computers began to be used widely for commercial and academic purposes several forms of physical storage media have been developed. In the earlier days of computing, when the large mainframe computer was the most common type of installation, magnetic tape was the main exchangeable storage medium. With the advent of desktop personal computers the floppy disk largely replaced magnetic tape for everyday storage purposes, but no single standard was adopted for disk size, storage density or data formats. As a result, several different standards still exist. Magnetic tape cartridges or cassettes are still used in some personal computer systems, but mainly for large scale storage, security copies and so on.

Many older computers use 5¼ inch diameter disks, while the modern standard size is 3½ inch. Other sizes have also been used on comparatively recent models, and each different size of disk needs a physically different disk drive. Even within the 3½ inch standard there are two main storage densities, allowing 0.72 or 1.44 megabytes of data to be stored, and a very similar situation exists in 5¼ inch disks. In addition to this, the two main types of personal computer which are currently most widely used – the IBM-compatible PC and the Apple Macintosh – use completely different storage formats on the same physical disk. Disks formatted for use on IBM-compatible machines can only be used in Apple Macintosh disk drives using special software, and disks formatted for use on the Macintosh range cannot be handled by the disk drives on IBM-compatible PCs. Computers running the Unix operating system often use storage formats which are totally different from either of these, but may be able to access disks written under MS-DOS.

This rather complex situation means that you must make sure that the texts that you intend to use for your research are available on an appropriately sized medium in a format which is accessible by your hardware and operating system. If this is not the case, you will need to convert them to the appropriate format. The main conversion methods are dealt with below. Whichever method seems likely to be most appropriate for your individual data problem, a quick check with a local expert will save a great deal of frustration and wasted time and effort.

4.1.1(a) Dual disk drives If the text is available on a different size of disk to the one used by your own computer, but is in the same data format, you need to gain access to a computer compatible with your own which has disk drives catering for both sizes. Storage densities will also be important: drives capable of handling higher storage densities can normally read and write disks with the same format but with a lower density, but you must ensure that you use the appropriate type of disk. If, for instance, you intend to use an IBM-compatible computer which has a low density 3½ inch disk drive, and the data is currently available on high density 5¼ inch disks produced on another IBM-compatible machine, you will need to use an IBM-compatible computer with both a high density 5¼ inch drive and a 3½ inch drive. Both disk drives on such a machine would probably be capable of handling both high and low density disks, and you would need to ensure that the disk used in the 3½ inch drive was a low density disk and was properly formatted as low density before copying the data to it.

In a case like this, the lower storage capacity of the disks to which the data was being copied might mean that more disks would be needed than the original number. If any individual files were larger than the maximum capacity of the new disks they would need to be divided up, using either a text editor or a file-splitting utility, to allow them to fit.

4.1.1(b) Communication software Where you need to convert the file format to one used by a completely different type of computer, or where a machine with dual disk drives of the appropriate types is not available, the data can be transferred directly from one computer to another. This involves the use of a special lead to connect the two computers, or the connection of both of them to the same network or to an appropriate communications link. This is the technique that would be used to collect text files from an archive site through the internet, but it can equally well be used to convert from one format to another with the two computers side by side on the same desktop. Communications software exists for almost all types of computer, and is generally sufficiently standardised to allow data to be transferred between them, if it is in a suitable form. The main points to consider in information interchange between computers are outlined in section 4.1.2 below.

4.1.1(c) Special disk-formatting software In some cases special software is available which allows computers to handle disks formatted for other operating systems. For example, as already mentioned in section 4.1.1, some Apple Macintosh machines, running the appropriate software, can read and write disks formatted for the MS-DOS operating system which runs on IBM-compatible PCs, and many computers running Unix have similar software to enable MS-DOS file systems to be accessed. More specialised software also exists to allow formats based on older operating systems to be converted, usually to MS-DOS format, but these are becoming less easy to obtain. If local resources are not adequate for your needs, it is still possible to find specialist data transfer firms who can carry out the conversion for you.

4.1.2. Logical formats

Once the text files are in the correct physical format for use on your computer system, it is important to ensure that they are also in an appropriate logical format. Most of the text exploration software described in the following chapters, and most of the programs that you might write yourself, assume that the text is in the approximately standardised ASCII (American Standard Code for Information Interchange) format, sometimes referred to as ANSI standard. This is a very old standard, whose origins lie in the earliest days of computing, when the composition of the individual computer character meant that only 128 different characters were available.

There are implications of this for encoding any linguistic characters other than the standard unaccented roman alphabet. If characters outside this set occur in your texts they will need to be encoded using some other convention, often requiring two or more separate characters in the computer-readable version of the text to represent a single character in the original. As an example, the diachronic part of the Helsinki Corpus of English Texts contains texts in Old and Middle English which use additional characters no longer used in English. Because these are not provided for in the ASCII system it uses two- or three-character combinations to represent them. As an example, the character þ ('thorn') is represented by +t. Any software that you use to process the corpus would need to take special conventions like these into account, and if the software is not sufficiently adjustable, the text file may need to be modified so that it will not distort the results of your analysis.

It is also possible that the texts may not be in ASCII format to begin with. If they have been produced from a word processing or desktop publishing program they are likely to contain extra information relating to text formatting, page-layout information, illustrations contained in the text, and so on. Because of this the text encoding is likely to be very different from the simple

ASCII format, and before the file can be processed by the software you have chosen, it will probably need to be converted. Most modern word processing and desktop publishing software packages contain a facility for file format conversion, and ASCII is usually one of the options available. It is important to realise that the process of conversion will remove all the information relating to different typefaces, font sizes, paragraph indentation and so on. If any of this is important in your work, it may be necessary to find or develop software that can handle the file in its original form.

4.2. Text correction

For various reasons it is likely that your text, however it has been obtained, will contain errors. These could be individual typographical errors, caused by incorrect recognition during scanning, miskeying during text input or in the original creation of a document, or they could involve the omission, duplication or misplacing of sections of the text. It is obviously important to minimise the possibility of error during the input process, but however scrupulously it is carried out some mistakes are almost certain to creep in. Error correction is an important stage in the preparation of your text for use in research, and it can be a time-consuming and expensive process. Because of this, it is important to determine an acceptable level of error before you decide how to approach error correction. Errors which are unlikely to distort your results significantly are probably not worth correcting, and in many cases it will be worth carrying out a preliminary investigation to see how accurate the data needs to be. Once you have decided on the level of error detection and correction that you need, it may be possible to make it more efficient by using the computer to assist the process, or even, in some cases, to carry it out for you.

4.2.1. The spell checker

Perhaps the simplest way of using the computer to correct errors is to run the text file through a spell checker. Most word processing packages now contain this facility, and if the language in the text file conforms to the standard embodied in the spell checker a quick run-through could highlight many of the typographical errors. For obvious reasons, this would not have been a suitable method to use for the text of *Canterbury Tales* which formed the basis of the project described at the beginning of Chapter 1, and this will be true of any project which sets out explore spelling variation in texts. Equally obviously, it will only detect the errors that produce word forms which do not exist in the spell checker's dictionary. For example, if the text contains the word *tool* and it is somehow entered as *tolo* it is likely to be detected; if it is entered as *toll* it will almost certainly not be detected. In many cases, the second error could distort the results more seriously and would certainly be less likely to be picked up at a later stage.

4.2.2. Other computer-assisted methods

The computer can be used to carry out automatic error correction, but only where the error is consistent and capable of accurate identification. In the case of words split by hyphenation, for example, it may be possible to write a simple program which can detect the hyphen symbol at the end of a line and reconnect the remaining letters of the split word at the beginning of the next line. Such a program may need to check that the hyphen does not represent a dash, and will need a means of recognising the end of the word, but neither of these should present major problems. Section 2.1 of Chapter 8 provides a more detailed description of a practical example of the problem, and the program written to deal with it is described in Appendix 3.

Similarly, if a word has been systematically wrongly input because of scanning problems or human misunderstanding, all appearances of the incorrect version may be capable of automatic replacement by the correct form. Before this can be done with any confidence, of course, you need to be sure that it genuinely is a consistent error, and that none of the 'errors' could be the correct form of another word. Very often, a standard 'find and replace' utility within a word processor can be used, taking advantage of the opportunity to check the context before carrying out replacement if there is any doubt.

It is much harder to use the computer to detect the omission or duplication of sections of text, although if the number of lines in the original text is available, as it often is in editions of literary texts, a quick line count by the computer and a reconciliation of totals can provide a useful check. If a piece of text has simply been misplaced this check is unlikely to reveal the fact, but this may not distort results significantly so long as the text is complete.

4.2.3. Manual checking

Where the accuracy of the text is sufficiently important, you will almost certainly need to carry out manual checking instead of, or even as a supplement to, the use of the computer. Full proof-reading is probably the only certain way of achieving accuracy, and its usefulness will be entirely dependent on the skill and reliability of the proof-reader. It is also likely to be expensive in terms of time, money or both. In some cases, especially where the checking also needs to cover the addition of other information such as mark-up codes, significant judgement will be needed to determine the accuracy of the text, and the proof-reader will need to understand the project thoroughly and be capable of editorial decisions.

4.3. Mark-up codes

Apart from the need to correct errors, texts may need other information added to them before they are ready for analysis. It may be necessary, for example, to label the different structural levels of a text to ensure that particular forms of analysis are only carried out within an appropriate level. A fairly complex example of this can be seen in the computer-readable text of Johnson's *Dictionary*, mentioned earlier in section 3.2.2. During the process of keying in the entire text codes were added to it to identify the nature of the text within each dictionary entry. An example, taken from the early stages of the project, is given below for the word *abandon*:

@1 To <<a>>ABA<<'>>NDON.

@2 <cf2>v.a.<cf1>
@3 [Fr. <cf2>abandonner.<cf1> Derived, according to <cf2>Menage, <cf1> from the Italian <cf2>abandonare,<cf1> which signifies to forsake his colours; <cf2>bandum [vexillum] deserere. Pasquier<cf1> thinks it a coalition of <cf2>a ban donner,<cf1> to give up to a proscription; in which sense we, at this day, mention the ban of the empire. Ban, in our own old dialect, signifies a curse; and to <cf2>abandon,<cf1> if considered as compounded between French and Saxon, is exactly equivalent to <cf2>diris devovere.<cf1>]
@4 1. To give up, resign, or quit;
@9 often followed by the particle <cf2>to.<cf1>
@5 The passive gods behold the Greeks defile
Their temples, and <cf2>abandon to<cf1> the spoil
Their own abodes; we, feeble few, conspire
To save a sinking town, involv'd in fire.
@6 <cf2>Dryd.<cf1>
@7 <cf2>\AEneid.<cf1>
@4 2. To desert.
@5 The princes using the passions of fearing evil, and desiring to escape, only to serve the rule of virtue, not to <cf2>abandon<cf1> one's self, leapt to a rib of the ship.
@6 <cf2>Sidney,<cf1>
@8 <cf2>b. ii.<cf1>
@5 Then being alone,
Left and <cf2>abandon'd<cf1> of his velvet friends,
'Tis right, quoth he; thus misery doth part
The flux of company.
@6 <cf2>Shakesp.<cf1>
@7 <cf2>As you like it.<cf1>
@5 What fate a wretched fugitive attends,
Scorn'd by my foes, <cf2>abandon'd<cf1> by my friends.
@6 <cf2>Dryd.<cf1>
@7 <cf2>\AEn.<cf1>
@8 <cf2>2.<cf1>
@4 3. To forsake,
@9 generally with a tendency to an ill sense.

@5 When he in presence came, to Guyon first
He boldly spake, Sir knight, if knight thou be,
<cf2>Abandon<cf1> this forestalled place at erst,
For fear of further harm, I counsel thee.
@6 <cf2>Spenser's<cf1>
@7 <cf2>Fairy Queen,<cf1>
@8 <cf2>b. ii. cant. 4. stanz. 39.<cf1>
@5 But to the parting goddess thus she pray'd;
Propitious still be present to my aid,
Nor quite <cf2>abandon<cf1> your once favour'd maid.
@6 <cf2>Dryd.<cf1>
@7 <cf2>Fab.<cf1>

In the sample, each element of the original text is set on a separate line and preceded by a code consisting of '@' followed by a number. Each of these codes represents a different type of information contained within the dictionary entry. For example, '@1' signals the headword label, '@2' the grammatical information supplied by Johnson for this headword, '@3' the etymological information, '@4' the individual senses of the headword and so on. This is a very specific coding system developed for a very specific set of needs, but the general needs of those involved in text preparation, storage and investigation have led to the formation of a body to promote the development of a standard system, the Text Encoding Initiative (TEI), which has adopted as its starting-point a mark-up system called **SGML** (Standard Generalised Mark-up Language). SGML is now widely used in the preparation of texts for deposition in text archives.

The main problem involved in the addition of mark-up codes is the level of judgement that is needed, not only in the design or adoption of a specific coding system for the text, but also in its detailed application. If the codes are to be entered by the keyboard operators while they are keying in the data from the text, which may be the most efficient approach, they will need thorough training before data entry begins, and a high level of supervision during the input process. Even if this is provided, it is likely that the results will need significant manual checking before they can be used in a research project.

5. EXERCISES

1.   What types of text would you include in a corpus intended to be representative of the written language read by British schoolchildren?

2.   How would you set about designing and gathering a computer-readable corpus of casual conversational English?

3.   You want to create a corpus from medieval texts which are not yet available in computer-readable form. Describe the advantages and disadvantages of the various possible methods of entering the data.

FURTHER READING

Kytö, M., Ihalainen, O. and Rissanen, M. (eds) (1988) *Corpus Linguistics, Hard and Soft*, Amsterdam: Rodopi. The following papers are especially relevant: Kytö, M. and Rissanen, M. 'The Helsinki Corpus of English Texts: classifying and coding the diachronic part', pp. 169–79; Renouf, A. 'Coding metalanguage: issues raised in the creation and processing of specialised corpora', pp. 197–206.

Leech, G., Myers, G. and Thomas, J. (eds) (1995) *Spoken English on Computer*, London: Longman.

Leitner, G. (ed.) (1992) *New directions in Corpus Linguistics*, Berlin: Mouton de Gruyter. Part I, 'Corpus design and text encoding' (pp. 73–107) is especially relevant.

Renouf, A. (1987) 'Corpus development', in J. Sinclair (ed.), *Looking Up*, London: Collins ELT, ch. 1 (pp. 1–40).

Sinclair, J. (1991) *Corpus, Concordance, Collocation*, Oxford University Press, ch. 1 (pp. 13–26).

Svartvik, J. (ed.) (1992) *Directions in Corpus Linguistics: Proceedings of Nobel Symposium 82*, Berlin: Mouton de Gruyter. The 'Corpus design and development' section on pp. 129–209 is especially relevant.

Text archives and other sources of corpus data

Internet addresses, site holdings and World-Wide-Web pages vary so rapidly that any listings would be out of date long before publication. The best strategy, once you have connected yourself to the internet in the most convenient way, is to use one of the many search or directory programmes available to find the current addresses of archives and other useful sites. You may need to seek advice from local experts on the use of the software available to you.

The electronic edition of Johnson's *Dictionary*, referred to in sections 3.2.2 and 4.3, is now available on CD-ROM. It is edited by Anne McDermott of the University of Birmingham, and published by Cambridge University Press.

Examining the catch: the use of frequency lists

1. WHAT ARE FREQUENCY LISTS?

Once the corpus has been assembled and prepared for use it needs to be examined in outline before any detailed investigation can be carried out. The most useful way of carrying out a preliminary survey is to produce a **frequency list** of the contents of the texts. At its simplest, the frequency list shows the words which make up the texts in the corpus, together with their frequencies of occurrence. It can be produced in several different sequences and for language units other than words. Despite its apparent simplicity, it is a very powerful tool.

A word frequency list is produced by identifying each word form found in the text, counting identical forms and listing them with their frequencies (and any other relevant information) in a chosen sequence. None of these stages is entirely straightforward, but the potential problems will be dealt with later in section 2. For the moment, let us assume that the main problem, the concept of 'identical word forms', has been dealt with, and that they can be easily defined and identified. Simply as an example of the production process for a frequency list, consider the short text extract below, taken from a text of Mary Wollstonecraft Shelley's *Frankenstein, or the Modern Prometheus* obtained from the Gutenberg Project.:

> This is the most favourable period for travelling in Russia. They fly quickly over the snow in their sledges; the motion is pleasant, and, in my opinion, far more agreeable than that of an English stagecoach.

When this text fragment is put through a simple word frequency program it produces the list shown below:

agreeable	1	over	1
an	1	period	1
and	1	pleasant	1
english	1	quickly	1
far	1	russia	1
favourable	1	sledges	1
fly	1	snow	1
for	1	stagecoach	1
in	3	than	1
is	2	that	1
more	1	the	3
most	1	their	1
motion	1	they	1
my	1	this	1
of	1	travelling	1
opinion	1		

Details of the program are given in Appendix 3. This version of the frequency list has been produced in alphabetical order of word forms. Although this is convenient for some purposes, it is often more useful for a preliminary survey of the text to produce the list in descending order of frequency. This would produce the following rearrangement:

in	3	opinion	1
the	3	over	1
is	2	period	1
agreeable	1	pleasant	1
an	1	quickly	1
and	1	russia	1
english	1	sledges	1
far	1	snow	1
favourable	1	stagecoach	1
fly	1	than	1
for	1	that	1
more	1	their	1
most	1	they	1
motion	1	this	1
my	1	travelling	1
of	1		

Because this fragment is so small it is obviously rather uninteresting – only three word forms occur more than once – but it illustrates the basic concept. The next section explores the potential of this form of list in detail.

1.1. What the frequency list can show you

A list produced from the entire text of *Frankenstein* is obviously of rather more interest than the one based on the fragment above. The extract below shows the top thirty items in a version of the list arranged in descending frequency order:

the	4194	it	548
and	2976	his	535
I	2847	as	528
of	2641	not	510
to	2094	for	463
my	1777	by	460
a	1391	on	460
in	1129	this	402
was	1021	from	385
that	1018	her	374
me	866	have	365
but	687	be	360
had	686	when	328
with	666		
he	608		
you	575		
which	558		

The complete text contains 75,214 words, made up of 6,986 different word forms. The list above, in other words, shows only 30 lines from a list which is 6,986 lines long. The average number of occurrences for each word form (arrived at by dividing 75,214 by 6,986) is 10.8. Within the whole list, 5,999 of the word forms occur less often than ten times, and 2,996 of them only occur once.

The significance of these statistics is considered in a little more detail in section 1.3 below, but there are several points of interest within the list itself. All thirty items in it are purely grammatical words, crucial to the structure of the text but not contributing directly or independently to its meaning. In conventional word class terms they include articles (*the* and *a*), conjunctions (*and, but* and *when*), pronouns (*I, me, he,* etc.) and so on. The first word in the entire list which contributes any independent meaning is *man* with 137 occurrences, followed by *father* with 134, *life* with 115 and *time* with 98. The first proper name found is *elizabeth* with 92 occurrences, followed by *clerval* with 59 and *justine* with 55. None of these pieces of information is particularly useful by itself, but combined with a knowledge of the nature of the text or of similar pieces of information for other texts they can provide a very useful basis for a preliminary survey of the text and an exploration of its main features.

Frankenstein		COBUILD corpus	
Word	**Frequency**	**Word**	**Frequency**
the	4194	the	309497
and	2976	of	155044
I	2847	and	153801
of	2641	to	137056
to	2094	a	129928
my	1777	in	100138
a	1391	that	67042
in	1129	I	64849
was	1021	it	61379
that	1018	was	54722

Table 3.1 Ten most frequent words: *Frankenstein* and COBUILD

The frequency list becomes much more meaningful once it is compared with similar lists constructed from other texts. It is often particularly useful to compare it with the corresponding entries in a list compiled from a large general corpus. In Table 3.1, the top ten items from the *Frankenstein* list are shown alongside the top ten items from the COBUILD corpus word frequency list given in Sinclair (1991: 143):

The most striking feature of this comparison is perhaps the difference in the positions of *I* and *my* in the two lists. If you compare the top six words in the two lists you will see that in the Frankenstein list they have pushed *a* and *in* into seventh and eighth place. In the COBUILD list they occupy fifth and sixth. More surprisingly still, *I* is in third place in the Frankenstein list, compared to eighth place in the COBUILD list, while *my*, in sixth place in Frankenstein, is in an unimpressive fifty-sixth place in the full COBUILD list. A comparison of the frequencies of the words in the two lists is even more startling, although it is rather uninformative to compare their absolute values because of the huge difference in size of the two texts. If the relative frequency of *I* is calculated as a percentage of the frequency of the most common word, it amounts to nearly 68% in the Frankenstein list, compared to only 21% in the COBUILD list. The corresponding figures for *my* give 42% and 4% respectively. These begin to look like significant differences, although statistical analysis would be needed to establish the level of significance involved.

Even a nodding acquaintance with *Frankenstein* would suggest a good reason for these differences: it is constructed as a series of first person narratives. Any representative collection of English will contain some first person material, but it is unlikely that it will be made up entirely of texts which use this device. The frequency list has not necessarily revealed anything about this text which was not already known, but if a large number of texts were to be sorted into types of narratives, for example, this might provide a useful starting-point for the development of automatic classification procedures.

As it stands, then, the list can provide a useful general perspective of the basic features of the text. It is also extremely valuable as a basis for selecting words for further investigation. It can give a useful impression of the significance of individual words within the texts, and highlight any anomalies in distribution when compared to other corpora. Questions raised by the examination of the frequency list can then be pursued through other tools. The concordance listing, a particularly useful source of more detailed information about the behaviour of word forms in the texts, is discussed in detail in the next chapter: its use can be focused much more accurately by a careful examination of the word frequency list.

To make this simple tool as useful as possible, it is important to ensure that the information is presented in the most appropriate form, and the sequence of the words in the list is an essential consideration. Reasons for using sequences other than descending frequency order are considered in section 1.2.

1.2. Other possible sequences
1.2.1. Alphabetical order
Descending frequency order is probably the most useful basis for exploring the text or corpus as a whole and comparing the general characteristics of its components with those of other texts and corpora. It is not so useful, however, for examining the parts played by individual words, since the sequence of the list makes it difficult to find them. Because of this a list which is either produced in alphabetical order of word forms in the case of a paper copy, or capable of being searched by word form in the case of a computer-readable version, is often needed in addition to the frequency order list. The ability to browse the list in alphabetical order can also be very useful, since the words which are going to be of interest may only emerge from a consideration of the entire list.

As well as allowing easy reference to individual word forms, conventional alphabetical order brings together word forms which begin with similar sets of letters. This can be useful if you need to check whether other inflected forms of words under investigation are also present in the text. If, however, the research project is more concerned with types of words than with individual word forms, the endings of words will be more useful than their beginnings. In this case it will probably be more useful to arrange the list in alphabetical order of reversed word forms. The technical difficulties involved in this process are fairly trivial, and the results can be quite revealing. A programming suggestion is given in Appendix 3. Shown below is an extract from the complete *Frankenstein* list, part of which was used in section 1.1 above. It has been sorted into reversed alphabetical order, and this part of it comes from a section containing words ending in -ed:

resolved	32		approved	1
devolved	1		observed	21
revolved	5		deserved	1
loved	30		reserved	5
beloved	26		preserved	2
moved	14		bedewed	1
removed	4		viewed	4
proved	6		renewed	6
improved	8		strewed	2

Because sorting was carried out with the entire word reversed, the sequence of these words may appear counter-intuitive. This may become clearer if the reversed version of the first eight items of the list is shown:

devloser	32		devoleb	26
devloved	1		devom	14
devlover	5		devomer	4
devol	30		devorp	6

The special usefulness of this feature is that the list sequence reduces the influence of prefixes so that words like *devolved* and *revolved* are brought together, as are *loved* and *beloved*, *moved* and *removed*, and so on. This does not guarantee that the list can be relied upon as an exhaustive basis for such research, but it does provide rather more information in this area than any other sequence, and is almost certain to be useful as a starting-point.

1.2.2. Order of appearance
Frequency and alphabetic sequences both produce lists which give substantial information about individual words, but reveal little or nothing about text organisation. In some cases a third possible sequence may be useful, in which the words, rather like the characters in soap opera cast lists, are shown in the order of their first appearance in the text. The list given below is based once again on the text of *Frankenstein*, and the third column shows the word number of the first appearance of the word form within the text. This would not necessarily be printed as part of the list, but it may be useful for later cross-reference.

letter	28	1	petersburgh	3	7
to	2094	2	dec	1	8
mrs	4	3	th	15	9
saville	4	4	you	575	10
england	21	5	will	194	11
st	5	6	rejoice	1	12

hear	19	14	an	211	23
that	1018	15	enterprise	10	24
no	172	16	which	558	25
disaster	4	17	have	365	27
has	64	18	regarded	6	28
accompanied	9	19	with	666	29
the	4194	20	such	87	30
commencement	5	21	evil	23	31
of	2641	22	forebodings	2	32

This represents the original opening text:

Letter 1

TO Mrs. Saville, England

St. Petersburgh, Dec. 11th, 17-

You will rejoice to hear that no disaster has accompanied the commencement of an enterprise which you have regarded with such evil forebodings.

You will notice that nothing is omitted (except the numbers, which are ignored by this frequency list program) until word 13 is reached. This is another occurrence of the word *to*, which first appeared as word 2. The only other gap in this short extract is at word 26, a second occurrence of *you*. By the time we get another 5,000 words into the text, still only a fifteenth of the way through it, the omissions have become more frequent, so that the sentence:

Yesterday the stranger said to me, "You may easily perceive, Captain Walton, that I have suffered great and unparalleled misfortunes.

becomes:

perceive	7	5029
suffered	21	5035
misfortunes	17	5039

While a list produced in this way can be interesting to browse through it becomes more useful if it is used systematically. One of the main possible applications is in identifying changes in the nature of the text. Words which occur with similar frequency but appear for the first time in very different places may indicate the position of a change in topic or of the type of vocabulary used to discuss it. The investigation of this may be helped by producing a further list which is arranged first in frequency order, and which has words with equal frequencies arranged in order of first appearance. The extract below was taken from a list of this form produced from the *Frankenstein* text, and shows the words with a frequency of 25 in order of their first appearance:

sight	25	301	creatures	25	4701
cousin	25	700	died	25	6070
hour	25	730	desired	25	6619
others	25	957	head	25	6848
greater	25	1454	wretch	25	14907
spent	25	1784	william	25	18274
having	25	1899	rage	25	29880
sat	25	3020	safie	25	36803
spoke	25	4461			

Few of the words in this list are conclusive evidence of the nature of the textual organisation, and further investigation would be needed to establish the parts they play in the text, but the two proper names in the list, *William* and *Safie*, do show how the list can work. *William* appears first at word 18274, while *Safie* does not appear until word 36803. An examination of the text reveals that William is first introduced in chapter 6, mentioned in a letter to the narrator (by this point, Victor Frankenstein), while Safie does not appear until chapter 13, in the part of the narrative related by the monster to Frankenstein. A full list of proper names could easily be produced for the text and their first appearances mapped in a similar way to establish the patterns of their introduction. Further investigation of any of the words in the list would be best carried out using the concordance lists described in Chapter 4.

1.2.3. Lemmatised lists

The lists which have been considered so far have all been arranged in sequences based on individual word forms. This separates word forms which may be closely related in ways which are important for the project. The most common example of this situation is the need to group together different inflected forms of the same word, so that, for example, different parts of the same verb are shown together. The term normally used for this concept of a 'word' which includes all related inflected forms is **lemma**, and the process of producing a list which groups together all the forms belonging to each lemma is often called 'lemmatisation'.

Lemmatisation is independent of the basic sequence of the list: if it is carried out it groups word forms under the same lemma regardless of the position they would have occupied within that list. This is what the *Frankenstein* list extract shown in section 1.1 above could look like if it were treated like this:

I		5519				are		176
	I		2847		a		1602	
	my		1777		a			1391
	me		866		an			211
	mine		29	have			1140	
the		4194				had		686
and		2976				have		365
of		2641				has		64
to		2094				having		25
be		1864		in			1129	
	was		1021	that			1018	
	be		360	but			687	
	is		307					

This version of the extract has been produced manually by examining an alphabetic form of the entire list and adjusting it to include other forms of the lemmas. The frequency shown opposite the head item for the lemma is the total, which in this case has been used to adjust the position in this frequency-sorted list, and the indented lines show the frequencies for the individual forms. Lemmatisation can be performed automatically, although it is not a simple procedure, and possible approaches to the design of software to achieve this are discussed in section 2.

1.2.4. Project specific frequency lists

The list sequences described in the previous sections are likely to be appropriate for a wide range of research projects, although each will obviously be more suitable for some types of investigation than for others. In some cases, the project requirements will be rather more specific and may dictate other types of frequency list or other sequences. The selection of examples below should give you some idea of the possibilities.

1.2.4(a) Collecting related word forms Lemmatisation of frequency lists has already been discussed in section 1.2.3 above, but there are other possible groupings which might be needed by specific projects. Texts which contain significant spelling variation, such as the Chaucer texts described in Chapter 1, would be made significantly easier to analyse if frequency lists grouped variant spellings of the same word together, and any process of lemmatisation would be almost impossible without this. It is possible, if rather tedious and time-consuming, to do this manually, though there is no guarantee that the result will be correct or exhaustive. Some form of automatic grouping based on rules of spelling variation was one of the objectives of the project described both in Chapter 1 and, in more detail, in Chapter 8.

Groups of words which are related thematically or semantically could be very useful, but the process of automating this would probably be rather more

difficult. Using a text editor or word processor you could carry out a preliminary survey of the complete list (probably most usefully in alphabetical order)
and create the grouped lists as extracts from it. As an example of this approach,
the *Frankenstein* list was checked for nouns which could be used for the
organism created by Victor Frankenstein. Only words occurring ten times or
more were checked, and the following thematic group was extracted on the
basis of a detailed knowledge of the text:

being	97	enemy	23
horror	45	beings	22
creature	44	creation	19
fiend	34	daemon	16
monster	31	thing	11
creatures	25	devil	10
wretch	25		

The significance of these words within the text will be explored using
concordance lines in the next chapter. Their collection would have been
much more difficult, perhaps even impossible, without a frequency list.

1.2.4(b) Word length sequence This sequence may be a useful basis for
examining word form complexity, especially if combined with alphabetic or
frequency order within word length. It can also be used as a basis for the
calculation of statistics relating to word length, such as the mean figure and the
distribution of frequencies of words of various lengths, and as the starting-
point for detailed investigations arising from a study of these measures.
Appendix 3 contains a programming suggestion.

1.2.4(c) Other linguistic units The discussion so far has assumed that all
the individual words in the text are the units whose frequency is being investigated. Words, of course, are not the only units which make up texts, and
groups of words, clauses, sentences, and so on could be investigated in a similar way. The only requirement is that the boundaries of the units under investigation should be specified in some way that the computer can recognise, and
this may involve manual insertion of mark-up codes. The general considerations underlying the addition of mark-up codes to texts are discussed in
Chapter 2, section 4.3.

If the text is tagged with its grammatical characteristics or parsed in some
way, so that the structural patterns of groups, clauses, sentences or other units
are revealed, these patterns can also be used as the basis for frequency lists. If
individual words or phrases are labelled with their parts of speech or grammatical functions, the labels can be used in place of the words themselves as
the items to be counted. Computerised tagging and parsing is discussed in
some detail in Chapter 6.

1.3. What the frequency list doesn't show

I hope I have shown that even the simplest form of word frequency list can reveal important characteristics of the text that it was produced from. However, to use this simple but powerful tool effectively you also need to be aware of what it conceals.

The most obvious limitation derives from the basic nature of the word frequency list: by breaking the text into individual word forms it removes the words from their original contexts. One effect of this is that word forms which can have more than one meaning are gathered together and counted as one single word. The extracts from the *Frankenstein* list given above do not go far enough to show examples of this, but this extract may make it clearer:

place	59	placid	6
placed	28	placing	2
places	5		

This has been taken from the *Frankenstein* frequency list arranged in alphabetical order. The words *placed*, *placid* and *placing* are reasonably unambiguous. The word forms *place* and *places*, on the other hand, could represent elements of either the verb or the noun *place* and they can only be disambiguated by considering the contexts in which they occur. The problem is dealt with in some detail in section 2.2.3 below, and the use of concordance software to provide the necessary information is considered in section 1.3 of Chapter 4.

1.4. Types, tokens and statistics

The extracts given from the frequency lists so far have only shown the entries for individual words. Most word frequency software also produces useful totals, and sometimes offers a range of statistics based on them. The most common totals calculated for word frequency lists are usually referred to as **total tokens** and **total types**, and it is important to understand the distinction between them.

In this context, a token is an individual occurrence of any word form. The sentence:

> But I have one want which I have never yet been able to satisfy, and the absence of the object of which I now feel as a most severe evil, I have no friend, Margaret: when I am glowing with the enthusiasm of success, there will be none to participate my joy; if I am assailed by disappointment, no one will endeavour to sustain me in dejection.

This text contains altogether 67 words, or tokens, but these represent only 49 different word forms, or types. The frequency list shows the number of tokens found for each type. In this case, the following 10 types have more than one token:

I	6	which	2
have	3	am	2
to	3	will	2
of	3	no	2
the	3	one	2

Between them, these types account for 28 of the tokens. The other 39 types occur once only and make up the overall total of 67 tokens.

The distribution of tokens between the types in a text can provide a useful measure of the degree of lexical variety within it, and may even provide a starting-point for examining lexical differences between different types of text. Several statistics can be calculated from the information contained in the list The simplest is the ratio of tokens to types, in other words the mean frequency of each different word form. In the case of the sentence used above this is 69/49 or 1.41. This is an extremely low ratio, obviously caused by the smallness of the selected text. For the whole text of *Frankenstein* the ratio is 10.77. This figure is obviously affected by the overall number of tokens in the text, and comparisons between texts must be based on samples of the same size if they are to be useful

Cumulative frequency totals calculated from lists arranged in descending frequency order can give a useful indication of the relative importance of high and low frequency words. Applying this technique to the *Frankenstein* list shown in section 1.1 above would produce the figures in Table 3.2.

The program used to produce these figures from the original frequency list is described in Appendix 3. From them we can see that the 30 most frequent words in the text of *Frankenstein* account for over 40% of the total occurrences of all words. An examination of the entire list shows that the 62 most frequent words cover 50% of the total, but that the top 584 words need to be considered before 75% of the total number of words has been accounted for. These characteristics could be compared to other texts of a similar size as part of a preliminary investigation of relative lexical density.

Many other statistical measures can be calculated for word frequency lists, but their description belongs more properly in a textbook on statistics than in one devoted to the use of computers for language analysis.

2. HOW TO PRODUCE THEM

The production of frequency lists in any of the sequences discussed in section 1 is not an essentially difficult process. The usual methods adopted are described below together with the main problems that tend to be encountered and possible ways of tackling them. The method of production is only likely to be of interest to you if you are developing your own software or modifying existing programs to meet your needs, and if this does not apply you may want to skip section 2.1. However, the problems generally associated

Type	Frequency	Cumulative frequency	Percentage of total tokens
the	4194	4194	5.58
and	2976	7170	9.53
I	2847	10017	13.32
of	2641	12658	16.83
to	2094	14752	19.61
my	1777	16529	21.98
a	1391	17920	23.83
in	1129	19049	25.33
was	1021	20070	26.68
that	1018	21088	28.04
me	866	21954	29.19
but	687	22641	30.10
had	686	23327	31.01
with	666	23993	31.90
he	608	24601	32.71
you	575	25176	33.47
which	558	25734	34.21
it	548	26282	34.94
his	535	26817	35.65
as	528	27345	36.36
not	510	27855	37.03
for	463	28318	37.65
by	460	28778	38.26
on	460	29238	38.87
this	402	29640	39.41
from	385	30025	39.92
her	374	30399	40.42
have	365	30764	40.90
be	360	31124	41.38
when	328	31452	41.82

Table 3.2 Extract from *Frankenstein* cumulative frequency list

with frequency are likely to affect you even if you intend to use unmodified existing software, and sections 2.2 and 2.3 may help you to choose the most appropriate software package, or at least to understand any difficulties you may be having with the results. Section 2.4 extends the treatment of word frequency lists to cover the special demands of other linguistic units.

2.1. The general approach

The production of a word frequency list involves two main stages:

- splitting the text into words
- counting identical word forms.

The first stage demands the definition of word boundaries in a form that the computer can use. You need to make a clear distinction between characters which can be found within words, and those which can only be found between them. This is not quite as simple as it sounds, since some characters can be found in both positions, but this is discussed in more detail in the next section. For the time being, we could assume that all characters found in texts can be divided into these two categories, which can then be used to tell the computer how to recognise either the words themselves, or the gaps between them.

Once the text can be analysed into individual words they can be organised for counting. The way this is achieved often depends on non-linguistic considerations, such as the capacity of the computer's memory, the need for speed of operation and so on. Two main types of approach are common. The simpler method involves three subsidiary stages:

- producing a file containing each word found on a separate line

- sorting the word file into alphabetical sequence so that all identical forms are brought together

- counting the number of times that each word occurs in the sorted list.

Because the second stage of this method can usually be done perfectly adequately by existing sorting utilities, which do not need to be specially written for the purpose (unless special, non-standard characters are involved), and because the first and third stage involve relatively straightforward data manipulation, this approach is fairly accessible even to inexperienced computer users. This means that the most important part of the process from a researcher's viewpoint – the definition of word boundaries – can be completely under your control. The main disadvantage of this method is that it is rather slow and cumbersome, but this may not be of great importance since only computer time is being consumed, and you are left free to carry on with other work. A second advantage is that this approach makes only the lightest of demands on computer memory, and should allow you to handle fairly large text files using relatively modest equipment.

The main alternative uses space in the computer's memory to store the words found so far and their total occurrences to date. Every time another word is identified within the text the memory is searched to see whether a count already exists for that form. If it does, it is increased by 1, if not a new count is established and set equal to 1. This technique can also be fairly simple in some programming languages, but in others it may demand a detailed knowledge of database structures or memory handling routines. It also tends to make great demands on computer memory and may not be viable for large files except on relatively powerful computers. Its main advantage is its speed of operation.

Whichever basic approach is used, the sequence of the final list can be easily rearranged to suit your working needs using standard sort utilities. These are more sophisticated on some machines than on others, but where the programs supplied with the operating system are inadequate, commercial or public domain software is normally easily available to compensate for it.

2.2. Common problems

The major problems affecting the design of word frequency programs relate to the boundaries of the individual units in the text and the basis on which these units are regarded as being identical for counting purposes. The boundaries problem can be considered in two parts: the problem of the definition of the two character sets has already been mentioned in section 2.1, but even when this question has been settled there may be linguistic units which you want to treat as single words but which are conventionally represented as phrases. These two problems are dealt with in sections 2.2.1 and 2.2.2. The question of identity of units is considered in section 2.2.3.

2.2.1. Defining the character sets

The suggestion in section 2.1 that characters can be divided into those which are normally found within words and those which come between them is a slight oversimplification. Consider the following short extract, again taken from the text of *Frankenstein*:

> You may remember that a history of all the voyages made for purposes of discovery composed the whole of our good Uncle Thomas' library. My education was neglected, yet I was passionately fond of reading. These volumes were my study day and night, and my familiarity with them increased that regret which I had felt, as a child, on learning that my father's dying injunction had forbidden my uncle to allow me to embark in a seafaring life.

In this extract the character represented by the mark ' ' ', which appears in 'Thomas'' and 'father's', is used as an apostrophe, to signal the possessive of those two words. You would probably want to preserve this as part of the word, especially if your research aims included an investigation of the use of possessives. In the next extract from the same text its use is rather different:

> I learned and
> applied the words, `fire,' `milk,' `bread,' and `wood.' I learned also the names of the cottagers themselves. The youth and his companion had each of them several names, but the old man had only one, which was `father.' The girl was called `sister' or `Agatha,' and the youth `Felix,' `brother,' or `son.'

Here the apostrophe of the previous extract has been used together with the opening single quotation mark ' ` ' to enclose a string of quoted words which the creature has learned from his close observation of a family. It is unlikely that you would want these marks kept within the word, because this would separate the quoted and unquoted forms of the same words.

Similar problems arise with hyphens, which may also be used in some texts as dashes, and with full stops within abbreviations. In all these cases it seems that whichever character set you allocate them to the results will be imperfect. Possible approaches to this problem are suggested in section 2.3.1 below.

2.2.2. The nature of individual units

In my discussion of frequency lists so far, I have assumed that the basic unit being identified and counted is the word, a string of characters separated from other words by spaces or by other boundary characters. Despite the problems mentioned in the previous section this concept remains unchallenged. However, there are significant problems with this approach, since some units which behave as though they were indivisible units in their use in language are conventionally written as phrases containing more than one word. Some of these units are completely fixed phrases, such as *of course*, and cannot be used with this meaning with any intervening words. Others, including phrasal verbs such as *take up*, *put on*, and so on, are often found with other words set inside them. The normal word frequency list approach will not treat items like these as units unless the text is marked up to identify them or the software is adapted in some way. Possible ways of doing this are discussed in section 2.3.

2.2.3. Identity of units

Once the text has been broken into the appropriate units, the counting process depends on a comparison between them to ensure that the appropriate count is incremented. This may seem to be unproblematic, since identity between two units of the text is established by a full comparison of two strings of characters: if the sequences of characters are identical, the units are counted under the same item. To make this approach possible, upper and lower case versions of the same letter will usually be treated so as to make them appear identical. Two problems can undermine this apparent straightforwardness.

The first applies in almost all texts, and arises from the existence of homographs, words with identical written forms which have different meanings. If the comparison is carried out entirely on the basis of the strings making up the units items will be counted together despite their differing roles in the text.

As an example, the *Frankenstein* text contains 64 occurrences of the word *place* according to the word frequency list already described. On closer examination, 33 of these occurrences have the various meanings of the noun *place*, 26 of them form part of the verb *take place*, 4 form part of the verb *give place* and 1 represents the verb *place*. These distinctions are completely hidden by the counting process used in the production of the frequency list.

The other main problem arising from the basis of identity generally used in frequency lists is complementary to this blurring of distinctions between separate lexical items, and one aspect of it has already been described in the consideration of lemmatised lists in section 1.2.3 above. As an example of this problem the 26 occurrences of *place* in the *Frankenstein* text, already referred to in the previous paragraph, which form part of the verb *take place*, actually occur in the context of the following word forms, which are counted separately by the frequency list:

take	7
taken	13
takes	1
took	5

A similar but rather more specialised problem arises when dealing with texts which contain significant spelling variation, such as the Chaucer text described at the beginning of Chapter 1. Most modern samples of a single language variety follow standardised spelling systems, but the problem would be likely to arise in a collection of English texts produced by learners of the language, or one which contained both British and American forms of English, and not only in texts representing older, less standardised forms of English. As with the lemma problem, the variant forms of the same word would be counted separately unless the texts were given special processing.

2.3. Possible solutions

For most of the problems described in section 2.2 above there is a choice of approaches: either the processing which produces the frequency list can be modified in some way, so that problematic elements in the text are dealt with properly; or the text is modified in some way so that normal processing will handle it adequately.

2.3.1. Changing the processing

Unless you are writing the software yourself, or it is in a form in which you can alter the appropriate part of its operation, this will not be a possible option. Under these circumstances you will have to try to deal with the problem by making alterations to the text, and possible ways of doing this are discussed in the next section. If there is scope for changing the way in which the frequency list is produced, you will first need to make sure that you understand enough of the logic of the part of the processing being considered for alteration to appreciate the effects of the changes you are about to make. It is only possible to give very general guidance here.

If there is a problem in the definition of the two character sets – those within words and those between them – it should be possible to find the point in the software at which this distinction is defined and alter the basis of the distinction. In some word frequency programs this may not involve any changes to the software, since there may be a facility for setting new character

set definitions to allow for texts which contain special characters. The redefi-
nition of individual boundary characters will not, by itself, deal with the problems arising from the ambiguous uses described above, but if you are designing
the software from scratch you may decide to incorporate an algorithm that
tests the implications of something like the character "'", probably by examining the next character along in the text.

The recognition of phrases is a rather more complex business and the
frequency list program may not be the best place to deal with it. If you need
some form of automatic phrase recognition for your research, and can find or
write software which works adequately for your needs, it would probably be
better to adapt this software to provide some form of automatic mark-up
within the text, which could then be interpreted by the word frequency software so that it can count the units properly. The development of software
capable of recognising phrases in unmarked text would be a significant
research project in its own right, and would probably use frequency lists based
on single words as its starting-point.

The disambiguation of homographs, so that different meanings of the same
character string can be considered separately, is a complex matter. As a general
problem undermining the efficiency of automated natural language understanding systems, it still forms one of the main unrealised objectives of
researchers in that area. The context surrounding the individual word forms is
normally used as the basis for investigation, and in some cases it might be
possible to identify the main senses on the basis of other key words within the
immediate environment of the word itself. The formulation of software to
achieve this for a specific type of text is beyond the scope of this book
(although it is discussed a little further in Chapter 5), but if you were able to
develop it or to find existing software which was adequate for your purposes,
it would probably be best to use it on the text before applying the frequency
list software. The disambiguation algorithms could be use to apply distinguishing mark-up codes, and these could then be recognised by the frequency
list program so that the different meanings would be counted separately.

Automatic lemmatisation works reasonably well – it is used to rearrange
the word lists produced from COBUILD's Bank of English – and the recognition
of spelling variations is not entirely intractable, as section 2 of Chapter 8
shows. The best way to incorporate such algorithms into your own research is
probably to use them as a form of post-processing, which can be applied to a
frequency list produced using normal string comparisons. This has the twin
advantages of separating the mechanics of list production from the recognition
of like items, and restricting the processing to be carried out by the recognition algorithms. The simple layout of an appropriately sorted frequency list is
likely to cause fewer processing problems than the more complex form of the
original text. To use the algorithms in this way you would need to incorporate
them into a program which rearranged the original list, or else marked it so

that it could easily be rearranged by routine sorting. The most significant problem with this approach is likely to be the availability of recognition algorithms which are adequate for your purposes, and if you need great accuracy you may be better using the approach described in the next section.

2.3.2. Changing the text

The approaches suggested in the last section probably seem very attractive, because they enable the computer to deal with the problems automatically, and should make more efficient use of resources. But it is important to remember that the development of new software can in itself demand significant resources, and you must make sure that you are not going to spend more time attempting to develop an automatic process than you would spend doing the job manually. Before making the decision, you need to carry out a proper comparison of costs and benefits. If manual text mark-up or alteration is possible for the texts you are using and is likely to be more efficient, it is obviously a better approach, unless the development of the software which would perform the same tasks automatically is part of the point of your research. In many cases, of course, the scale of the project will make a manual approach impossible. If this is the case, and adequate software cannot be made available, you will need to consider the possible implications of any inaccuracy that will be introduced into your results.

The problems of character set definition, identification of phrases and homograph disambiguation need to be dealt with by altering the text or marking it up before the frequency list program is run, while the problems of lemmatisation and spelling variation can be tackled by rearranging the list once it has been produced. In both cases, the string-searching facilities of text editors and word processors are likely to be a great help. Any mark-up codes used must, of course, be recognisable by the frequency list software you are using.

2.4. Other linguistic units

So far I have assumed that frequency lists will use the single word as a basis, although the complications discussed above may alter this slightly. In practice, you may want to produce frequency lists based on other units of language. If so, two stages of processing will probably be needed:

- identifying the units and marking them in the text
- producing the frequency list based on the marked units.

The first stage may be either manual or computerised, depending on the nature of the problem. You may want to identify and count some of the phrasal structures within a text in addition to single words. If the phrases were fixed sequences of words, such as the phrases *of course*, *in due course* or *all in good time*, with no variation at all, a simple program could be written which would find these sequences in the original text and join the individual words of the phrase together.

As an example, the phrase *take place* occurs several times in the *Frankenstein* text. These are the original lines of the text file which contain the phrase, allowing for the combination of *place* with the whole range of possible forms of the verb *take*:

> hoping that some change would take place in the atmosphere and weather.
> takes place in science and mechanics, I was encouraged to hope my
> has taken place since you left us. The blue lake and snow-clad
> around me. Since you left us, but one change has taken place in
> change had taken place; but a thousand little circumstances
> open country. A great fall of snow had taken place the night before,
> that joy had taken place of sadness in the countenances of my friends.
> "The Turk allowed this intimacy to take place and encouraged the hopes
> taken place since I awoke into life. My attention at this time was
> "For some days I haunted the spot where these scenes had taken place,
> union with Elizabeth should take place immediately on my return.
> If this journey had taken place during my days of study and
> coincidences that had taken place during this eventful night;
> scenes that had taken place in Ireland and never alluded to them
> certainly take place. We were affectionate playfellows during
> Well, be it so; a deadly struggle would then assuredly take place,
> and terror to you the day after our marriage shall take place,
> that if my cousin would consent, the ceremony should take place
> Great God! what a scene has just taken place! I am yet dizzy

A very simple text manipulation program, described in Appendix 3, can replace the space in these phrases by some other symbol, in this case the underscore:

> hoping that some change would take_place in the atmosphere and weather.
> takes_place in science and mechanics, I was encouraged to hope my
> has taken_place since you left us. The blue lake and snow-clad
> around me. Since you left us, but one change has taken_place in
> change had taken_place; but a thousand little circumstances
> open country. A great fall of snow had taken_place the night before,
> that joy had taken_place of sadness in the countenances of my friends.
> "The Turk allowed this intimacy to take_place and encouraged the hopes
> taken_place since I awoke into life. My attention at this time was
> "For some days I haunted the spot where these scenes had taken_place,
> union with Elizabeth should take_place immediately on my return.
> If this journey had taken_place during my days of study and
> coincidences that had taken_place during this eventful night;

scenes that had taken_place in Ireland and never alluded to them
certainly take_place. We were affectionate playfellows during
Well, be it so; a deadly struggle would then assuredly take_place,
and terror to you the day after our marriage shall take_place,
that if my cousin would consent, the ceremony should take_place
Great God! what a scene has just taken_place! I am yet dizzy

Once this identification has been carried out the frequency list program
needs to be set so that it does not treat the symbol used for joining the phrase
components together as a word boundary. The identification process is obviously fairly easy in this case because of the simple nature of the phrase, with
no intervening words and almost no variation in form. More complex examples may require manual or manually assisted processing.

Frequency lists are also likely to be based on units other than individual
words in the case of tagged or parsed texts. The nature of tagging and parsing
and the further possibilities that they can create are dealt with in Chapter 6.

3. SUMMARY

The frequency list is a powerful tool for carrying out the initial survey of a
corpus. It can be produced in a variety of sequences to suit the particular
emphases of the research and can be applied to words or to other linguistic
units. It can be particularly helpful in the selection of items for further investigation through concordance listings or other techniques. A wide variety of
existing software is available for producing frequency lists, and programs can
be constructed fairly easily if your special requirements demand it or if you
need to ensure that you have full control over the basis of list production.

4. EXERCISES

1. You want to produce a word frequency list from a set of texts which
    includes the following passage, which is typical of the set as a whole:

    > After the man from the B.B.C. had left, Mario threw his glass at the
    > wall in a rage. It shattered, and wine stained the dining-room carpet.
    >   "They can't do this! They're not getting away with it!"
    >   "So what are you going to do about it?" drawled Erica. "You heard
    > what he said – 'We've got you where we want you. We're in complete
    > control'". She imitated the strange squeaky voice of the minor exec-
    > utive. "Face it. It's all over."

    Which characters should form the word boundaries in your program?
    Are there any problems with your choice?

2. The extract given below is from a word frequency list arranged in alpha-
    betical order:

abhominable	1	abreggynge	1	accepteth	3
abhomynable	6	abreyde	2	accident	2
abhomynacion	1	abroche	1	accidental	1
abhomynacions	1	abrood	1	accidie	18
abhomynacioun	1	absalon	1	acciouns	2
abiden	1	absence	7	accomplice	3
abideth	2	absent	2	accompliced	3
abidyng	2	absolon	30	accompte	1
abidynge	1	absolucion	1	accord	12
able	17	abstinence	9	accordant	2
ablucions	1	abstinent	1	accorde	6
ably	1	abusioun	2	accorded	5
aboght	2	abyd	2	accorden	1
aboghte	1	abyden	2	accordeth	3
abood	1	abydeth	1	accordynge	1
aboughte	1	abye	4	accuse	1
abouten	5	abyen	1	accused	1
above	44	abygail	1	accusen	3
aboven	16	ac	2	accusest	1
abowndone	1	acceptable	1	accusynge	1
abrayde	1	accepte	4	achaat	1
abregge	5	accepted	1	achatours	1

What problems would you face in lemmatising the list manually?

3. These are the top fifteen lines of a frequency list produced for the rhyming schemes of nursery rhymes (from the project described in section 4 of Chapter 1). 'X' represents long complex schemes which do not fit a straightforward pattern, such as the cumulative rhyme 'This is the house that Jack built'. What would you do to investigate further?

ABCB	132	AAAA	20	AABC	7
AABB	125	AABBCC	19	AAAB	6
ABAB	43	AA	15	ABCCB	6
AABCCB	31	AABA	13	AABCB	5
X	31	AABBA	13	ABBA	5

FURTHER READING

Clear, J. (1987) 'Computing', in J. Sinclair (ed.), *Looking Up*, London: Collins ELT, Ch. 2 (pp. 41–61).

Renouf, A. (1992) 'What do you think of that? A pilot study of the phraseology of the core words in English', G. Leitner (ed.), *New Directions in English Language Corpora*, Berlin: Mouton de Gruyter, pp. 301–17.

Sinclair, J. (1991) *Corpus, Concordance, Collocation*, Oxford: Oxford University Press, Ch. 2 (pp. 27–36).

Studying the environment:
using concordances

1. SEEING WORDS IN CONTEXT

The great benefit of the frequency lists described in Chapter 3 is their ability to separate the words in a text from each other so that the texts are reduced to summaries of their components. This allows you to consider the general profile of the words making up the texts, but you lose the contextual information which would show you the full nature of those words. The concordance provides a simple way of placing each word back in its original context, so that the details of its use and behaviour can be properly examined. This chapter describes the usual features of concordance programs and their output and the benefits and problems involved in using them as a basic part of your language analysis toolbox.

1.1. Exploring texts

Every research project which uses texts as a basis for investigating features of language will have its own special needs and methodology, but they will probably all share certain characteristics. The texts are usually being used as evidence that certain linguistic units within them behave in a particular way. Where the units involved are individual words, the evidence being sought could relate to their syntactic or semantic behaviour, spelling, pronunciation, and so on. In almost all cases, the context in which each word is found will almost certainly need to be included in the investigation. As an example of the use of a concordance program to provide access to this context, I want to take some of the thematically related items which were selected from the *Frankenstein* frequency list in section 1.2.4(a) of Chapter 3.

1.2. The use of frequency lists for selecting items

The items listed in Chapter 3 were picked from the frequency list because they could be used as labels for the organism created by Victor Frankenstein. The frequency list is very useful as a means of isolating words from the surrounding detail of the text so that they can be surveyed in this way, but the lack of this detail also prevents us from seeing precisely how these potential labels are actually used. This may seem slightly paradoxical, but you must remember that the frequency list is only the first stage in the exploration of the text. It is important to strip the words of their surrounding context so that we can concentrate on them as individual words and make decisions based on their potential linguistic behaviour. Once the selections have been made the next stages of the exploration must be carried out back in the words' original textual environments. The concordance program allows you to find the words you have selected in this environment, and to explore the ways in which they relate to the other words around them.

The original list contained the words:

being	enemy
horror	beings
creature	creation
fiend	daemon
monster	thing
creatures	devil
wretch	

Some of these, like *fiend, monster, daemon* and *devil*, seem to be intrinsically negative. Others, such as *being, creature* and *creation* (and their plural forms, where they are also included) have a more neutral feel to them. It is not certain yet, of course, that any of these words is used in the way that has been suggested: only the context can confirm that. The frequency list has simply provided a way of focusing the investigation.

1.3. The use of concordance lines
Once the words have been selected the concordance program can be used to show their context. As an example, here are the first 20 lines extracted (using MicroConcord, written by Mike Scott and Tim Johns and published by Oxford University Press) for the word *being*:

```
1   felt myself peculiarly fortunate in being able to secure his services. I heard
2   iend reassured the suppliant, and on being informed of the name of her lover, in
3   less seas, the very stars themselves being witnesses and testimonies of my trium
4   h, at the distance of half a mile; a being which had the shape of a man, but app
5   emained alive; but there was a human being within it whom the sailors were persu
6   a noble creature in his better days, being even now in wreck so attractive and a
7   , he appeared to despise himself for being the slave of passion; and quelling th
8   usness of what they owed towards the being to which they had given life, added t
9   of a vale attracted their notice as being singularly disconsolate, while the nu
10  g on her as of a distinct species, a being heaven-sent, and bearing a celestial
11  ght. On the evening previous to her  being brought to my home, my mother had sai
```

```
12 the hands of the infidels. No human    being could have passed a happier childhood
13 tudy appertaining to that science as being built upon secure foundations, and so
14  Henry deeply felt the misfortune of being debarred from a liberal education. He
15 hed which formed the mechanism of my being;chord after chord was sounded, and s
16 not my eyes that night. My internal   being was in a state of insurrection and tu
17 rs at Ingolstadt, my residence there being no longer conducive to my improvement
18 bodies deprived of life, which, from being the seat of beauty and strength, had
19 r I should attempt the creation of a being like myself, or one of simpler organi
20 that I began the creation of a human being.As the minuteness of the parts form
```

This example shows the main features of this type of concordance. Each occurrence of the word *being* in the text is shown in the centre of each line, surrounded by a fixed number of characters of its original context. In this case each line is 80 characters long, including the word which was used as the basis for the production of the concordance, often referred to as the **search-word** or **keyword**. The 'Keyword in Context' (or KWIC) concordance is not the only possible form, but it is the most commonly used. Section 2.2 describes other possible contexts. In many KWIC programs (including the software used to produce this listing) the extent of the context either side of the keyword is variable.

The other main feature of the set of lines shown is that they are arranged in their original order of occurrence within the original text file. Concordance programs are often equipped with sophisticated built-in sort facilities which allow the lines to be rearranged into alternative sequences. The use of alternative sequences is discussed in more detail in section 2.4.

Definite patterns emerge from a detailed examination of the concordance lines for *being*. We are investigating possible uses of the word as a label for Frankenstein's creation, which means that we are only interested in it if it is used as a noun. Lines 1 to 3, 6, 7, 9, 11, 13, 14, 17 and 18 are all verbal uses, and can be disregarded. If the same exercise is repeated over all 97 of the occurrences of *being*, 50 of them can be discarded in this way by a brief examination of the concordance lines. In a similar way, it can be seen from the context that the occurrences in lines 5, 10, 12, 15 and 16 do not apply to Frankenstein's creation. This leaves lines 4, 8, 19 and 20 as possible references from this brief extract:

```
4  h, at the distance of half a mile; a being which had the shape of a man, but app
8  usness of what they owed towards the being to which they had given life, added t
19 r I should attempt the creation of a being like myself, or one of simpler organi
20 that I began the creation of a human being. As the minuteness of the parts form
```

If the same exercise is repeated for all the noun uses of *being* it leaves 30 lines which seem worthy of further investigation. In many cases the 80 character context provided by the concordance line is not quite enough to identify the use completely, and the options within the program for exploring a wider stretch of surrounding text would need to be invoked. A similar approach could then be used for all of the other words in the list. The information provided by the relevant concordance lines should enable you to carry out a detailed comparison between the possible terms.

The ability to distinguish uses of individual words in this way from their context is the basis of the use of concordance information. The examples used in the description of the normal features of concordance software in section 2 below are intended to suggest possible approaches to the interpretation of the output and to introduce you to the features of concordance software which make these approaches easier.

2. CONCORDANCE SOFTWARE

This section describes the range of approaches that can be adopted in the design of a concordance program. Several excellent concordance software packages are currently available, and it is quite likely that one of these would be suitable for all but the most demanding research purposes, so that you are relatively unlikely to need to write your own software. Despite this, it is important to understand the operating methods of the software available for your selection to ensure that you choose wisely, or, in extreme cases, that you correctly identify the need for a specially written program.

The two main tasks that a concordance program needs to perform are:

● finding all the occurrences of the keyword in the texts

● presenting the results of the search in an appropriate format.

Section 2.1 describes the main alternative approaches for the first of these tasks, and sections 2.2 to 2.6 describe the main options commonly found for the second.

2.1. Finding keywords

The choice of methods for finding occurrences of keywords in their texts is generally made on the basis of processing efficiency. Most of the commercial concordance programs involve a pre-processing stage which indexes all of the words in the text. In other words, the text is analysed into individual words in a similar way to the approach used for the creation of a frequency list, and a file is created which contains a list of all the words found together with a note of the location of each occurrence within the original text file. In some cases the original text is no longer used, but is replaced by a database containing all of the original text plus structural information designed to optimise the search routines. The details of the organisational methods adopted are not important, but you need to assess the relative advantages and disadvantages of this approach within your own project.

The indexing approach should allow faster processing times, since the index file will be smaller and easier to search than the original text file. Concordance software which uses this technique may also generate frequency lists as a by-product, so avoiding the need for separate software. The main disadvantages arise from the need for pre-processing. This introduces an extra stage into the operation, and may be inconvenient if the text needs to be changed. Changes are sometimes needed to correct errors which are revealed by the exploration process, and any alterations will probably involve the complete re-indexing of the text file. This can take a significant amount of time where large texts are involved, but the saving in processing time in the search for keywords will also be most marked when dealing with large texts.

It is of course possible to index the text file on the basis of units other than words. More sophisticated concordance programs often allow you to describe the mark-up codes used within your corpus so that the information contained in them can be incorporated in the database. This can be particularly useful where the texts in a corpus have a significant structure, which can then be reflected in the concordance output. For example, the ability to incorporate references to acts, scenes and characters can be useful in corpora based on the texts of dramas.

If your specialised processing needs mean that you need to develop your own software, searching methods based on the original unindexed text files will be much easier to design. Any resulting slowness of operation will need to be set against the cost of developing more sophisticated programs.

2.2. Types of context

The method of presentation already mentioned in section 1.3 above – the Key Word in Context (or KWIC) – forms the standard display option in many general-purpose concordance packages. The overwhelming advantage of this format is the ease with which it can be read and with which changes in the context can be detected. The central block of the display, occupied by the keyword, seems to keep the reader's eye in the best position for scanning the lines and noting context patterns. The example shown in section 1.3 shows how this works. In that example the lines are arranged in the order of their occurrence in the original text files: the example in section 2.4 below shows how the effect is intensified if the lines are sorted on some part of the imme-diate context.

Despite these advantages of the basic KWIC layout, other extents and forms of context may occasionally be more appropriate, and many concordance packages include among their display options:

- variable length KWIC format

- sentence context

- paragraph context

- whole text browsing.

The first of these simply allows adjustment of the size of the stretch of text within which the keyword is centred. Restrictions caused by display sizes may make it impossible to see the entire context on the screen at one time, and the program will often allow the line to be 'scrolled' horizontally, so that both ends of the context can be read. Once it is printed out the data is easier to cope with, and context lengths of over 160 characters can be accommodated in a fairly legible form while preserving the central position of the keyword, which makes it so much easier to read the lines.

Sentence and paragraph context simply place the keyword in the sentence or paragraph in which it occurs. The boundaries of the sentence or paragraph are normally obtained from an examination of the text. This may seem a more strictly linguistic arrangement than any based simply on context length, but interactions between words often operate beyond sentence and paragraph boundaries, and the use of these divisions may prejudge important questions of the nature of textual organisation.

The facility for browsing the whole text – moving backwards and forwards from the point of occurrence of the keyword – allows access to as much context as you may need for checking the details of word usage. Unlike the other three options, this one is only available as an interactive process on the screen, but in some packages it may be possible to select the stretch of text which interests you and print it out.

2.3. Keyword specification

The concept of the keyword in concordance programs has been assumed, so far, to be straightforward. A string of characters is input to the concordance program as the pattern to be searched for, and concordance lines are produced for occurrences of that string and that string only. In practice, things are rarely so simple. For one thing, most words are capable of occurring at the beginning of a sentence with an initial upper case letter. For another, if the word is a noun or a verb, you may be as interested in occurrences of its other possible forms as you are in the base form. To allow you to deal with problems like these as conveniently as possible, concordance software often includes facilities for adjusting its pattern–matching characteristics, and the options most commonly found are described in the following two sections.

2.3.1. Case sensitivity

The problem of upper case letters in text handling has already been mentioned in the description of frequency lists (see Chapter 3, section 2.2.3). Because it is generally assumed that you would want to ignore case in searching for a particular keyword, most concordance software is set up so that insensitivity to case – for example recognising *the* and *The* as the same word – is the standard procedure. However, because there are times when case sensitivity is needed – perhaps in the exploration of proper names – this can normally be selected as a separate option.

2.3.2. Multiple keyword patterns

The ability to search for multiple forms of a word is usually provided either through some form of wild card symbol or, in more sophisticated systems, as a facility for specifying the keyword as a regular expression. These terms may need a little more explanation to bring out the similarities and differences between them.

2.3.2(a) Wild cards In the case of many nouns and verbs in English, forms other than the base form are made up of a word stem which does not alter, to which various endings are added in a regular system of morphology. For example, the plural of *tree* is *trees*. A wild card symbol allows this regularity to be exploited by replacing part of the keyword with a symbol which is interpreted by the software as meaning any other character or characters. If the symbol were '*' (as it often is), entering the keyword *part** would make the concordance program find all words which began with the letter sequence *part*. This would obviously include the plural form *parts*. Similarly, if the keyword entered were *enter** the forms *enter*, *enters*, *entering* and *entered* would all be searched for. This could be a useful way of finding the other relevant forms of a word, although it does suffer from a certain crudeness of approach.

As an example, the output produced by using the keyword *part** in a search of the *Frankenstein* text includes the following lines:

```
the cottage had formerly occupied a part of it, but the panes had been filled u
my arms, hastened towards the deeper parts of the wood. I followed speedily, I
```

Overall the concordance list contains 39 occurrences of *part* and 3 of *parts*. However, it also contains the following lines:

```
I cannot do in your absence." Having parted from my friend, I determined to visi
udgement from heaven to chastise her partiality. She was a Roman Catholic; and
philosopher knew little more. He had partially unveiled the face of Nature, but
urn to my native country. I did not  participate in these feelings, for to me th
eing overflowed, that I wished to be participated. But now that virtue has beco
r house at Belrive. This change was  particularly agreeable to me. The shutting
o understanding; I had forgotten the particulars of what had happened and only f
hey proceeded to search the country, parties going in different directions among
ilosophy. I replied carelessly, and  partly in contempt, mentioned the names of
irteen years of age we all went on a party of pleasure to the baths near Thonon;
```

Together these non-relevant lines account for 28 lines in a total set of 70, of which only 42 represent the words which were actually required. Similarly, using *enter** as the keyword produces rather more output than you would want. The first ten lines produced for this keyword from the *Frankenstein* text are:

```
1  s accompanied the commencement of an enterprise which you have regarded with suc
2  ich I dedicated myself to this great enterprise. I commenced by inuring my body
3  et a second step is taken towards my enterprise. I have hired a vessel and am o
4  e, is a man of wonderful courage and enterprise; he is madly desirous of glory,
```

```
5   I easily engaged him to assist in my enterprise. The master is a person of an e
6    whom the sailors were persuading to enter the vessel. He was not, as the other
7   ars uneasy when anyone except myself enters his cabin. Yet his manners are so c
8   unicated to him without disguise. He entered attentively into all my arguments i
9   every hope, to the furtherance of my enterprise. One man's life or death were b
10  street near the Reuss. But when he    entered, misery and despair alone welcomed
```

There are lines for *enter* (6), *entered* (8 and 10) and *enters*, but it has also retrieved *enterprise* (1 to 5 and 9). Other lines in the output contain *entering*, but they also contain *entertain* and *entertained*.

Many concordance programs allow the use of wild cards to be fine-tuned to reduce the scale of this problem. In the program used to produce these concordance lines there is an alternative wild card symbol, '?', which can be used to represent a single occurrence of any character. If *part?* is used as the keyword instead of *part**, it produces only 45 lines of output. 42 of these are the desired forms *part* and *parts*, and the other three are occurrences of the word *party*. To make the search still more accurate, a more sophisticated form of pattern specification is needed.

2.3.2(b) Regular expressions Regular expressions are a more highly developed form of the wild card approach. They are widely used in many areas of computing, and the facilities available in concordance programs are often modified versions of more general notation systems. At their simplest level they may allow the entry of alternative keywords. In the example described above in which the various forms of the verb *enter* were needed, you would simply key in all of the forms required. So that the program can recognise that all of these forms are needed some special form of separator will be used for the list. In the MicroConcord program, used for the output examples used in this chapter, the list for the verb forms of *enter* would be:

enter\enters\entering\entered

The use of this pattern successfully retrieves all occurrences of the forms of the verb *enter* without the unwanted lines described in the previous section. In some concordance packages the regular expression notation is more versatile and can specify a wider range of patterns in a more efficient form, which often imitates the general notations used in other programs. More complex specification systems use **metacharacters**, a development of the wild card, to specify the relationships between different elements of the pattern. Because these metacharacters vary from one package to another you will need to read the manual carefully to discover how they are used within the software you are using. As an example of a possible format, here is the specification of the forms of *enter* listed above in the regular expression notation used in the programming language awk and in many standard Unix utilities:

^enter(s|ing|ed)?$

This pattern specifies that the string must begin (^) with *enter*, followed by zero or one (?) occurrences of one of the alternatives (separated by |) enclosed within the parentheses (), and that this must then form the end of the string ($). In this expression the symbols '^', '(', '|', ')' and '$' are all metacharacters and describe the relationship between the other characters in the string.

2.4. Sorting options

When a keyword has a large number of occurrences it may be difficult to detect patterns in the set of concordance lines as it comes from the text files. Many concordance packages include a sorting facility so that the sequence of concordance lines output to the screen or a file can be altered to suit the investigation that you are performing. The range of options available in a particular package varies, but the basis of ordering of the output could include the following:

- the sequence in which the lines occurred in the original texts

- the keyword, for cases where wild cards or regular expressions are used

- a word which appears a specified number of words to the right or left of a keyword

- a category allocated by the user after the lines have been extracted.

One of these sequences will probably form the default option, and the others may be available interactively, so that lines are rearranged while you wait and displayed on the screen in their new order, or as part of a file or printer output facility. The choice of sequence for the concordance lines will be dictated by your research needs, but it is possible to make some general points.

2.4.1. Order of occurrence

Arranging the lines in their order of occurrence within the original text is useful if, for example, you wish to investigate changes of usage patterns in different sections of the text. It would be possible to annotate the list so that it is divided into the sections which you want to compare, and then to examine any differences of usage between them. In some programs this is the default sequence, and it is likely to be the initial order in which output is produced if you develop your own concordance software.

2.4.2. Keyword sequence

Keyword sequence is extremely useful where multiple keywords have been specified by the use of wild cards or other regular expressions. As an example of its potential, here are the first 20 lines produced from the *Frankenstein* text by using *enter**★** as the keyword, as already mentioned in section 2.3.2(a) above:

```
 1  s accompanied the commencement of an enterprise which you have regarded with suc
 2  ich I dedicated myself to this great enterprise. I commenced by inuring my body
 3  et a second step is taken towards my enterprise. I have hired a vessel and am o
 4  e, is a man of wonderful courage and enterprise; he is madly desirous of glory,
 5  I easily engaged him to assist in my enterprise. The master is a person of an e
 6   whom the sailors were persuading to enter the vessel. He was not, as the other
 7  ars uneasy when anyone except myself enters his cabin. Yet his manners are so c
 8  unicated to him without disguise. He entered attentively into all my arguments i
 9  every hope, to the furtherance of my enterprise. One man's life or death were b
10   street near the Reuss. But when he  entered, misery and despair alone welcomed
11  fin weeping bitterly, when my father  entered the chamber. He came like a protec
12  nevolent disposition often made them enter the cottages of the poor. This, to m
13  singular talent and fancy. He loved  enterprise, hardship, and even danger for i
14  He tried to make us act plays and to enter into masquerades, in which the charac
15  hat seemed to keep human beings from entering the citadel of nature, and rashly
16   the guidance of my new preceptors I entered with the greatest diligence into th
17   and excited by this catastrophe, he entered on the explanation of a theory whic
18   deformed and abortive creation, and entertained the greatest disdain for a woul
19  ed up in one place and had longed to enter the world and take my station among o
20  the lecturing room, which M. Waldman entered shortly after. This professor was v
```

Because the different keywords are jumbled together it is difficult to tell which lines are relevant and which are not. If the lines are ordered by keyword the position becomes much clearer. Here are some extracts from the complete set of 80 occurrences, ordered by keyword, showing the division of the list into blocks of the same keyword form. The numbering in the leftmost column indicates the position in the re-ordered list:

```
 1  He tried to make us act plays and to enter into masquerades, in which the charac
 2  to laugh and talk with strangers or  enter into their feelings or plans with the
                            . . .
20     in a few minutes before the fire.'"`Enter,' said De Lacey, `and I will try in w
21  on her knees. She rose on seeing us  enter, and when we were left alone with her
22  the young woman joined him and they  entered the cottage together. "The old man
23  to complete the negotiation they had entered into for his Indian enterprise. He
                            . . .
58  curiosity. Finding the door open, I  entered. An old man sat in it, near a fire
59  t. While I was thus engaged, Ernest  entered: he had heard me arrive, and haste
60  ath them. Thus I returned home, and  entering the house, presented myself to the
61  tep on the white plain. To you first entering on life, to whom care is new and a
                            . . .
64  e of either journeying to England or entering into a long correspondence with th
65  o prevent her but she persisted, and entering the room where it lay, hastily exa
66  s accompanied the commencement of an enterprise which you have regarded with suc
67  singular talent and fancy. He loved  enterprise, hardship, and even danger for i
                            . . .
74  I easily engaged him to assist in my enterprise. The master is a person of an e
75  e, is a man of wonderful courage and enterprise; he is madly desirous of glory,
76  ars uneasy when anyone except myself enters his cabin. Yet his manners are so c
77  der. But as brother and sister often entertain a lively affection towards each o
78  kindness and gentleness which I had  entertained but a few moments before gave p
79  deformed and abortive creation, and  entertained the greatest disdain for a woul
80  tioned in my last letter the fears I entertained of a mutiny. This morning, as I
```

In this sequence the set of concordance lines is much more easily read because of the separation of the individual word forms.

2.4.3. Other words in the concordance lines

Where there is a large number of occurrences of a keyword the context needs to be examined to distinguish different usages. Many packages allow sorting by specified words of the context to facilitate this process. As an example of the potential value of this sequence here are the first 20 lines from the *Frankenstein* text containing the word *entered* arranged in their original sequence:

```
1   nicated to him without disguise. He entered attentively into all my arguments in
2   street near the Reuss. But when he  entered, misery and despair alone welcomed h
3   in weeping bitterly, when my father entered the chamber. He came like a protect
4   the guidance of my new preceptors I entered with the greatest diligence into the
5   and excited by this catastrophe, he entered on the explanation of a theory which
6   he lecturing room, which M. Waldman entered shortly after. This professor was ve
7   ber on what occasion Justine Moritz entered our family? Probably you do not; I
8   as about five in the morning when I  entered my father's house. I told the servan
9   . While I was thus engaged, Ernest  entered: he had heard me arrive, and hasten
10  nnocent." At that instant my father entered. I saw unhappiness deeply impressed
11  an appearance of courage. When she  entered the court she threw her eyes round i
12  to me, yet I could not refuse. We   entered the gloomy prison chamber and beheld
13  n that overhangs it. Soon after, I  entered the valley of Chamounix. This valley
14  the rain again began to descend; we entered the hut, the fiend with an air of ex
15  uriosity. Finding the door open, I  entered. An old man sat in it, near a fire,
16  petite. One of the best of these I  entered, but I had hardly placed my foot wit
17  t it was dry; and although the wind entered it by innumerable chinks, I found it
18  the young woman joined him and they entered the cottage together. "The old man h
19  ndured in the first village which I  entered. "My days were spent in close attent
20  andate. "A few days after, the Turk entered his daughter's apartment and told he
```

A close examination of these lines shows that in some cases the keyword is used without a direct object, as in lines 2 and 9, while in others the direct object follows immediately, as in lines 3 and 7. If the first word to the right of the keyword is used as the basis for sorting, the patterns become slightly easier to identify. Here is the complete set of lines containing the keyword sorted in this way:

```
1   ing a more secluded hiding-place, I entered a barn which had appeared to me to b
2   uriosity. Finding the door open, I  entered. An old man sat in it, near a fire,
3   nded admission into the cabin. They entered, and their leader addressed me. He
4   nicated to him without disguise. He entered attentively into all my arguments in
5   petite. One of the best of these I  entered, but I had hardly placed my foot wit
6   . While I was thus engaged, Ernest  entered: he had heard me arrive, and hasten
7   andate. "A few days after, the Turk entered his daughter's apartment and told he
8   apartment was opened and Mr. Kirwin entered. His countenance expressed sympathy
9   nnocent" " At that instant my father entered. I saw unhappiness deeply impressed
10  o complete the negotiation they had entered into for his Indian enterprise. He c
11   but pausing near the cottage, they entered into conversation, using violent ges
12  t it was dry; and although the wind entered it by innumerable chinks, I found it
13  lizabeth, and my father reposed. I  entered it and approached the tomb which mar
```

```
14  my nurse, and in a moment my father entered it. Nothing, at this moment, could h
15  street near the Reuss. But when he  entered, misery and despair alone welcomed h
16  which I had received. The ball had  entered my shoulder, and I knew not whether
17  t I am a blasted tree; the bolt has entered my soul; and I felt then that I shou
18  as about five in the morning when I  entered my father's house. I told the servan
19  at town and a good harbour, which I entered, my heart bounding with joy at my un
20  ndured in the first village which I  entered. "My days were spent in close attent
21  and excited by this catastrophe, he entered on the explanation of a theory which
22  ber on what occasion Justine Moritz entered our family? Probably you do not; I
23  ?' said the old man. `Come in.' "I  entered. `Pardon this intrusion,' said I; †`
24  he lecturing room, which M. Waldman entered shortly after. This professor was ve
25  o the consequences of the affair. I entered the room where the corpse lay and wa
26  I paused to collect myself and then entered the chamber. With trembling hand I
27   final and wonderful catastrophe. I  entered the cabin where lay the remains of m
28   to me, yet I could not refuse. We  entered the gloomy prison chamber and beheld
29  n that overhangs it. Soon after, I  entered the valley of Chamounix. This valley
30  the rain again began to descend; we entered the hut, the fiend with an air of ex
31  an appearance of courage. When she  entered the court she threw her eyes round i
32  in weeping bitterly, when my father entered the chamber. He came like a protect
33  he said this. He and his companion  entered the cottage, in which they remained
34  the young woman joined him and they entered the cottage together. "The old man h
35  ence we proceeded to Oxford. As we  entered this city our minds were filled with
36  pened, and Felix, Safie, and Agatha entered. Who can describe their horror and
37  the guidance of my new preceptors I entered with the greatest diligence into the
38  t the anxiety that preyed there and entered with seeming earnestness into the pl
```

Although this rearrangement has not completely separated the two patterns, it has made them easier to identify in many places. In the first 11 lines, only lines 1 and 7 have a following direct object, and lines 12 to 14, 16 to 19 and 25 to 34 form coherent groups with similar structures. While this facility may not completely distinguish linguistically significant patterns, it can make them much easier to detect. It is also worth noting that the type of sorting being carried out here, which depends on the positions of individual words in the lines of text relative to the keyword, is rather difficult to achieve using standard sorting utilities. Within the concordance software, the information already held to allow the lines to be displayed properly can also be used to specify the positions of the relevant pieces of data.

2.4.4. User-allocated categories

When you use concordance output you generally distinguish keyword usage patterns within individual lines on the basis of the contextual information provided by the other words in the line. The sorting options shown so far make this process easier, but they may still leave the output sorted in a less than perfect way. Some packages allow you to make your own decisions about the categories to which individual lines belong, and to incorporate these decisions into the output as the basis for sorting it. In section 1.3 above the concordance lines for *being* in the *Frankenstein* text were considered, and it was found that out of 97 occurrences of the word only 47 were noun uses rather than verb uses. It is always rather difficult to keep track of deliberations like these unless they can be recorded somewhere, and a facility which allows you to allocate each line to a category (in this case, noun or verb) and record that fact so that the set of lines can be sorted into the categories makes the process much more reliable. In the extracts shown below, the complete set of lines for *being* has been marked in this way, so that an entry of '0' in the second column from the left represents the noun use, and an entry of '1' the verbal use, and has then been sorted according to these categories:

```
1  0  nly attempted to gain from any other being that wore the human form. "My trave
2  0  proportion. I had never yet seen a  being resembling me or who claimed any in
                                    . . .
46 0  ssion. I approached this tremendous being; I dared not again raise my eyes to
47 0  e." Must I then lose this admirable being? I have longed for a friend; I have
48 1  rsons, to the inn. I could not help being struck by the strange coincidences
49 1  eeded to consummate the series of my being and accomplish that which must be d
                                    . . .
```

Once the lines are sorted in this way it becomes much easier to check the allocation. if an error is found it can be corrected, the lines can be sorted again and the output will be much easier to use.

2.5. Output options

For most concordance programs the standard output option is the screen display, and in many cases this can be rearranged, annotated, even edited to a certain extent before it is made more permanent by choosing some other form of output. The usual options are:

● direct output to a printer

● output to a text file.

The second of these is often the most convenient, partly because the file can be manipulated through a word processor to make printing easier and more flexible, and partly because once the information is available in a text file it can be put through further processing stages. As an example, Chapter 5 describes the calculations that can be made from concordance lines to assess the significance of collocational patterns found in texts. Even if the program only has direct printer output available as an option, it is often possible to use redirection facilities within your computer's operating system to pass the information to a text file instead.

Most concordance packages allow some control over output, often including the ability to choose:

● context length, which can often be much greater than can be easily displayed on a screen

● line numbering

● text references.

Line numbering makes the location of individual occurrences much easier, and text references can range from the name of the text file from which the line was taken – useful where several files are being processed in the same run – to precise details of the position of the occurrence within its text. In order for this detailed positional information to be available it must be specified in the original text file in a form which the concordance program can process.

2.6. Other information

Some concordance packages provide other information about the texts they process in addition to the individual concordance lines. Statistics relating to the size of the file and the number of occurrences of the keyword can easily be calculated and displayed, and packages which index their texts often incorporate full frequency list provision as part of their display options. This also enables them to produce the word frequency statistics already discussed in Chapter 3. Even where these facilities are not available, particularly in packages which process unindexed texts, some information is often produced relating to **collocation** and phrase structures.

2.6.1. Collocation

Chapter 5 describes in some detail the use of concordance lines as the basic source of information for the investigation of collocation patterns. Some concordance programs carry out basic collocation calculations and can report the results in their output. In most cases the information provided is unlikely to be as detailed or as rigorous as that which can be produced by the type of full analysis described in Chapter 5, but it may provide a useful guide for further investigation.

As an example, part of the collocation information provided by a concordance program for the word *being* is shown below. This list shows all the words occurring within a distance of three words either side of *being* with a frequency greater than 10:

of	32
the	32
a	28
to	22
I	21
and	16
my	14
human	14
in	13

Little can be concluded from this, except perhaps that the word *human* may be of some significance. This is a very crude basis for assessing collocation, but it may be useful as a starting-point.

2.6.2. Identification of phrases

The identification of phrasal structures within a text can be made a great deal easier using concordance lines. In the first place, patterns which might provide evidence of the existence of phrases are likely to appear more obviously within concordance lines than in continuous text. In section 2.4.3 the concordance lines for *entered* were sorted by the word immediately to the right of the keyword. In the extract shown from the sorted output lines 10 and 11 are:

```
10  o complete the negotiation they had entered into for his Indian enterprise. He c
11   but pausing near the cottage, they entered into conversation, using violent ges
```

This suggests *entered into* as a possible phrase worth investigating. Many concordance programs have a simple option for detecting possible phrases, which allows a second word to be specified alongside the keyword. Occurrences of the keyword will only be selected for output if this word is also found within an appropriate number of words of it. Often the direction of the co-occurrence can also be specified. In this case, if *entered* is given as the keyword, with *into* as the second word to be found within five words to the right, the following output is produced:

```
1   nicated to him without disguise. He entered attentively into all my arguments in
2    but pausing near the cottage, they entered into conversation, using violent ges
3   o complete the negotiation they had entered into for his Indian enterprise. He c
4   the guidance of my new preceptors I entered with the greatest diligence into the
5   t the anxiety that preyed there and entered with seeming earnestness into the pl
```

This simple device has now revealed five occurrences of this phrase, including three which are interrupted by other text. Coupled with detailed collocation work this can provide a powerful additional tool for investigating phrasal structures.

3. USING NON-SPECIALIST UTILITIES

The example used in section 1.3 was based on concordance lines produced by a piece of commercial software specially developed for that purpose. While specially written software is almost certain to be more efficient and more flexible, it is possible to produce similar contextual information using more standard text handling utilities. This section describes the ways in which some of them can be used in the initial stages of text exploration.

3.1. Facilities within text processing programs

What the concordance program effectively does for you is to find the occurrences of the word or words you are investigating and list them out in an appropriate form. The first part of this exercise, finding the occurrences, can be achieved using the search facilities built into most text editors and word processors. As an example, the word processor that I used to write this book has a facility which will find the next occurrence of any word that you type in, moving either up or down the text, as you decide, from your current position. Once the next occurrence has been found the search-word is highlighted within its surrounding text. You can explore the context, and, if you wish, copy an appropriate part of it to another file to build up your own concordance list. The procedures are not automated as they are in a dedicated concordance program, and the process of building up the list is likely to take far longer, but there may be some small advantages.

In the first place, you will probably already have access to word processing software and no extra expense will be incurred. If the use of the concordance program is likely to be fairly small scale this may be an important consideration. If the text contains a large number of special characters there may be a more significant benefit. If the word processor can handle the special characters for text input and editing, its search utility should be able to handle them equally well. This would give you the chance to use texts prepared using the word processor directly, without any further processing to convert them into plain text format.

These benefits are unlikely to outweigh the difficulties imposed by the lack of automation for anything other than the smallest scale of investigation, but the approach may be useful in the preliminary stages of a project, especially if the word processor has a macro facility which will allow you to automate some of the tasks involved.

3.2. Separate search utilities

The general text search utilities available for most computer operating systems may also be useful for preliminary investigation. They allow files to be searched for particular pieces of texts, usually displaying the line of the file which contains the specified string of characters. Many of them are extremely simple and can only be used to search for explicitly specified character strings, while more powerful utilities make it possible to search for text patterns on the basis of sophisticated regular expression descriptions.

The most powerful of these utilities can be significantly more effective in the early stages of text exploration than the search facilities built into word processors, while the simplest of them are generally rather less useful. But however powerful they are, they are unlikely to provide the same degree of help as a specialist concordance program because of their lack of control over the context supplied with the keyword or text pattern. The reasons for this are explored in the next section. A practical example of the use of a search utility in an application is described in section 3.2.3 of Chapter 8.

3.3. The nature of text files

In linguistic terms, the hierarchy of units making up a text could be summarised as:

- letters
- words
- phrases
- clauses
- sentences
- paragraphs.

A computer-readable text file has the same logical organisation, but its physical form is based on a three level hierarchy:

- characters
- words
- lines.

The last of these three units, the lines of text, do not necessarily correspond to any of the units in the language-based hierarchy, and they can be thought of as an artefact of the conversion process. In many cases, especially where text has been scanned to convert it to computer-readable form, they correspond to the lines of text in the original printed edition which was used in the text input process, but this is not necessarily the case. Line breaks may be introduced into the text simply to make it easier to handle, since some software cannot deal with lines beyond a certain length. An example showing typical line breaks in a computer text file has already been shown in section 3.2.2 of Chapter 1, which includes some discussion of the general effect of this form of file organisation on text handling.

The main implication of line breaks for the text search utilities described in the previous section is that the context that they provide is often limited to the line of text in which the pattern was found. Consider the following set of lines containing the word *being*, extracted from the *Frankenstein* text file using a version of grep, a standard text search utility. The individual occurrences of the word are the same as those shown in the concordance example in section, but the context is simply the text line in which each appears:

```
1. fortunate in being able to secure his services. I heard of him
2. My generous friend reassured the suppliant, and on being informed
3. stars themselves being witnesses and testimonies of my triumph.
4. the distance of half a mile; a being which had the shape of a man,
5. human being within it whom the sailors were persuading to enter the vessel.
6. better days, being even now in wreck so attractive and amiable.
7. despise himself for being the slave of passion; and quelling the
8. what they owed towards the being to which they had given life,
9. as being singularly disconsolate, while the number of half-clothed
10. species, a being heaven-sent, and bearing a celestial stamp in all
11. my pride and my delight. On the evening previous to her being
12. No human being could have passed a happier childhood than myself.
13. that science as being built upon secure foundations, and so worthy
14. the misfortune of being debarred from a liberal education.
```

```
15. keys were touched which formed the mechanism of my being; chord after
16. I closed not my eyes that night. My internal being was in a state
17. being no longer conducive to my improvements, I thought of returning
18. deprived of life, which, from being the seat of beauty and strength,
19. whether I should attempt the creation of a being like myself,
20. feelings that I began the creation of a human being. As the
```

Some of the complexity of concordance software lies in the need to extract the appropriate context from the original text file despite intervening line breaks and other structural problems.

4. PROBLEMS OF USING CONCORDANCE SOFTWARE

The main problems that tend to arise when using concordance programs have already been mentioned in the discussion of keyword specification in section 2.3. There are two major types of problem: output that omits occurrences of words that you are interested in, and output that includes occurrences of words that you are not interested in. They are both dealt with in the following sections, together with some suggestions for reducing their impact on your work.

4.1. Including too little

One of my undergraduate students wanted to explore the semantic changes that are alleged to have taken place in various common English words. One of them was the word *flour*. A concordance list was produced for the word *flour* from the diachronic part of the Helsinki Corpus of English Texts. The results, 29 occurrences altogether, showed some confirmation of the changes described in the literature, but they seemed rather inconclusive and sketchy. One important feature of the development of the word had been overlooked: its spelling had varied significantly during the period under investigation. The *Oxford English Dictionary* lists several other forms for the word *flour.*

flure, floure, flowre, flower

If these are taken into account in the search a rather more useful concordance list is produced. The new listing showed 52 occurrences and provided a more useful basis for the research.

Spelling variation is not the only possible source of this problem: morphological changes also produce different word forms, and concordance software will not usually allow for them in searching for a keyword. Ways round this problem have already been considered in section 2.3.2 as part of the discussion of wild cards and regular expressions. These are relatively primitive ways of dealing with variation in word forms, but they should generally be effective in situations where you can produce an exhaustive list of the forms that interest you. If the scale of the research project justifies it, you may want to develop special concordance software which can generate its own search patterns from a set of rules, but this is likely to be rather complex and may not produce significantly better results.

4.2. Including too much

The listing produced for *being* which is described in section 1.3 contains 97 occurrences of the word. On closer examination, only 30 of these, or just over one third, were of interest for the purpose for which the investigation was carried out. Many of the other occurrences represented a different part of speech, the verbal use of *being* rather than the noun use. In many cases occurrences of words which have more than one meaning are only wanted in a restricted range of those meanings. Generally speaking, concordance software, like frequency list software, uses simple pattern-matching techniques, and cannot readily distinguish different syntactic or semantic properties when searching for keywords, and so is equally badly affected by problems such as homographs.

If this extra sensitivity is needed, it can be provided either by changing the data, or by changing the processing, in a rather similar way to the suggested solutions to the equivalent problems in the use of frequency lists. The original text can be marked up with the extra information needed to distinguish the occurrences of the word form, or special software could be added to the concordance program to detect the differences automatically. Some of the possibilities arising from both approaches are discussed in Chapter 6.

5. SUMMARY

The basis of the use of concordance lines as a source of linguistic evidence is their ability to show the context in which individual occurrences of words are found. The options found within modern dedicated concordance software are designed to facilitate the process of observing and distinguishing the patterns found in the textual contexts of the individual occurrences. By themselves, the concordance lines for a particular keyword or set of keywords can provide a detailed picture of linguistic behaviour, and they can also be used as the basis for further processing to assess the significance of collocation patterns.

6. EXERCISES

1. What keywords would you need to enter into a concordance program to retrieve all the occurrences of different parts of the verb *to go*?

2. The extract below is from a concordance for the word *good* from Dickens' *A Christmas Carol*:

```
1  it. And Scrooge's name was    good upon 'Change, for a
2  ce upon a time - of all the   good days in the year, o
3  , then, said Scrooge. Much    good may it do you! Muc
4  h good may it do you! Much    good it has ever done you! There
5   which I might have derived    good, by which I have not profit
6   n be apart from that - as a  good time: a kind, forgiving, ch
7  believe that it has done me   good, and will do me good; and I
8   done me good, and do me      good; and I say, God bless it!
9  us than a merry Christmas.    Good afternoon!Nay, uncle, but y
```

```
10  reason for not coming now?   Good afternoon, said Scrooge.
11   why cannot we be friends?   Good afternoon, said Scrooge. I
12   A Merry Christmas, uncle!   Good afternoon! said Scrooge. An
13  oge. And A Happy New Year!   Good afternoon! said Scrooge. Hi
14  ine occupies me constantly.  Good afternoon, gentlemen! Seei
15  rching, biting cold. If the  good Saint Dunstan had but nippe
16  riving a coach-and-six up a  good old flight of stairs, or th
17  ss into eternity before the  good of which it is susceptible
18  s I! But you were always a   good man of business, Jacob, fau
19  benezer. You were always a   good friend to me, said Scrooge.
20  ey sought to interfere, for  good, in human matters, and had
21  with snow upon the ground.   Good Heaven! said Scrooge, clasp
22  upon merry Christmas! What   good had it ever done to him? T
23  brimful of glee. Home, for   good and all. Home, for ever an
24  ldren bade the schoolmaster  good-bye right willingly; and ge
25  g. Top couple, too; with a   good stiff piece of work cut out
26  content to be so, until, in  good season, we could improve ou
27   by observing that they are  good for anything from pitch-and
28  eve that he was ready for a  good broad field of strange appe
29  xes, or that everything was  good to eat and in its Christmas
30  ut soon the steeples called  good people all, to church and c
```

How many different uses of the word *good* can you find in the extract?

3.   The concordances below are taken from the *Frankenstein* text and show
      two of the words from the 'thematic set' collected in section 1.2.4(c) of
      Chapter 3, *being* and *creation*. Are there any major differences between
      the textual environments and thematic associations of the two words?

being

```
1   h, at the distance of half a mile; a being which had the shape of a man, but app
2   emained alive; but there was a human being within it whom the sailors were persu
3   usness of what they owed towards the being to which they had given life, added t
4   g on her as of a distinct species, a being heaven-sent, and bearing a celestial
5    the hands of the infidels. No human  being could have passed a happier childhood
6   r I should attempt the creation of a being like myself, or one of simpler organi
7   that I began the creation of a human being. As the minuteness of the parts form
8   y to my first intention, to make the  being of a gigantic stature, that is to say
9   altogether free from blame. A human  being in perfection ought always to preserv
10   Unable to endure the aspect of the  being I had created, I rushed out of the ro
11   sacrifice of the dignity of a human  being. "Justine, you may remember, was a gr
12   evil and despair. I considered the  being whom I had cast among mankind, and en
13   on the story that I had to tell. A  being whom I myself had formed, and endued
14  that Justine, and indeed every human being, was guiltless of this murder. I had
15  ot consent to the death of any human being, but certainly I should have thought
16  ceased to fear or to bend before any being less almighty than that which had cre
17  y all the feelings which can arm one being against the existence of another. He
18  ge that I, an imperfect and solitary being, should be wretched. Yet why were th
19  t honour that can befall a sensitive being; to be base and vicious, as many on r
20  s relationships which bind one human being to another in mutual bonds. "But wher
21   proportion. I had never yet seen a  being resembling me or who claimed any inte
22  thought Werter himself a more divine being than I had ever beheld or imagined; h
23  ently united by no link to any other being in existence; but his state was far d
24   ask information from a single human being; but I did not despair. From you onl
25  nly attempted to gain from any other being that wore the human form. "My travels
```

26 f encountering the visage of a human being. Nature decayed around me, and the s
27 my benevolence! I had saved a human being from destruction, and as a recompense
28 ies and have the same defects. This being you must create." Chapter 17 The bein
29 ing you must create." Chapter 17 The being finished speaking and fixed his looks
30 are the cause of its excess. If any being felt emotions of benevolence towards
31 ent, neither you nor any other human being shall ever see us again; I will go to
32 l feel the affections of a sensitive being and became linked to the chain of exi
33 ges of inaccessible precipices was a being possessing faculties it would be vain
34 re so eminently deserving. He was a being formed in the "very poetry of nature.
35 ow exist? Is this gentle and lovely being lost forever? Has this mind, so repl
36 have interested the most unfortunate being. Clerval did not like it so well as
37 se. I was now about to form another being of whose dispositions I was alike ign
38 re been moved by the sophisms of the being I had created; I had been struck sens
39 mangled the living flesh of a human being. I paused to collect myself and then
40 ttered wreck- the shadow of a human being. My strength was gone. I was a mere
41 ed my narration I said, "This is the being whom I accuse and for whose seizure a
42 e." Must I then lose this admirable being? I have longed for a friend; I have s
43 stil '; I must pursue and destroy the being to whom I gave existence; then my lot
44 kenstein! Generous and self-devoted being! What does it avail that I now ask t
45 ssion. I approached this tremendous being; I dared not again raise my eyes to h
46 not thus   thus," interrupted the being. †"Yet such must be the impression co

creation

1 year lived in a paradise of my own creation; I imagined that I also might obtai
2 progeny as a deformed and abortive creation, and entertained the greatest disda
3 the world the deepest mysteries of creation. I closed not my eyes that night.
4 desire of the wisest men since the creation of the world was now within my gras
5 first whether I should attempt the creation of a being like myself, or one of s
6 ith these feelings that I began the creation of a human being. As the minutenes
7 rcase, I kept my workshop of filthy creation; my eyeballs were starting from the
8 omised myself both of these when my creation should be complete. Chapter 5 It wa
9 ole train of my progress toward the creation; the appearance of the works of my
10 ed just at the time that I dated my creation, and which would give an air of del
11 d devil! You reproach me with your creation, come on, then, that I may extingui
12 chosen few! And what was I? Of my creation and creator I was absolutely ignora
13 of the four months that preceded my creation. You minutely described in these pa
14 the materials necessary for my new creation, and this was to me like the tortur
15 mply with a compact made before her creation. They might even hate each other; t
16 victim to me and the monster of m creation. I repassed, in my memory, my whol
17 nthusiasm that hurried me on to the creation of my hideous enemy, and I called t
18 d completed, no less a one than the creation of a sensitive and rational animal,
19 conceived the idea and executed the creation of a man. Even now I cannot recoll

FURTHER READING

Clear, J. (1987) 'Computing', in J. Sinclair (ed.) *Looking Up*, London: Collins ELT, ch. 2 (pp. 41–61).

King, P. and Johns, T. (eds) (1991) *Classroom Concordancing. English Language Research Journal* Vol. 4, Birmingham: Centre for English Language Studies, University of Birmingham.

Krishnamurthy, R. (1987) 'The process of compilation', in J. Sinclair (ed.) *Looking Up*, London: Collins ELT, ch. 3 (pp. 62–85).

Sinclair, J. (1991) *Corpus, Concordance, Collocation*, Oxford: Oxford University Press, chs 2, 3 (pp. 27–49).

The sociology of words: collocation analysis

1. THE BASIS OF COLLOCATION ANALYSIS

The use of concordance lines described in the last chapter is an essentially qualitative technique: you use them to assess the behaviour of individual occurrences of keywords within their contexts in the corpus. Because of the complexity of their behaviour and of the ways of describing it, most forms of automatic numerical analysis are difficult, if not impossible, to apply. Any form of quantitative assessment is normally possible only after you have made the crucial decisions which distinguish one type of behaviour from another. Concordances are still an immensely useful source of information, but it would be much more satisfying if you could analyse the contexts of words automatically without having to use your own judgement. At least one aspect of the analysis can be dealt with both automatically and, to some extent, quantitatively. The technique that makes it possible is known as collocation analysis.

Collocation has been defined as 'the occurrence of two or more words within a short space of each other in a text' (Sinclair 1991: 170). In collocation analysis, interest normally centres on the extent to which the actual pattern of these occurrences differs from the pattern that would have been expected. Any significant difference can be taken as at least preliminary evidence that the presence of one word in the text affects the occurrence of the other in some way. This chapter examines the ways in which actual and expected patterns of co-occurrence can be computed and compared, and the measures that can be applied to the results to assess their significance and explore their implications. Some concordance packages include forms of collocation analysis as part of their display options, and section 2 examines the possibilities of using this information in your research. Section 3 discusses the considerations involved in designing your own collocation software, and Section 4 describes the interpretation and use of the results.

2. FACILITIES WITHIN CONCORDANCE PACKAGES

Concordance lines already contain the basic information needed for collocation analysis, and some concordance packages include facilities for investigating it. The approach may range from the simple provision of frequency
information for words which are near to the keyword, to the inclusion of
sophisticated statistical routines which calculate the figures needed for the
comparison and use them to produce measures of significance. The two
examples described below give some idea of the range of possibilities.

2.1. Simple frequency information

The most basic form of collocation information provided by concordance
packages is a list of the frequencies of all the words found within predetermined proximity limits. These can easily be calculated from the concordance
lines currently displayed by the program and reported to the user. As an example, the following information was produced by MicroConcord for the occurrences of *place* in the *Frankenstein* text. It uses a fixed span of three words either
side of the keyword:

THE	19	FROM	7
TO	16	IT	5
IN	16	TOOK	5
HAD	15	WHERE	5
A	15	HAS	5
AND	14	GAVE	4
TAKEN	13	BEFORE	4
I	13	CHANGE	4
MY	10	WAS	4
THIS	9	SAFETY	3
OF	9	IS	3
THAT	8	BUT	3
TAKE	7		

The main problem with this information is that the use of raw frequencies
foregrounds the very common words such as *the, to*, and *in*, despite the fact that
their comparatively high frequencies of occurrence within the specified
distance from the word *place* are unlikely to provide conclusive evidence of
significant collocation patterns. These are words which, on the basis of
frequency of co-occurrence alone, would be found to collocate strongly with
most keywords. Some of the words in the list do seem interesting, and it can
perhaps be read more usefully if the purely grammatical words are discarded.
This would leave:

TAKEN	13	GAVE	4
TAKE	7	CHANGE	4
TOOK	5	SAFETY	3

All of these could form fairly strong patterns with *place* and would be worth investigating further.

2.2. Statistical significance measures

The second example also uses the word *place* taken from the *Frankenstein* text. This output, produced by the concordance program TACT using an adjustable span of five words either side of the keyword, is rather more sophisticated. It uses the frequencies of co-occurrence within the span of words as the start-ing-point for calculating their significance. The calculations involved are explained in section 3.4 below. In Table 5.1 the second column shows the frequency of the listed word within the span, the third its frequency within the entire text, and the final column shows the z-score, the measure of statis-tical significance calculated for the word from a comparison of the other two figures. The figures shown represent the top 30 items in the output.

Collocate	Span frequency	Text frequency	z-score
taken	13	33	25.023
take	7	22	16.421
alluded	1	1	11.191
breakers	1	1	11.191
casualties	1	1	11.191
chairs	1	1	11.191
coincidences	1	1	11.191
concealment	1	1	11.191
cooped	1	1	11.191
deposited	1	1	11.191
desolating	1	1	11.191
distraction	1	1	11.191
eventful	1	1	11.191
fitting	1	1	11.191
gnashing	1	1	11.191
guards	1	1	11.191
household	1	1	11.191
inhabits	1	1	11.191
intimacy	1	1	11.191
jumped	1	1	11.191
likely	1	1	11.191
mechanics	1	1	11.191
playfellows	1	1	11.191
shocking	1	1	11.191
swell	1	1	11.191
takes	1	1	11.191
safety	3	10	10.421
change	5	28	10.191
alteration	2	5	9.891
took	5	36	8.870

Figure 5.1 Collocates of *place* in *Frankenstein*: top 30 z-scores

Collocate	Span frequency	Text frequency	z-score
taken	13	33	25.023
take	7	22	16.421
safety	3	10	10.421
change	5	28	10.191
took	5	36	8.870
gave	4	32	7.476
where	6	77	6.938
has	5	64	6.343
town	3	26	6.186
since	3	27	6.053
this	12	402	4.987
had	15	686	4.157
before	5	146	3.600
in	19	1128	3.430
during	3	67	3.410
our	4	126	3.027
that	14	1017	2.139
if	4	194	2.007
what	3	132	1.929
some	3	147	1.718

Table 5.2 Collocates of *place* in *Frankenstein*: top 30 z-scores with a frequency threshold of 3

Because a significance measure is now being used to order the potential collocates the frequent grammatical words have been largely eliminated. This has brought *taken* and *take* to the top of the list, and *takes* and *took* are also reasonably significant. The results are still distorted to some extent by the large number of single occurrence words producing spuriously high significance levels, and it may be useful to look at the list with these removed. A frequency of three within the span is often used as a threshold to avoid this effect. Table 5.2 shows the top twenty lines once words occurring less than three times have been removed.

The items at the top of this adjusted list are now beginning to look very interesting, and it is important to remember that this list has been produced completely automatically. Once the span and the low frequency threshold are set the calculations are made entirely by the computer. The next section looks at the details of the calculations involved in the production of similar information.

3. INVESTIGATING COLLOCATION: THE MAIN CONSIDERATIONS

The calculation of the information needed for collocation analysis is not difficult, although several alternative approaches are available. The starting-point for the calculations is a set of concordance lines for the words under investigation, long enough to contain the required span of words. The length of the span represents the first element of choice.

3.1. The span

After the definition of collocation already quoted in section 1, Sinclair goes on to describe the notion of a 'short space' between the word and its collocates as 'a maximum of four words intervening'. This gap between the words can perhaps be better understood by looking at an annotated concordance line. The word under investigation, the keyword used to generate the concordance lines, is often referred to as the **node**. The words around the node can be thought of in terms of their distance from it in words. The example below shows a concordance line for the keyword *place* extracted from the *Frankenstein* text. Below the concordance line the positions of the words to the left of the node word are expressed in negative numbers, those to the right in positive numbers.

```
sail directly towards the town, as a place where I could most easily procure nou
                    -5   -4  -3 -2 -1 node +1 +2  +3  +4  +5
```

The numbered words, those between *towards* on the left and *easily* on the right, represent the maximum distance expressed in Sinclair's description. Between *towards* and *place* and between *place* and *easily* four words intervene. The total distance between *towards* and *easily* is normally referred to as the span, and would be expressed as within five words either side of the node. Other spans than this could of course be used. In some situations an asymmetric span could be more appropriate. Once the span has been established, the concordance lines can be truncated to fit it as the starting-point for the analysis. The programming needed for this is described in Appendix 3. The line shown above would be reduced to:

```
towards the town, as a place where I could most easily
```

To make the frequency calculations easier, the node word could be omitted, producing the set of co-occurring words:

```
towards the town, as a where I could most easily
```

The set of lines truncated in this way to the selected span is then used as the basis for calculating actual and expected frequencies of co-occurrence.

3.2. Calculating actual frequencies of co-occurrence

Once the concordance lines have been truncated so that only the words within the span are left, their frequencies of occurrence can be calculated. This exercise is very similar to the creation of word frequency lists described in Chapter 3, and similar considerations, including word boundaries, lemmatisation and spelling variation, would apply. The frequency list algorithm could be incorporated in a set of routines which also carry out the other calculations, although this is not strictly necessary, since they could easily be carried out on a list produced by an ordinary frequency list program.

The extract below shows part of the result of carrying out this exercise on the 64 concordance lines produced for *place*:

the	37	taken	13
i	24	this	12
and	23	you	8
in	20	from	8
to	19	but	7
a	19	take	7
of	19	where	6
that	15	which	6
had	15	it	5
my	14	change	5

The ordering by raw frequency again shows the distortion caused by high frequency items, although, as suggested in section 2.1, the elimination of the purely grammatical words would make the list more useful. The use of a 'stop-list' of the words that you want to eliminate could automatically produce a frequency list which would be of more interest for collocation analysis. Any differences between the list shown above and the figures shown in section 2.1 are caused by the difference in the span, since the concordance lines were produced by the same program.

3.3. Calculating expected frequencies

At this point significant choices must be made, both of which affect the calculation of the expected frequency figures which will be compared to the actual frequencies to assess their significance. The choices relate to two main areas: the hypothesis to be used for predicting the distribution of words in the text, and the texts to be used as the source of numerical data for the hypothesis.

3.3.1. The distribution hypothesis

To calculate an expected frequency for the words occurring in the span there must be a theoretical language model which predicts how those words would be distributed if there were no particular pattern of collocation between them and the node word. In other words, if we want to check whether the node word is exercising some influence over the distribution of those words, we need to know how we would expect them to behave in the absence of that influence. The simplest model, and perhaps the only one practically available, is random distribution. This says in effect that in the absence of any significant collocation between the node and the other words in the text, those other words will occur around it at random in the same proportions as they occur throughout the text as a whole.

As you will see in more detail when we consider the calculation of expected frequencies, this model considerably simplifies the calculation. Unfortunately, it is also quite obviously incorrect as a description of the behaviour of language. Even if the specific word being used as the node had no collocational effect on the words around it, the grammar of the language would constrain the types of words in different ways depending on the grammatical properties of the node word. Ideally the language model should incorporate the relevant parts of these grammatical constraints so that they can be taken into account in the calculations, but they are unlikely to be sufficiently well-formulated for this to be possible. There is also at least one advantage of the random language model: it makes no assumptions about the behaviour of the words and so should allow their behaviour to be assessed in an unbiased way.

3.3.2. The source of distribution data

There are two possible ways of obtaining the data on which expected frequency distribution figures can be calculated. The most straightforward source is the entire text from which the concordance lines have been taken, but this may not provide a sufficiently representative sample for comparison. The overall frequency figures for a large reference corpus would provide a better source. If you want to investigate the general patterns of collocation in the language as a whole, you would need to use a large reference corpus for all of the data.

3.3.3. The calculation

Once the distribution model and the source of comparative data have been selected, the expected frequency can be calculated. The example calculations given below represent an assumed random distribution model, using the over-all frequencies for the entire *Frankenstein* text. The examples are shown in detail, as though being worked manually, purely for the sake of illustration. While it would be theoretically possible to carry out the calculations manu-ally from the type of frequency list described in section 3.2, the task would be extremely tedious and probably impossible when very frequent node words were under investigation. It would be relatively simple to write software which would accept the frequency lists as input and perform all the necessary calculations. Examples of calculation programs are shown in Appendix 3.

The starting-point for these calculations is the frequency list produced from the truncated concordance lines. For each of the words in the list whose frequency of co-occurrence is regarded as significant an expected frequency must be calculated. The simplest basis for this is to take each word's overall frequency in the entire corpus and to use the size of the sample formed by the truncated concordance lines to scale this figure down. The first item in the frequency list shown in section 3.2 is *the*. Its overall frequency in the entire *Frankenstein* text, which consists of 75,214 tokens altogether, is 4,194. If this word is randomly distributed throughout the text, then its expected frequency in a 640 word sample (64 lines containing 10 words each) should be:

$$\frac{4194}{75214} \times 640 = 35.69$$

Collocate	Text frequency	Expected span frequency	Observed span frequency
the	4194	35.69	37
i	2847	24.23	24
and	2976	25.32	23
in	1129	9.61	20
to	2094	17.82	19
a	1391	11.84	19
of	2641	22.47	19
that	1018	8.66	15
had	686	5.84	15
my	1777	15.12	14

Table 5.3 Collocates of *place* in *Frankenstein*: extract from expected frequency calculations

This compares with its actual frequency in the set of truncated lines of 37, and the two figures can then be used to assess the significance of the difference between them.

Table 5.3 shows the expected frequency calculation for the first ten items in the list of words found in the truncated concordance lines. The second column shows the actual frequency in the entire text, and the third the expected frequency in a random sample of 640 words. The final column shows the actual frequency within the set of truncated concordance lines for comparison with the expected frequencies:

Some of the differences between the expected and actual frequencies seem interesting in this extract from the list, particularly the words *in*, *that* and *had*, but their importance cannot be properly assessed without applying an appropriate measure of significance to the results. The next section considers the main alternatives.

3.4. Measures of significance

The idea of significance, which has already been mentioned several times in this description of collocation analysis, relates directly to the concept of probability. In simple terms, a result is statistically significant if the probability of its chance occurrence is sufficiently low. The various measures which are described below allow this probability to be calculated or reflected in some way so that the statistical significance of a particular result, in this case an observed frequency of co-occurrence within the selected span, can be assessed. The statistical theory underlying the measures is generally rather complex, and beyond the scope of a description of analytical methods like this, but once a formula has been selected the calculations involved are generally fairly simple. The next four sections describe the mechanics of the three most commonly used measures and compare the results of applying them. Their statistical justification is not analysed, although section 3.4.4 summarises some of the main differences between their approaches. Programming examples demonstrating the calculation of these measures by the computer are given in Appendix 3 (sections 10–12).

3.4.1. z-score

The z-score is probably the most familiar of the statistical significance measures commonly used, although there is some controversy over its application in this form of linguistic analysis. The calculation is reasonably straightforward. It can be represented by the formula:

$$z = \frac{O - E}{\sigma}$$

where:

O = the observed frequency of occurrence of the word within the span

E = the expected frequency of occurrence of the same word

σ = the standard deviation of the occurrence of the word in the whole text

So for each of the co-occurring words in the list the difference between the observed and expected frequencies is divided by a standard statistical measure of variation, its standard deviation. The result is called the z-score, and it can be used in conjunction with standard statistical tables as a significance measure.

The two figures which need to be calculated for this formula are:

- E, the expected frequency of co-occurrence

- σ, the standard deviation of the co-occurring word.

The calculation of E has already been described in section 3.3.3. For the word *the* in the example used there it is 35.69.

The calculation of the standard deviation uses the formula:

$$\sigma = \sqrt{N(p(1 - p))}$$

where:

p = the probability of occurrence of the co-occurring word in the whole text, as above

N = the number of tokens in the set of truncated concordance lines

If a word occurs x times in the entire text, and the text contains y tokens altogether, the word's probability, p, of occurring at any point in the text is simply x/y. For the word *the*:

$$p = \frac{4194}{75214} = 0.05576$$

The number of tokens in the set of truncated lines is 64 x 10 = 640. The standard deviation for the occurrence of *the* in a sample taken from the entire text, which consisted of 640 words would be calculated as:

$$\sqrt{640 \times 0.05576 \times (1 - 0.05576)} = 5.80$$

The z-score for *the*, the difference between the observed and expected frequencies expressed as a number of standard deviations , is given by:

$$\frac{37 - 35.69}{5.80} = 0.2259$$

This figure is very low, and does not demonstrate any significant variation between the occurrence of *the* within a ten-word span of *place* and its occurrence throughout the rest of the text. z-scores can be calculated for all of the words in the span frequency list to see whether any of them are significant, or can simply be used to arrange them in order of likely significance. If the calculations are carried out for all the words in the span frequency list, and the results are sorted by the z-scores, the result looks like this:

taken	24.01	should	1.49
take	15.75	you	1.41
safety	9.99	more	1.35
change	9.76	would	1.15
took	8.48	one	0.94
gave	7.15	which	0.58
where	6.61	but	0.48
has	6.04	to	0.28
town	5.91	is	0.24
since	5.78	the	0.23
this	4.65	it	0.16
had	3.81	i	−0.05
in	3.38	not	−0.16
before	3.37	my	−0.29
our	2.83	and	−0.47
from	2.62	he	−0.52
that	2.17	of	−0.75
a	2.10	me	−0.88
if	1.83	with	−1.13
what	1.77	was	−1.26
some	1.57		

A useful (though not very precise) cut-off measure for significance in this type of test is around 3, so that the following words are almost certainly worth more detailed investigation:

taken	has
take	town
safety	since
change	this
took	had
gave	in
where	before

A detailed comparison of these results with those from the other two measures is given in section 3.4.4.

3.4.2. t-score

The *t*-score is in many ways similar to the *z*-score, but it is calculated in a slightly different way. The change to the calculation is said to provide more accuracy in dealing with co-occurring words with relatively low overall frequencies. The *t*-score formula is very similar to the *z*-score formula, with a significant change to one of the elements. The standard deviation used in the bottom half of the formula is calculated for the node word in combination with the co-occurring word rather than for the co-occurring word by itself. In other words, while the formula for calculating standard deviation for *z*-score is:

$$\sigma = \sqrt{N(p(1-p))}$$

p is replaced by the probability of the occurrence of the node word and the co-occurring word together within the selected span. In the practical application of this formula, as used by Church *et al.* (1991), Clear (1993) and Stubbs (1995), the usual calculation of the standard deviation is considered to be unnecessary, and a useful approximation[1] is used instead, which makes the overall formula:

$$t = \frac{O - E}{\sqrt{O}}$$

where *O* and *E* have the same values as were used in the *z*-score formula: observed and expected frequencies of co-occurrence.

Using the word *the* as an example once again, the calculation would be:

$$\frac{37 - 35.69}{\sqrt{37}} = 0.2154$$

If the *t*-score is calculated for the span frequency list for *place*, and is then used to sort the results, we get:

taken	3.53		some	1.01
take	2.57		should	0.98
this	2.48		more	0.92
had	2.37		would	0.83
in	2.32		one	0.72
where	2.18		which	0.51
change	2.13		but	0.44
took	2.10		to	0.27
has	1.99		the	0.22
gave	1.86		is	0.22
before	1.68		it	0.15
safety	1.68		i	−0.05
from	1.67		not	−0.17
a	1.64		my	−0.30
that	1.64		and	−0.48
since	1.60		he	−0.59
town	1.60		of	−0.80
our	1.46		me	−1.06
if	1.17		with	−1.54
you	1.10		was	−1.65
what	1.08			

Absolute statistical significance is harder to assess with the *t*-score, but the words with a score of 2 or over are likely to be the most interesting. From the above list this would select:

taken	in
take	where
this	change
had	took

These results are compared with those from the other measures in section 3.4.4.

3.4.3. Mutual Information

The mutual information measure, unlike the *z*- and *t*-scores, does not express the difference between observed and expected frequencies in terms of a standard deviation. Instead it seeks to represent the amount of information that each of the two words, the node and its collocate, provide about each other by comparing the observed probability of their co-occurrence with the expected probability assuming that they were distributed randomly. The formula is normally given as:

$$I = \log_2 \frac{O}{E}$$

where O and E once again represent the observed and expected frequencies of co-occurrence.

Performing the calculation once again for the word *the*, we get:

$$\log_2 \frac{37}{35.69} = 0.052$$

If the mutual information value is calculated for all the words in the span frequency list and used to order them, it produces the following results:

taken	5.53	would	0.94
take	5.22	that	0.79
safety	5.14	one	0.78
change	4.39	you	0.71
took	4.03	a	0.68
gave	3.88	which	0.34
town	3.76	but	0.26
since	3.71	is	0.20
has	3.20	it	0.10
where	3.19	to	0.09
before	2.01	the	0.05
our	1.90	i	−0.01
this	1.81	my	−0.11
what	1.42	not	−0.12
had	1.36	and	−0.14
from	1.29	of	−0.24
if	1.28	he	−0.37
some	1.26	me	−0.56
should	1.20	was	−0.80
more	1.10	with	−0.92
in	1.06		

Some users (for example Stubbs (1995)) have suggested that the conversion of the basic ratio to a base-2 logarithm masks what is really going on, and it is certainly less straightforward to consider an I figure of 1.58 than to think of the observed frequency being three times the expected level. 1.58 is roughly the logarithm of 3 to the base 2, and this result for I means that the observed figures were literally three times as high as would be expected by chance. Strict statistical significance is not really available, but a ratio of 3:1 could be used as a cut-off point. This would leave the following words:

taken	since
take	has
safety	where
change	before
took	our
gave	this
town	

The differences between these results and those from the other two methods are discussed in the section 3.4.4.

3.4.4. Significance measures compared

Each of the significance measures described above can be used to order the list of words, to highlight those which appear to be most strongly collocated with the node word. If the top fifteen lines from each sorted list produced for the word *place* in the *Frankenstein* text are placed side by side, we can compare the results and investigate any differences (see Table 5.4).

The sorted lists may be easier to compare if they are rearranged into alphabetical order, so that differences in their contents are easier to spot. In Table 5.5 the three lists have been numbered to show their ranking when sorted by the three measures.

There are two major types of difference shown here: words which are included in one list but not in another, and words whose ranks differ between the lists. The first thing noticeable from the table is the remarkable similarity at the top of the lists: *taken* and *take* are in the same positions in all three lists. This suggests that they are strong collocates, and of course when they do occur in the concordance lines they generally form part of the phrasal verb *take place*. The other part of the same verb found in the lists, *took*, is also in a similar position in all three lists.

z	t	I
taken	taken	taken
take	take	take
safety	this	safety
change	had	change
took	in	took
gave	where	gave
where	change	town
has	took	since
town	has	has
since	gave	where
this	before	before
had	safety	our
in	from	this
before	a	what
our	that	had

Table 5.4 Collocates of *place* in *Frankenstein*: significance measures compared

z		t		I	
Word	**Rank**	**Word**	**Rank**	**Word**	**Rank**
		a	14		
before	14	before	11	before	11
change	4	change	7	change	4
		from	13		
gave	6	gave	10	gave	6
had	12	had	4	had	15
has	8	has	9	has	9
in	13	in	5		
our	15			our	12
safety	3	safety	12	safety	3
since	10			since	8
take	2	take	2	take	2
taken	1	taken	1	taken	1
		that	15		
this	11	this	3	this	13
took	5	took	8	took	5
town	9			town	7
				what	14
where	7	where	6	where	10

Table 5.5 Collocates of *place* in *Frankenstein*: comparative alphabetical list

Three words – *our, since* and *town* – occur in both the *z*-score and *I* lists but are not found in the *t* list. All of these have relatively low frequencies in the *Frankenstein* text (126 for *our*, 27 for *since* and 26 for *town*). Both the *z*-score and the mutual information measure *I* artificially inflate the significance of low frequency co-occurring words because of the nature of their formulae. This point is reinforced by the fact that three other words – *a, from* and *that* – only appear in the *t* list. All have relatively high frequencies in the whole text, and so are downgraded by the other two measures. One word, *what*, is unique to the *I* list, again probably because of its relatively low frequency in the text.

Similar reasons lie behind the main differences in rank of the words which are found in all three lists. As an example, the word *safety* comes third in both the *z* and the *I* list, but is eleventh in the *t* list. The word only occurs three times within the span, but because of its low frequency, 10, in the entire text, it is made to seem more significant by the *z* and *I* measures.

There are, then, important differences between the information provided by the three measures: more, perhaps, between *t* and the other two than between *z* and *I* themselves. It is difficult, if not impossible, to select one measure which provides the best possible assessment of the collocates, although there has been ample discussion of their relative merits (in, for example, Church *et al.* 1991; Clear 1993; and Stubbs 1995). It is probably better to use as much information as possible in exploring collocation, and to take advantage of the different perspectives provided by the use of more than one measure.

4. INTERPRETING THE OUTPUT

The main value of the techniques described in this chapter is that they can focus your attention on specific aspects of the contexts of words already selected for investigation through concordance lines. They can help you to organise the context into its major patterns, and to use your knowledge of those patterns to assess the general behaviour patterns of the language or the uses being made of particular words within the text. This can make it much easier to identify phrases and idioms without the need for prior knowledge or manual manipulation. It might also be possible to use this information to differentiate between the various meanings of a single word form or its range of syntactic features. It could allow you, for example, to differentiate between the various phrasal verbs in the *Frankenstein* text which include the word *place*, such as *take place*, *give place* and so on, or between the noun and verb uses of the word. The following sections discuss some of these applications in more detail.

4.1. Identifying phrases

In the examination of the results in section 3.4.4 the most significant collocates appeared to be *take* and *taken*, with *took* also featuring in the lists. An examination of the concordance lines in which these collocates occur shows the general pattern:

```
my union with Elizabeth should take  place immediately on my return. My father's
, hoping that some change would take place in the atmosphere and weather. About
e Turk allowed this intimacy to take place and encouraged the hopes of the youth
ld consent, the ceremony should take place in ten days, and thus put, as I imagi
y struggle would then assuredly take place, in which if he were victorious I sho
he day after our marriage shall take place, for, my sweet cousin, there must be
s an event that would certainly take place. We were affectionate playfellows du
losophers. If this journey had taken place during my days of study and happiness
 strange coincidences that had taken place during this eventful night; but, know
memory of the scenes that had taken  place in Ireland and never alluded to them
e than the alteration that had taken place in my feelings since the night of the
owth of our dear children, has taken place since you left us. The blue lake and
ou left us, but one change has taken place in our little household. Do you reme
try. A great fall of snow had taken  place the night before, and the fields were
e sole alteration that joy had taken place of sadness in the countenances of my
te to me. A change indeed had taken  place in me; my health, which had hitherto
 revolution of the seasons had taken place since I awoke into life. My attentio
eat God! what a scene has just taken place! I am yet dizzy with the remembrance
he spot where these scenes had taken place, sometimes wishing to see you, someti
dden and desolating change had taken place; but a thousand little circumstances
errupted by the casualties that took place around them. The more I saw of them,
 the cottage. Some conversation took place between him and his father, and the y
veral changes, in the meantime, took place in the cottage. The presence of Safie
or five months before the trial took  place, the result of which deprived them of
th its waters. This frequently took  place, but a high wind quickly dried the ea
```

All of the occurrences are quite clearly instances of the phrasal verb *take place*. This pattern would have emerged fairly clearly from the sorted concordance lines alone, but this is not always the case. Consider another reasonably highly placed collocate from the three lists: *change.* The lines containing *change* are:

```
by bodily exercise and by change of place, some relief from my intolerable sens
, hoping that some change would take place in the atmosphere and weather. About
ou left us, but one change has taken place in our little household. Do you reme
te to me. A change indeed had  taken place in me; my health, which had hitherto
dden and desolating change had taken place; but a thousand little circumstances
```

Four of the five occurrences are forms of the phrase *change ... take place.* The frequency of co-occurrence in this individual text is probably too low• for any definite conclusion to be drawn, but there does seem to be a wider pattern at work in which one of the main things that *take place* is some form of *change*.

The use of this form of analysis for identifying phrases and idioms can be directed more closely by a progressive analysis of collocation, using phrases which have already been established as the node word and examining collocations with the entire phrase so as to build up phrases which may consist of several words incrementally. Its scope could also be widened by replacing the current node word with one of its main collocates and identifying its collocation patterns. As an example, having established that *take* is one of the principal collocates of *place*, concordance lines for *take* could be processed in the same way to establish other phrases which contain the word and to establish the relative importance of *place* as a collocate of *take*.

4.2. Disambiguating meanings

Because the meanings of words are generally determined by the contexts in which they are found the information provided by collocation analysis can also be used as a major source of evidence for the allocation of a specific meaning to an occurrence of a word within a stretch of text, removing the ambiguity surrounding the word. This could form a basis for the automatic semantic tagging outlined in section 3.3 of Chapter 6, which could make it possible to construct frequency lists automatically in which different senses of words were properly separated. Even within the rather limited text used to illustrate the mechanics of the analysis process, the meaning of *place* within the phrasal verb *take place* can be fairly easily separated from its more general noun uses. With larger corpora more precise disambiguation should be possible.

4.3. Identifying syntactic features

Because the collocation patterns surrounding a node word may signal syntactic differences as well as semantic differences, the analysis could also be used in some cases to differentiate between, for example, the same word form being used as a noun and being used as a verb. There is a form of this in the analysis of collocation with *place*, in the sense that the phrasal verbs identified by the analysis, *take place* and *give place*, are syntactically distinct patterns from the normal noun use exemplified by the concordance line:

```
ssed me in French, "I fear that this place is very shocking to you; can I do any
```

5. PROBLEMS AFFECTING COLLOCATION ANALYSIS

The problems that beset the use of frequency lists and concordances can also affect collocation analysis, and may be capable of being dealt with in a similar way. Homographs are dealt with in 5.1, and the double set of problems created by spelling variations is explained in 5.2. Lemmatisation raises rather different issues, and these are considered in section 5.3. Section 5.4 deals with a more complex problem, where the syntactic categories of the collocating words form the main point of interest rather than the forms of the words themselves.

5.1. Homographs

The problems that homographs cause for frequency lists and concordances, documented in section 2.2.3 of Chapter 3 and section 4.2 of Chapter 4, are repeated in collocation analysis. The problem can affect both the node word and the collocates, and can only be overcome if enough information is available to distinguish the usages of the individual occurrences of the words. Because collocation is one of the main hopes for developing automatic disambiguation the situation may seem hopelessly circular. In fact, the problem for the node word is not as serious as it might seem, since different collocation patterns should help to distinguish its various usages. A potentially greater problem lies in the possible distortion of these patterns that could be caused by homographs within the collocates. Even this can be overcome if the results of the initial collocation analysis are explored using more precise positional information (rather than an undifferentiated span) or if the lines used for the analysis are marked up to distinguish the homographs. It may even be possible to carry out some or all of this marking up automatically, as discussed in section 3.3 of Chapter 6.

5.2. Spelling variation

If you ignore the details of the calculations involved, which vary from one significance measure to another, collocation effectively combines the use of concordance lines with the use of frequency lists. The results of both of these techniques will be affected by spelling variations, and any combination of the two will be doubly affected. As an example, I wanted to examine the collocates of the word *blood* in a historical corpus, to see if there were any differences between the patterns found in Old English, Middle English and Early Modern English. I was using the diachronic part of the Helsinki Corpus of English Texts, which can be accessed in three subcorpora corresponding to these language stages. Because the original spelling is preserved in the corpus, there is considerable variation in the word form representing *blood*. It seems from a frequency list produced from the corpus that it can be written in any of the following forms:

blod	bloude
blode	blot
blood	blota
bloode	blud
bloud	blude

To produce concordance lists from which collocation information could be extracted, all of these spellings were entered as alternative keywords. This dealt with half of the problem. The calculations involved in collocation analysis are based on a frequency list created from the truncated concordance lines. This frequency list will also be affected by spelling variations, this time in the collocates, and unlike the variations in the node word, these cannot be explored and adjusted in advance. It may be possible to annotate the frequency list afterwards, but the effort involved is much greater than in situations where spelling variation does not occur, and the problem will almost certainly reduce the accuracy of the results.

5.3. Lemmatisation

The usual problems caused for frequency lists and concordances by the need for lemmatisation are less clear-cut for collocation analysis. In the case of both the node word and the potential collocates, it may not be immediately clear whether all the forms of the lemma should be treated as one node for collocation analysis, or whether you should keep them separate and analyse their patterns individually. Different patterns may be found for different parts of the lemma. The patterns found for *place* in the *Frankenstein* text, for example, in which it formed part of the phrasal verb *take place*, would not be found for *places*, but all forms of the verb *take* were relevant in examining the significance of the phrase. You will probably need to carry out detailed investigations before you can decide whether to group lemma forms or keep them separate, and the default separation produced by basic forms of collocation analysis may not be a disadvantage.

5.4. Colligation

The analysis process described so far has concerned the actual word forms found in the context of the node word. You may be more interested in the syntactic surroundings of the word rather than its lexical patterns, in which case collocation analysis will provide you with little useful information. **Colligation**, the syntactic patterning found around node words, can only be detected if you can go beyond the word forms of the surrounding text and gain access to information relating to its word classes or other syntactic features. This is unlikely to be possible without further input, and methods of making linguistic information like this available are discussed in Chapter 6.

6. SUMMARY

Collocation analysis allows the automatic quantitative investigation of context patterns associated with selected keywords, or node words. Generally a span of words either side of the node word is established which is best fitted for the type of investigation being performed, and observed and expected frequencies of the co-occurring words within the span are used as the basis for calculating significance measures. The significance measures can then be used to direct further examination of the patterns or as a basis for the automatic identification of phrases, meanings or syntactic features.

FURTHER READING

Church, K., Gale, W., Hanks, P. W. and Hindle, D. (1991) 'Using statistics in lexical analysis', in U. Zernick (ed.), *Lexical Acquisition: Using On-Line Resources to Build a Lexicon*, Englewood Cliff, NJ: Lawrence Erlbaum, pp. 115–64.

Clear, J. (1993) 'From Firth principles: computational tools for the study of collocation' in M. Baker, G. Francis, and E. Tognini-Bonelli (eds), *Text and Technology*, Amsterdam: John Benjamins, pp. 271–92.

Sinclair, J. (1991) *Corpus, Concordance, Collocation*, Oxford, Oxford University Press, Ch. 8 (pp. 109–121).

Stubbs, M. (1995) 'Collocations and semantic profiles: on the cause of the trouble with quantitative studies', *Functions of Language*, 2(1), pp. 23–55.

NOTE

1. The explanation of this is fairly simple, but you certainly do not need to understand it to be able to use the *t*-score successfully. In the expression for the standard deviation:

$$\sigma = \sqrt{N(p(1 - p))}$$

p, the overall probability of co-occurrence of the two words, is assumed to be fairly small. In this case, $1 - p$ approximates to 1, and $p(1 - p)$ approximates to p. This means that the expression can be approximated to:

$$\sigma = \sqrt{N(p)}$$

and since $N(p)$ is equal to O, the observed frequency of co-occurrence, this can be further re-stated as:

$$\sigma = \sqrt{O}$$

Putting them in their place: tagging, parsing and so on

1. INCORPORATING LINGUISTIC INFORMATION

The analytical tools which have been described so far have been remarkably free of linguistic content. Frequency lists and concordance programs both use pattern-matching techniques to produce their output, and collocation analysis simply takes the results of using a concordance program, makes a frequency list out of part of it and then performs some relatively simple statistical calculations on the results. The use of linguistic models or descriptive methods is generally restricted to the interpretation of the results. Despite this, possibly even because of it, all of these tools are very powerful and effective in the general exploration of texts. Their lack of specific involvement with the language or type of text under investigation means that the same types of software can be used for a wide range of languages and text types: they are effectively language independent tools. What they cannot do, however, without further input, is to provide a detailed analysis of the language of a corpus on the basis of a specific language model, or use the information that would be provided by this type of analysis. This limitation has already been noted in the descriptions of the basic tools in Chapters 3, 4 and 5. Some form of lemmatisation, for example, has been suggested as a useful basis for reorganising frequency lists, and the incorporation of rules to ensure the correct treatment of spelling variations throughout the three techniques has also been discussed. Both of these would involve adding detailed information about the language of the text to the basic software. The exploration of colligation, syntactic patterning rather than lexical patterning, demands extra information about the words in the corpus.

In general, more complex forms of investigation may only be possible if the computer has access to some form of detailed linguistic analysis of the text. This chapter discusses some of the approaches which can be adopted to make this type of information available to the computer, and some of the ways in which it can be used. Section 2 describes the main types of analysis and considers how they can be performed manually. Section 3 deals with the automation of the analysis and some of the problems involved. Section 4 describes the sublanguage approach and the contribution it can make to getting round these problems. Finally, section 5 looks at the contribution that the extra information can make to text exploration techniques.

2. THE MAIN AREAS OF ANALYSIS

For general research purposes the most important areas of additional linguistic information are those relating to syntax and semantics. The complete set of possible meanings and syntactic structures of the text in the corpus can be thought of as the ultimate additional information that the computer could be given. Any approach to this, however tentative, would need to begin with the fullest possible account of the syntactic and semantic properties of the language making up the texts. Section 2.1 describes the general principles of syntactic analysis, and section 2.2 outlines the approach to semantic disambiguation.

2.1. Syntactic analysis

If you want to carry out any form of syntactic analysis you will need a detailed description of the language model that you want to use, and of its relationship to the text that you want to analyse. The tasks involved in carrying out syntactic analysis can be considered independently of the level of computer involvement. First, you need to define the type of analysis that you want. The following sentence has been taken from the text of *Frankenstein*, already used as a source of examples in earlier chapters:

> You will smile at my allusion, but I will disclose a secret.

Before this sentence can be analysed a linguistic model must be chosen. To make the description as straightforward as possible I am going to use a simple clause analysis model, based on Halliday, in which each clause within a sentence is considered as consisting of some of the following components:

- predicator
- subject
- complement
- adjunct.

For a detailed explanation of the model and these terms see either Halliday (1961) or Malmkjær (1991). The analysis of the sentence would determine how many clauses it contains and would allocate the words in each clause to their appropriate component headings.

Before we can begin the analysis we need a detailed knowledge of the linguistic properties of the individual words in the text. This is available to all users of the language, because they need it to process the language every time they use it. Unless they have studied linguistics, however, they may not be conscious of the details of this knowledge and would almost certainly have problems in describing it explicitly. The detailed processing performed in the everyday use of language is still largely undocumented despite extensive research. Despite this it is possible to devise a practical approach to this form of analysis.

In the first place, it is often useful to divide the analysis into two stages. They involve the identification of the linguistic properties of the individual words, followed by the assessment of the functions of the words in relation to each other. The first stage is often called **tagging**, and the second stage **parsing**. The terms are generally used with these meanings throughout this chapter, but 'tagging' can also be used to describe the addition of other information, for example during the process of semantic disambiguation described in section 3, and 'parsing' is often used by other writers to describe the entire analysis process.

2.1.1. Tagging

The information attached to the individual words during the tagging process is usually its word class or the part of speech that it represents. First of all, the text needs to be divided into individual words:

You
will
smile
at
my
allusion
,
but
I
will
disclose
a
secret
.

Because punctuation is often important in the analysis of text, the comma and full stop have been treated as separate words. For each of these items, word class information can now be allocated. The simplest source of this information is probably the entry in a dictionary for each of the words, and the following word classes have been established using the grammar codes in *Collins Cobuild English Dictionary* (1995):

You	PRONOUN
will	MODAL/NOUN/VERB
smile	VERB/COUNT NOUN
at	PREPOSITION
my	POSSESSIVE DETERMINER
allusion	NOUN
,	PUNCTUATION
but	CO-ORDINATING CONJUNCTION
I	PRONOUN
will	MODAL/NOUN/VERB
disclose	VERB
a	DETERMINER
secret	ADJECTIVE/COUNT NOUN
.	PUNCTUATION

The word class information has been given in upper case to make it easier to distinguish from the original words. The dictionary has no entry for the punctuation (except as the nouns 'comma' and 'full stop'), so it has simply been labelled as 'PUNCTUATION' for the time being.

You will no doubt have noticed that not all of the words have single word class labels attached to them: *smile* can be either a verb or a count noun; *secret* can be a noun or an adjective; *will* can be a modal, a noun or a verb. This potential ambiguity may be important later when we attempt to parse the sentence.

2.1.2. Parsing

The word class information added to the words in the tagging process describes their potential roles as individual words. To parse the sentence we need to identify their functions as parts of a clause. The most important component of the clause is the predicator, and it is probably best to identify this first. The presence of the comma followed by the word *but*, tagged as a co-ordinating conjunction, makes it likely that there are two clauses in the sentence, so two predicators are needed. The predicator is realised by a verbal group, so it would be useful to identify any of those within the words. The possibilities are:

will	MODAL/UNCOUNT NOUN/COUNT NOUN/VERB
smile	VERB/COUNT NOUN

and:

will	MODAL/UNCOUNT NOUN/COUNT NOUN/VERB
disclose	VERB

For the user of the language the ambiguities in the word class tags will cause few problems. For the computer they could cause severe difficulty unless some method of disambiguation is provided. There are sources of information within the text which may make this possible.

Looking first at the possibilities for the first occurrence of *will*, the word *You*, tagged as a pronoun, coming immediately before it, suggests that it is a verb rather than a noun. The presence of *smile*, potentially a verb, immediately after it, makes the modal interpretation possible. The alternative possibility, that *smile* is a count noun, is made less likely by the fact that if it were the complement of *will* it would need some sort of determiner, such as *a* or *the*. This suggests that the first predicator is *will smile*. The word *I* immediately before the second *will* works in the same way as the pronoun *You*, and the unambiguous verb *disclose* following it makes it most likely to be a modal. The second predicator is therefore *will disclose*.

Once the predicators of the clauses have been identified, the tags of the remaining words make further parsing reasonably straightforward. The subjects *You* and *I* have already been identified as part of the disambiguation of *will*. The preposition *at* immediately after *smile* looks like a probable introduction to an adjunct, and the possessive determiner *my* and the noun *allusion* seem most likely to complete it before the comma marks the end of the first clause. The only remaining words in the second clause, the determiner *a* and the noun or adjective *secret* are reasonably easy to deal with. Following a determiner, and with no noun following it, *secret* can be identified as a count noun, and the nominal group *a secret* as the complement of *will disclose*. The final parse could be represented as:

> ⌈ [You] *Subject* ⌉
> | [will smile] *Predicator* | *Clause 1*
> ⌊ [at my allusion] *Adjunct* ⌋
> [, but] *Clause linker*
> ⌈ [I] *Subject* ⌉
> | [will disclose] *Predicator* | *Clause 2*
> ⌊ [a secret] *Complement* ⌋
> [.] *Sentence end*

If this level of analysis were needed for a large text or corpus the time and effort involved in carrying it out manually would be very significant. This was, after all, a very simple sentence.

2.2. Semantic disambiguation

Syntactic structure is not the only information which may be needed. The existence of homographs in English is one of the major problems affecting the usefulness of basic corpus exploration tools. Section 2.2.3 of Chapter 3 describes the problems that they can cause for frequency lists, section 4.2 of Chapter 4 does the same for concordances, and section 5.1 of Chapter 5 describes their implications for collocation analysis. To overcome this problem, the software needs some way of differentiating between different senses of the same character string. For smaller texts the simplest method would be the manual encoding (or 'tagging') of each occurrence of the word with a clear disambiguation.

As an example, consider the following sentences taken from the *Frankenstein* text:

1.   I profited of this time to rest for a few hours.

2.   Among these there was one which attracted my mother far above all the rest.

3.   For this I had deprived myself of rest and health.

Each contains the word form *rest* used in a different sense. The definitions provided for these senses in a *Collins Cobuild English Dictionary* (1995) are:

1.   If you **rest** or if you **rest** your body, you do not do anything active for a time. (**rest 2**, sense 1)

2.   The **rest** is used to refer to all the parts of something or all the things in a group that remain or that you have not already mentioned. (**rest 1**, sense 1)

3.   If you get some **rest** or have a **rest**, you do not do anything active for a time. (**rest 2**, sense 2)

Once the appropriate sense had been identified for each occurrence in the text, it could be signalled by a code added to the word form. In the annotated examples below, given in their original order of occurrence in the text, a simple number code has been used, relating to the three senses identified in the sample sentences. The tagged word form has been set in bold type simply to make it easier to spot.

> I took refuge in the courtyard belonging to the house which I inhabited, where I remained during the **rest_2** of the night, walking up and down in the greatest agitation, listening attentively, catching and fearing each sound as if it were to announce the approach of the demoniacal corpse to which I had so miserably given life.

> Mingled with this horror, I felt the bitterness of disappointment; dreams that had been my food and pleasant **rest_3** for so long a space were now become a hell to me; and the change was so rapid, the overthrow so complete!

> We returned again, with torches; for I could not **rest_1**, when I thought that my sweet boy had lost himself, and was exposed to all the damps and dews of night; Elizabeth also suffered extreme anguish.

As with large scale syntactic analysis, this can obviously be a fairly complex and time-consuming process, particularly if something more than the disambiguation of a few word forms is needed. Some useful short-cuts may be available. For example, sense 1 in the above examples is grammatically different from senses 2 and 3, and if the text had been through a process of syntactic tagging this would already have achieved part of what was needed. It would still not provide disambiguation between senses 2 and 3, of course, and this would need to be done manually. Semantic disambiguation can become much more efficient if you use a concordance program as an aid to the identification of senses, as suggested in section 2.4.3 of Chapter 4, but any large scale exercise in manual disambiguation is likely to involve significant time and effort.

3. AUTOMATING THE ANALYSIS

The analyses described in section 2 were performed manually. In the process of syntactic tagging, the dictionary was consulted for each word in the sentence and the range of possible word classes was entered. For the parsing process these word classes were then used to identify clause boundaries and to allocate the words to the potential clause components. To achieve semantic disambiguation each occurrence of the ambiguous word form was matched against its possible senses, one was selected on the basis of context and the word was labelled appropriately. It would obviously be very useful if these tasks could be performed automatically. Sections 3.1 to 3.3 examine some of the problems involved in trying to achieve this.

Several different levels of computer involvement can be considered. At one extreme the detailed linguistic analysis could be performed manually. The computer would then be used simply to collate and summarise the results or to make them available for further investigation. If this approach were adopted no extra software would be needed. The frequency list, concordance and collocation tools described in Chapters 3 to 5 would be modified to make them able to recognise the manually applied codes. At the other extreme, the computer could carry out some or all of the analysis automatically. This approach demands relatively complex language specific software. The next three sections outline the main possible approaches.

3.1. Tagging

The automation of the manual process described in section 2.1 would not, at first sight, seem to involve too many difficulties. The dictionary information could be stored in computer-readable form, and for each word in the text the grammar code would simply be retrieved and used as the tag. This would produce the same sort of result as is shown in section 2.1, with more than one tag assigned to some words, and this may be a problem. If unambiguous tags are needed, the software will need to do a little more work. There is another possible complication. Looking up words in a dictionary is fine if all the words you need are in there and have enough detail in their grammar codes for your purposes. For the sentence which was analysed in section 2.1 this was not a problem, but no dictionary can contain all the words that could be encountered in a text.

As an extreme example, consider the first stanza of the poem 'Jabberwocky' from Lewis Carroll's *Through the Looking-glass*:

> 'Twas brillig, and the slithy toves
>   Did gyre and gimble in the wabe;
> All mimsy were the borogoves,
>   And the mome raths outgrabe.

Some of the words in this text would not be found in any dictionary, because they were invented specially for the poem. Even *The Oxford English Dictionary* does not include all of them. It has *slithy* and *toves*, for example, but not *brillig* or *borogoves*.

This may seem a rather unfair example, but consider the following text:

> The output power of each carrier divided by the intermodulation noise temperature in the frequency bandwidth of the carrier is the C/T intermodulation ratio that is used in link budget calculations.

The sentence is taken from chapter 2 of the *Handbook on Satellite Communications*, part of the ITU corpus. It is rather specialised, but certainly not nonsense. Again, few general-purpose dictionaries would have all of the terms used in this sentence. The creation of new dictionaries to cope with all the words that could be encountered in texts would be a mammoth task, if indeed it were possible. To overcome this problem taggers often have routines built into them which allow them to guess the word classes of words which are not covered by their dictionaries.

To show the results of using an automatic tagger both on known and unknown words, here are some samples of the output of a tagging program developed during the early days of the COBUILD dictionary project. First, the sentence from *Frankenstein* used as an example of manual tagging in section 2.1:

PN	You	LNK	but
MOD	will	PN	I
VB	smile	MOD	will
PREP	at	VB	disclose
D	my	D	a
N	allusion	ADJ	secret
#	,	.	.

The labels used are rather more abbreviated than in the manual version, but they are essentially the same. The abbreviations used stand for:

#	punctuation other than full stop	N	noun
ADJ	adjective	PN	pronoun
D	determiner	PREP	preposition
LNK	linker	VB	verb
MOD	modal	.	full stop

They are also, of course, unambiguous. *will* has been tagged definitely as a modal, *smile* equally definitely as a verb. The tagging of *secret* may seem rather odd, but its mistaken identification as an adjective in this case is unlikely to affect the parsing process.

Taking the Lewis Carroll nonsense sentence next, the tagger managed to produce tags, although the analysis is not complete:

-S	Twas	#	;
??	brillig	D	All
#	,	N	mimsy
LNK	and	COP	were
D	the	D	the
ADJ	slithy	NPL	borogoves
NPL	toves	#	,
VB	Did	LNK	And
??	gyre	D	the
LNK	and	ADJ	mome
VB	gimble	NPL	raths
PREP	in	??	outgrabe
D	the	.	.
N	wabe		

There are two new definite tags in this analysis:

COP	the verb *to be* used as a copulative
NPL	plural noun

and two ambiguous ones:

-S	a word ending in -s, which could be a plural noun or the third person singular of a verb
??	unknown

Given the nature of the input, the tagging process seems to have gone remarkably well. Among the nonsense words *slithy, toves, gimble, wabe, borogoves, mome* and *raths* all seem to have the correct tags. It is, of course, possible to assess the correctness despite the fact that these are invented words because there is enough structure left in the text for word classes to be reasonably obvious. The tagger has given up on *brillig*, partly because of the ambiguity surrounding *twas*, on *gyre*, probably because of confusion caused by the preceding word *did*, and on *outgrabe*. The determiner tag allocated to *all* seems to be an error, and this has made it tag *mimsy* as a noun rather than an adjective. Distorted word order is probably partly responsible for this.

The program could have had similar problems with the tagging of the technical sentence. Here is the output:

D	The	D	the
N	output	N	carrier
??	power	COP	is
PREP	of	D	the
ADJ	each	ADJ	C
N	carrier	N	T
VB	divided	N	intermodulation
PREP	by	N	ratio
D	the	CJ	that
N	intermodulation	AUX	is
N	noise	PAP	used
N	temperature	PREP	in
PREP	in	ADJ	link
D	the	N	budget
N	frequency	NPL	calculations
??	bandwidth	.	.
PREP	of		

Three new tags are introduced in this example:

AUX	auxiliary verb
CJ	conjunction
PAP	past participle

Only two words have been given the unknown tag '??': *power* and *bandwidth*. Their position immediately after nouns may be responsible for this. The only other peculiarity is the tagging of the first part of the ratio *C/T* as an adjective, and the second part as a noun, and the tagging of *link* as an adjective. As with the first example sentence neither of these is likely to cause major problems at the parsing stage.

A reasonable level of automatic tagging seems to be achievable. Some programs, like the one demonstrated above, attempt to produce unambiguous tags, and the selection process can be fooled by unusual context or unfamiliar words. Programs which simply allocate the range of possible word classes, in the same way as the manual tagging shown in section 2.1, tend by their nature to produce more accurate results, but they obviously leave rather more problems for the parsing stage. The major advantage of automatic tagging is the enormous amount of time that it can save, especially in a large corpus. Its major disadvantage is the potential of the software for systematic errors if it is not properly designed to cope with your text's characteristics.

3.2. Parsing

The automation of the parsing process tends to be rather more complex than the automation of tagging. The automatic parser which is capable of dealing accurately and unambiguously with completely unrestricted English texts has not yet been developed, although many systems can now boast reasonable accuracy levels within some textual restrictions.

Section 2.1 shows that, even for a relatively simple sentence, the decisions involved in parsing can be both complicated in themselves and difficult to formulate rigorously. Even the identification of clause boundaries demanded a certain amount of juggling with the number of potential predicators and the presence of a co-ordinating conjunction, and was performed in a slightly *ad hoc* way which did not cover the possibilities that could arise in other cases. The complexity arises partly from the number of stages involved in the parsing process, each of which operates at a different level of analysis. For the grammar model used in section 2.1 they could be summarised as:

● identification of clause boundaries

● identification of group boundaries

● allocation of groups to clause components.

To reduce the complexity of the parsing process we can consider the boundary-marking stage separately. The output shown below was produced by the Boundary Marker program described in Coniam (1995). It marks the types of boundary found between each of the words in the sentence from *Frankenstein* used in section 2. The software used to produce it was designed as a partial parser. It identifies all of the boundaries found within the sentence, but does not makes the final allocation to clause components.

```
[ ( main clause bdry
                                    You    )
    ( group bdry
                                    will   )
    ( word bdry
                                    smile  )
    ( group bdry
                                    at     )
    ( prepositional bdry
                                    my     )
    ( word bdry
                                    allusion   )
    ( group bdry
```

```
                                           ,    )
(  main clause bdry
                                    but   )
(  group bdry
                                     I    )
(  group bdry
                                    will  )
(  word bdry
                                  disclose )
(  group bdry
                                     a    )
(  word bdry
                                   secret )
(  main clause bdry
                                     .    )    ]
```

This may seem, at first sight, slightly difficult to interpret. The line between each pair of words contains a description of the type of boundary identified for them. The main types of boundary shown in this analysis are 'main clause' (for example between the comma and *but*), 'group' (for example between *You* and *will*) and 'word' (for example between *will* and *smile*). There is also something called a 'prepositional' boundary (between *at* and *my*). These boundaries can be used to produce a summarised list of the clauses and the groups within them. In the list below, word and prepositional boundaries are treated as subdivisions within their groups:

Main clause 1:
        Group 1: You
        Group 2: will smile
        Group 3: at my allusion
        Group 4: ,
Main clause 2:
        Group 1: but
        Group 2: I
        Group 3: will disclose
        Group 4: a secret.

The final full stop forms the sentence boundary and ends the second main clause.

The program has effectively carried out the first two stages of parsing described above. The allocation of the groups to clause components can probably also be achieved using this analysis, but some other information is needed, mainly so that the types of group found within the clauses can be established. This information can also be extracted from the output produced by the program. As part of the work needed in the identification of the boundaries it tags the words in the text with their syntactic properties, and these tags can be used, together with the boundary markers, to help in making the allocation decisions. The list below (extracted from output produced by the program) combines this information:

```
main clause bdry        subj_pron               You
group bdry              aux/modal               will
word bdry               non_fin_verb_base       smile
group bdry              preposition             at
prepositional bdry      determiner              my
word bdry               noun_count              allusion
group bdry              comma                   ,
main clause bdry        but_conj                but
group bdry              subj_pron               I
group bdry              aux/modal               will
word bdry               non_fin_verb_base       disclose
group bdry              a_determiner            a
word bdry               noun_count              secret
main clause bdry        clause_punc             .
```

Taking the boundary markers and the tags together it is relatively easy to rearrange this data to make it easier to process. Clause boundaries are marked with an asterisk:

```
subj_pron                             You
aux/modal;non_fin_verb_base           will smile
preposition;determiner;noun_count     at my allusion
comma                                 ,
*
but_conj                              but
subj_pron                             I
aux/modal;non_fin_verb_base           will disclose
a_determiner;noun_count               a secret
*
```

From this point it is a straightforward matter to use the tags to determine the types of group involved.:

```
You                     NOMINAL
will smile              VERBAL
at my allusion          PREPOSITIONAL
,
*
but
I                       NOMINAL
will disclosure         VERBAL
a secret                NOMINAL
*
.
```

Finally, this classification of the groups allows them to be allocated to the clause components:

```
You                     SUBJECT
will smile              PREDICATOR
at my allusion          ADJUNCT
```

```
                                    END OF CLAUSE 1
but
I                                   SUBJECT
will disclose                       PREDICATOR
a secret                            OBJECT
                                    END OF CLAUSE 2
```

The information provided by the partial parser has now been used to parse the sentence fully according to the grammatical model adopted. The final allocation technique is extremely crude, and will only produce reliable results from unproblematic sentences which follow a fairly fixed word order, but it provides an example of what can be done. The simple programs which carry out the various stages of the allocation process are described in Appendix 3.

3.3. Semantic disambiguation

Although semantic disambiguation is a relatively complex process, it may be possible to automate at least some of it and achieve reasonable levels of accuracy. The text surrounding the word form under investigation question should contain enough information to identify the correct usage, but the machine will need a set of routines which can make this information available to it in a form that it can use. The collocation analysis techniques described in Chapter 5 could provide a suitable basis for beginning the process. Comparative collocation data would be needed for all the possible senses of the word so that the patterns found in the immediate neighbourhood of the word in the text could be checked for their implications. This could perhaps be provided from a reference corpus which has already been disambiguated, or from information extracted from a machine readable dictionary.

As a fairly obvious example of the use of context for disambiguation, consider the following sentence taken from the *Frankenstein* text:

> We accordingly lay to, hoping that some change would take place in the atmosphere and weather.

The presence of the verb *take* immediately before *place* allows it to be interpreted as part of the phrasal verb *take place*. Collocation analysis can provide a good basis for the identification of phrases, and the possibilities are described in sections 4.1 and 4.2 of Chapter 5. Once phrases have been identified they can be used to help disambiguate the meanings of different phrasal occurrences of the same word form.

The following sense of *place* can also be disambiguated from its context, but it may require a knowledge of a greater range of potential collocates, or the use of other information:

> I replied that I could not answer with any degree of certainty, for the ice

had not broken until near midnight, and the traveller might have arrived at a place of safety before that time; but of this I could not judge.

In a case like this the disambiguation process can be made easier if some syntactic analysis has already been carried out. The tagger described in section 3.1 produced this output for the relevant part of the sentence:

D	the	N	place
N	traveller	PREP	of
??	might	N	safety
AUX	have	PREP	before
PAP	arrived	D	that
PREP	at	N	time
D	a	#	;

The word *place* is unambiguously tagged as a noun, and its immediate context includes the determiner *a* and the preposition and noun *of safety*. The 'noun of noun' pattern found in *place of safety* may now be capable of identification with other similar collocational patterns, allowing the sense to be identified correctly.

4. SCALING DOWN THE PROBLEM: THE USE OF SUBLANGUAGES

The development of taggers, parsers and semantic disambiguators capable of dealing with unrestricted English text is an enormously complex task, and one which is beyond the scope of this book to describe. But there is a technique which can allow you to explore restricted areas of a language much more easily. The sublanguage approach described below can make it possible for you to disregard, at least temporarily, many of the complications which arise if you try to deal with the unrestricted totality of a 'natural' language.

In this context the word 'natural' differentiates the type of language used by human speech communities from the artificial languages created as potential world languages or for computer programming, formal logic and so on. It also highlights the main problem involved in dealing with it. Natural language is intrinsically more complex than artificial language because it is formed by dynamic, unconscious agreement within its user community, and is not deliberately designed for a specific and limited set of tasks. The details of its operation are probably not capable of being fully documented, whereas artificial language is fully specified within its design. It also changes constantly as the speech community adapts to different linguistic needs, often in unpredictable and apparently inconsistent ways. If the area of language that you are investigating is susceptible to the sublanguage approach, many of these inherent complexities can be significantly reduced.

4.1. What is a sublanguage?

The concept of a sublanguage has been used by several researchers as the basis for investigating and manipulating specific types of natural language. The features that distinguish a sublanguage have been described (in Lehrberger 1982: 102) as including:

- limited subject matter

- lexical, syntactic and semantic restrictions

- 'deviant' rules of grammar

- a high frequency of certain constructions

- unusual features of text structure

- the use of special symbols.

These characteristics tend to be found in texts produced for specialised purposes, including descriptions of scientific processes, medical records, aviation maintenance manuals, weather forecasting and so on. The recognition of their special features can usefully restrict the scope and nature of the tasks involved in analysing them. This in turn means that activities like tagging and parsing become much easier. Obviously, only certain types of language lend themselves to this approach. In the second case study described in Chapter 8, for example, the technique is applied to dictionary definition sentences.

4.2. Using the sublanguage approach

The main difference between the general language approach and the sublanguage approach lies in the extent and nature of the linguistic features that you need to take into account. If you are dealing with a sublanguage, you may simply need to cope with its restricted set of realisations for very specific communicative purposes, instead of tackling the fundamental nature of a language's operation over its full range of potential uses. In these circumstances syntactic tagging and parsing no longer need to be carried out on a universal general language basis, but can be modified to cover just the functions and relationships actually used in the sublanguage. At least three of the distinguishing features of sublanguages described above – limited subject matter, lexical, syntactic and semantic restrictions, and the high frequency of certain constructions – tend to reduce the overall possibilities of variation within them, while the 'deviant' rules of grammar, unusual features of text structure and the use of special symbols should represent elements of the structural framework which are already partly documented.

As already mentioned, the second case study in Chapter 8 describes the use of this approach in the development of a parser for dictionary definition sentences. The restrictions on lexis, syntax and semantics allowed a grammar to be built up which applied only to the definition sentences. This grammar is based on a structural taxonomy which was developed for the definition sentences. The taxonomy contains 17 sentence structure types which together provide a basis for the complete functional analysis of over 31,000 definition sentences in the *Collins Cobuild Student's Dictionary*. Full details are given in section 3.3 of Chapter 8.

5. ENHANCING CORPUS EXPLORATION TECHNIQUES

The text investigation tools described in Chapters 3, 4 and 5 are all rather crude, largely because they rely on the recognition of strings of characters to make their processing decisions. Earlier discussions of the problems affecting the output of word frequency, concordance and collocation software suggest that the extra information provided by syntactic tagging and parsing and semantic disambiguation could remove some of these problems and enhance corpus exploration techniques. Section 5.1 considers the advantages of tagging corpus texts with syntactic or semantic information and section 5.2 deals with the uses that can be made of parsed texts.

5.1. Using tags

The main problems affecting the use of word frequency, concordance and collocation software arise from their inability either to distinguish between different uses of the same word form or to treat different word forms as representative of the same item. For example, the word *thought* occurs 74 times in the *Frankenstein* text. An extract from the concordance lines shows that this word form can represent several different linguistic units:

```
 1  I wished sometimes to shake off all thought and feeling, but I learned that ther
 2  ed, I felt a wish for happiness and thought with melancholy delight of my belove
 3  re no injustice in this? Am I to be thought the only criminal, when all humankin
 4  no need of a remoter charm,        By thought supplied, or any interest        Unbor
 5  , and I banished from my mind every thought that could lead to a different concl
 6  inually falling on the head. Every  thought that was devoted to it was an extrem
 7  , and dark melancholy clouded every thought. The rain was pouring in torrents, a
 8  nquietude and impatience, my father thought it best to yield. We took our passa
 9  he schools of Geneva, but my father thought it necessary for the completion of m
10  How could you suppose that my first  thought would not fly towards those dear, de
11  ned to my father's house. My first   thought was to discover what I knew of the m
12  leep did not afford me respite from thought and misery; my dreams presented a th
13  reat God! If for one instant I had  thought what might be the hellish intention
14  of fifteen. It is true that I have   thought more and that my daydreams are more
15  rehensions. For a long time I have  thought that each post would bring this line
16  being, but certainly I should have  thought such a creature unfit to remain in t
17  ather a severe tone, "I should have thought, young man, that the presence of you
18   pleased the magistrate; perhaps he thought that my former exclamation was a mom
19  to banish my despair. Sometimes he  thought that I felt deeply the degradation o
20  wledge. I had often, when at home,  thought it hard to remain during my youth co
21  and ascertain my fate. Sometimes I  thought that the fiend followed me and might
22  ger conducive to my improvements, I thought of returning to my friends and my na
23  ting my hands before my eyes, for I thought I saw the dreaded spectre glide into
24  otonous yet ever-changing scene. I  thought of Switzerland; it was far different
25  tried to stifle these sensations; I thought that as I could not sympathize with
```

Eight of these twenty-five lines (1, 4–7 and 10–12) are occurrences of one of the noun senses of *thought*, while the remaining seventeen represent the past form of the verb *to think*. The confusion of these separate linguistic units within the word frequency list and the concordance lines distorts the results of using these techniques. If they could be distinguished by a combination of syntactic and semantic tagging these tools and the collocation analysis derived from them could be used more effectively.

5.1.1. Syntactic tags

The general approach used in syntactic tagging has already been described in section 2.1. Whether the analysis process is completely manual, completely automatic or a combination of the two, the normal result will be an annotated version of the original text in which individual words are tagged with information which shows their syntactic properties. The text exploration software may need slight modifications to make use of the information contained in these tags, but the overall effect would be that both the frequency list and the concordance lines could be organised on a basis that goes beyond character-string recognition. If the process had been applied to the *Frankenstein* text, the frequency list and the concordance program could have separated *thought* as a verb from *thought* as a noun simply on the basis of the tags.

Some corpora which have been developed as general research resources have been comprehensively tagged so that this can be done. The Lancaster-Oslo/ Bergen (LOB) corpus, for example, is available in both tagged and untagged form. It was tagged using the CLAWS (Constituent-Likelihood Automatic Word-tagging System) combined with post-editing. The process is described in Garside, Leech and Sampson (1987). The tags make the text rather more difficult to read for the human researcher, but they provide the information needed by the computer to differentiate between identical word forms which are being used as different parts of speech. Here is a sample taken from the beginning of the corpus:

```
A01    2 ^ *'_*' stop_VB electing_VBG life_NN peers_NNS **"_** ._.
A01    3 ^ by_IN Trevor_NP Williams_NP ._.
A01    4 ^ a_AT move_NN to_TO stop_VB \0Mr_NPT Gaitskell_NP from_IN
A01    4 nominating_VBG any_DTI more_AP labour_NN
A01    5 life_NN peers_NNS is_BEZ to_TO be_BE made_VBN at_IN a_AT meeting_NN
A01    5 of_IN labour_NN \0MPs_NPTS tomorrow_NR ._.
A01    6 ^ \0Mr_NPT Michael_NP Foot_NP has_HVZ put_VBN down_RP a_AT
A01    6 resolution_NN on_IN the_ATI subject_NN and_CC
A01    7 he_PP3A is_BEZ to_TO be_BE backed_VBN by_IN \0Mr_NPT Will_NP
A01    7 Griffiths_NP ,_, \0MP_NPT for_IN Manchester_NP
A01    8 Exchange_NP ._.
A01    9 ^ though_CS they_PP3AS may_MD gather_VB some_DTI left-wing_JJB
A01    9 support_NN ,_, a_AT large_JJ majority_NN
A01    10 of_IN labour_NN \0MPs_NPTS are_BER likely_JJ to_TO turn_VB down_RP
A01    10 the_ATI Foot-Griffiths_NP
A01    11 resolution_NN ._.
```

The tags used in this extract are fairly detailed: even this relatively small extract uses over 30 different tags. A full explanation of the tags is provided with the corpus on the CD-ROM which contains the ICAME Collection of English Corpora, referred to in section 3.1.3 of Chapter 2. A frequency list produced from the corpus which incorporates the tags has three distinct entries for the word *thought*:

thought_nn	112
thought_vbd	106
thought_vbn	61

These three tagged word forms can also be searched for separately using the concordance software, so that concordance lines can be produced for *thought* as a noun (nn), as the past tense of the verb *think* (vbd) and as its past participle (vbn). The first five concordance lines produced for each of these items are shown below:

NOUN

```
1  A30 79 and_CC sincerity_NN of_IN   thought_NN ._. A30 80 ^ \0Clr_NPT Brook_N
2  iven_VBN it_PP3 much_AP serious_JJ thought_NN ._. **'_**' A40 76 ^ if_CS he_
3  X are_BER two_CD schools_NNS of_IN thought_NN about_IN B18 54 the_ATI advantage
4  coherent_JJ body_NN G60 9 of_IN    thought_NN about_IN society_NN related_VBN to
5  ,_, J52 75 without_IN taking_VBG   thought_NN about_IN it_PP3 ._. ^ when_WRB J52
```

PAST TENSE

```
1  BD ._. ^ when_WRB Alan_NP P26 150  thought_VBD about_IN it_PP3 ,_, it_PP3 seemed_
2  65 melt_VB away_RP if_CS he_PP3A    thought_VBD about_IN her_PP3O now_RN ._. ^ K27
3  crushed_VBN ._. ^ he_PP3A K27 78    thought_VBD about_IN that_DT sort_NN of_IN dea
4  Gallery_NPL ._. ^ K27 67 he_PP3A    thought_VBD about_IN K27 68 Rosemary_NP ,_, b
5  ._. **'_**' K27 86 ^ he_PP3A        thought_VBD about_IN Rosemary's_NP$ house_NN .
```

PAST PARTICIPLE

```
1  e_PP10 her_PP$ husband_NN had_HVD  thought_VBN A33 51 of_IN going_VBG to_IN Amer
2  15 130 my_PP$ plate_NN ,_, and_CC  thought_VBN about_IN \0Mr_NPT Raoul_NP N15 130
3  ge_NN has_HVZ R08 112 to_TO be_BE  thought_VBN about_IN to_TO be_BE believed_VBN
4  was_BEDZ at_RB first_RB" J73 13    thought_VBN advisable_JJ to_TO run_VB the_ATI
5  would_MD have_HV been_BEN D02 190  thought_VBN an_AT intrusion_NN ._. ^ the_ATI D
```

If necessary, the lines could be processed after extraction to remove the tags and make them easier to read.

These tags can also be used in a rather different way, so that your exploration of the text can concentrate on the syntactic patterns represented by word sequences rather than on the words themselves. The analysis software could be set up to recognise only the tags, or a new version of the text could be produced composed entirely of sequences of tags. If we did this to the first part of the tagged LOB corpus shown above it would become:

    ★'VB VBG NN NNS ★★' .

    IN NP NP .

```
AT NN TO VB NPT NP IN
VBG DTI AP NN
NN NNS BEZ TO BE VBN IN AT NN
IN NN NPTS NR .
NPT NP NP HVZ VBN RP AT
NN IN ATI NN CC
PP3A BEZ TO BE VBN IN NPT NP
NP , NPT IN NP
NP .
CS PP3AS MD VB DTI JJB
NN , AT JJ NN
IN NN NPTS BER JJ TO VB RP
ATI NP
NN .
```

The tag sequences in the text are now available for conventional frequency list and concordance software to work on. The units need no longer be the individual words: either entire sentences or smaller groups of tags could be investigated to establish frequencies of occurrences of particular patterns. The simple program used to reduce the text to a string of tags is described in Appendix 3.

5.1.2. Semantic tags

Semantic tagging can provide the same advantages as its syntactic equivalent when you are investigating words which are used in more than one sense within a text. Going back to the example of the word *thought* in the *Frankenstein* text, the concordance lines for the noun in the extract used in section 5.1.1 are:

```
1  I wished sometimes to shake off all thought and feeling, but I learned that ther
2  ed, I felt a wish for happiness and thought with melancholy delight of my belove
4  no need of a remoter charm,   By    thought supplied, or any interest   Unbor
5  , and I banished from my mind every thought that could lead to a different concl
6  inually falling on the head. Every  thought that was devoted to it was an extrem
7  , and dark melancholy clouded every thought. The rain was pouring in torrents, a
10 How could you suppose that my first  thought would not fly towards those dear, de
11 ned to my father's house. My first   thought was to discover what I knew of the m
12 leep did not afford me respite from thought and misery; my dreams presented a th
```

Two senses of the word seem to be present here, the general activity of thinking, shown in lines 1, 2, 4 and 12, and the individual ideas that occur to the thinker, shown in lines 5, 6, 7, 10 and 11. If the text had been tagged with this distinction a similar separation to that suggested for the different syntactic manifestations of the word could have been achieved.

5.1.3. Parsed texts

The main difference between text which has been parsed and text which has simply been tagged is the scope of the analysis. With some possible exceptions in the case of phrasal structures, tagging provides information about individual words. Parsing, on the other hand, should identify the structural relationships of groups of words. This changes the potential research perspective in an important way. Instead of being restricted to text exploration at word level, you should be capable of dealing with larger, potentially more significant linguistic units. The extra information provided by the parsing process should also remove much of the ambiguity from the text, so that your investigation can be more closely focused and more efficient.

Because of this shift away from the individual word in parsed texts, the approach suggested in section 5.1.1, where the syntactic tags replace the word forms as the basis of the investigation, could be very useful. The structural units of the parsed text could form the basic chunks for defining the boundaries of tag sequences.

6. NATURAL LANGUAGE PROCESSING AND NATURAL LANGUAGE UNDERSTANDING

The detailed language analysis processes involved in syntactic tagging, parsing and semantic disambiguation are often gathered together with other similar tasks under the general heading of Natural Language Processing (or NLP). If texts can be analysed automatically to reveal both their syntactic structures and their semantic features it should be possible to take the process a stage further. The difficulties arising from the use of computers in the investigation of texts can generally be ascribed to their inability to 'understand' the information contained in them in any human sense. The basic analysis tools depend on matching patterns formed by the character strings which represent the words. They cannot access the meanings of words themselves, or of the texts that they form. If NLP could be developed to the point where computers become capable of 'understanding' the meaning of a text and acting on it, both text exploration techniques and the applications which exploit them could be enormously improved.

The nature of this 'understanding' perhaps needs to be established a little more clearly. It is not the same process as humans are capable of, but it should allow the computer to perform at least some of the same operations as a human who has understood the same piece of text. The most important of these operations from a practical viewpoint is probably the ability to infer other information correctly from the contents of the text. As an example, consider the following sentence (taken from *The Realms of Gold*, by Margaret Drabble 1977, p.146):

> Her mother made the tea, while Janet finished the chicken, and started the sauce.

The human reader would have no difficulty, given the preceding text, in identifying *her* as referring to Janet. The sense of *made* appropriate to *tea* would be easily disambiguated from others in the range of possible meanings. The word *tea* itself would be easily interpreted as the hot drink rather than the meal because of the earlier sentences (on p. 145 of the same text):

> 'Would you like a cup of tea, Mummy?' said Janet. 'Would you mind putting the kettle on? My hands are all chickeny.'
> 'Don't let me hold you up,' said her mother, going to fill the kettle.

For similar reasons there would be few problems involved in interpreting *finished* and *started* as descriptions of different stages of the processes of preparing food. Readers with little or no experience of cookery might not have a clear picture of the details underlying the preparation of the chicken or the sauce, but as the text is not a cookery book this will probably have little real effect on their appreciation or 'understanding' of the text.

If the same sentence is considered from the computer's viewpoint, the same degree of linguistic appreciation of the text's implications should be perfectly adequate for most purposes. The ability to replace the possessive *her* with the name of the person to whom it refers, and to disambiguate words like *made, tea, finished* and *started*, should allow the computer to 'understand' the linguistic relationships defined by the text, to report accurately on their implications and to react appropriately.

The complexity inherent in natural language has already been described in section 4, and for all of the reasons given there most of the techniques currently being developed as part of the quest to enable computers to achieve fully automatic natural language understanding are themselves extremely complex and demand significant computational resources. Chapter 7 outlines some of the main applications which use these techniques or which could be enhanced by using them.

7. SUMMARY

Syntactic tagging, parsing and semantic disambiguation can provide valuable extra information which can significantly enhance your exploration of corpus texts. The major problems involved in using them are:

- they are time-consuming to carry out manually on large volumes of text

- they can be difficult to automate with sufficient accuracy.

If the language under investigation has the appropriate characteristics it may be possible to reduce the linguistic complexity which causes these problems by using the sublanguage approach.

FURTHER READING

Coniam, D. J. (1995) 'Boundary Marker: a partial parser', unpublished Ph.D. thesis, School of English, University of Birmingham.

Garside, R., Leech, G. and Sampson, G. (eds) (1987) *The Computational Analysis of Engish*, London: Longman.

Grishman, R. and Kittredge R. (eds) (1986) *Analyzing Language in Restricted Domains: Sublanguage Description and Processing,* Hillsdale: Lawrence Erlbaum Associates.

Grune, D. and Jacobs, C. J. H. (1990) *Parsing Techniques: A Practical Guide,* Chichester: Ellis Horwood.

Halliday, M. A. K. (1985) *An Introduction to Functional Grammar,* London, New York, Melbourne and Auckland: Edward Arnold.

The leading edge: applications of natural language processing

1. WHY DO COMPUTERS NEED TO UNDERSTAND LANGUAGE?

The desire to give computers the ability to process and understand natural language is not a purely academic goal directed towards obscure research objectives. It is a crucial requirement of many commercial applications currently under development, and would significantly enhance many processes already in use. This chapter outlines some of the most important areas in which the existing or potential future ability of computers to analyse natural language is involved.

The extent to which each of the areas described below currently make use of NLP capability varies greatly. Word processing and lexicography are conducted reasonably effectively without using it to any great extent, although it would greatly enhance important aspects of their operation. Data retrieval is rather cumbersome and inefficient without it, although it is certainly possible. Even computer assisted language learning gets along without it, although the lack of it is often sorely felt. The development of expert systems, machine translation and speech recognition are unlikely to be fully effective on any practical level until NLP has developed to a much higher stage than currently appears possible.

2. WORD PROCESSING

Although most word processing software contains rudimentary concordancing facilities, so that text patterns can be searched for and, if necessary, replaced with other patterns, they make little real use of language analysis techniques. Section 2.1 investigates the enhancements that could be made to the spell checking software used in word processing packages through the use of these techniques, 2.2 considers grammar and style checkers, and 2.3 and 2.4 consider other facilities which could be incorporated into word processing software if automatic natural language understanding were fully developed.

2.1. Better spelling

The spell checking routines found in most major word processing packages would benefit greatly from an ability to disambiguate the senses of the words being verified. If a misspelling in a document is the correct form of another word the spell checker will normally accept it, since they usually operate purely on the basis of a comparison of the forms found in the text with a list of acceptable forms. Because of this the software would not detect, for example, the incorrect substitution of *loose* for *lose*, or *their* for *there*.

The use of a semantic disambiguator within the spell checking software would make it possible for the computer to carry out something much closer to automatic proof-reading. The incorporation of a parser could bring the software sufficiently close to a form of machine understanding of the text for full automatic checking of the contents. This facility could either be used in the same way as most current spell checkers, as a tool which examines the text once it has been created, or it could monitor text during the writing process and report problems as they occur. Some word processors already use this approach with their existing spell checking software.

2.2. Checking grammar and style

Many word processors already include primitive grammar checkers as part of their tools. These tend to be rather less useful than the spell checkers, probably because they are trying to do something rather more complex than they are capable of. As an example, the sentence below was checked using the grammar tool in a popular word processing package:

> The detailed language analysis processes involved in syntactic tagging, parsing and semantic disambiguation are often gathered together with other similar tasks under the general heading of Natural Language Processing (or NLP).

The sentence was highlighted with the warning message:

> The word **disambiguation** does not agree with are.

and the advice:

> Consider **is** instead of **are**.

The source of this error is fairly obvious. The subject of the sentence is not *disambiguation* but *the detailed language analysis processes involved in syntactic tagging, parsing and semantic disambiguation*, and the analysis tool has too short a span to be able to refer back properly to the plural noun *processes*. The tool provides only a very primitive approach to grammatical analysis and its comment seem rather unhelpful. Significant improvements to the technique will only be achieved if the program acquires a form of NLP capability which allows it to analyse the sentences fully and produce more useful and accurate guidance.

If this could be done, the word processing software would be able to detect:

- grammatical problems, giving a fully accurate description and useful suggestions for improvement

- departures from the style specified for the document or observed by the computer in the surrounding text

- repetition of ideas expressed within pieces of adjacent text, even where the words used to express them are significantly different.

As with the spell checker improvements suggested in section 2.1 above, these would all contribute to the automation of a significant part of the proof-reading process.

2.3. Checking textual consistency

Checking the consistency of substantial pieces of writing, including the accuracy of cross-references between different parts of the text, is often the most time-consuming element of proof-reading. Many word processing packages already include some measures to ensure that information included at several different points in the text is automatically changed throughout if it is altered at the point of first appearance. Many also allow the results of calculations to be entered as mathematical formulae rather than as numbers so that changes in the underlying data will automatically alter the value of the results. These facilities are extremely useful, but they cannot give you control over the meaning of the text, to ensure that changes in the contents of one text element are reflected in any comments and cross-references elsewhere in the text which are relevant to it.

A word processor equipped with the ability to understand natural language could:

- automatically identify cross-references and comments and the text elements that they relate to

- maintain a record of all the cross-references and comments in the text

- check the implications of changes to any text elements covered by these references.

If necessary it could then either issue appropriate warnings or even make the necessary changes whenever the validity of a comment or cross-reference is affected by changes in the text that they refer to. It would be particularly useful if this facility were constantly operating, so that effects of any changes were monitored and reported as they happened.

2.4. Text generation

If the computer can be given the capacity to 'understand' natural language, it should also be possible to reverse the process, so that meaning or logical content could be used to generate an appropriate text. Stylistic constraints could be built into the algorithms, and some routine writing tasks could be almost completely automated. A limited form of this process already exists in the 'merge' facility found in most word processors. This is most commonly used to create versions of 'form letters' which are automatically customised to their recipients' requirements using a standard form and a database. The text generator would simply take the process one stage further. Routines which are capable of doing this already exist within machine translation and speech synthesis systems, and this would simply require the development of the technique to cope with the wider needs of the word processor user.

3. LEXICOGRAPHY

The need for computer assistance in lexicography is now fully established, although it is a fairly recent development. The second edition of OED, published in 1989 but under development from about 1982, was conceived from the outset as a computer-based project. The entire texts of the first edition and its supplements were converted to database format (largely maintaining the original structure designed by Sir James Murray and his colleagues in the nineteenth century) to allow them to be integrated with each other and the new entries. Modern dictionaries, like most modern publications, depend on the technologies of word processing, desktop publishing and data manipulation that computers have made possible. But there is a further level of computer involvement in lexicography, more directly related to the language analysis techniques already described in this book.

The Cobuild range of dictionaries began with the first edition of the *Collins Cobuild English Language Dictionary* in 1987. They are produced on the basis of large scale corpus evidence, using frequency lists, concordance lines and collocation analysis to their limits. The current set of corpora used for the series, the Bank of English, amounted to 211,000,000 words of running text by the autumn of 1995 and is steadily expanding. It is also no longer alone. The British National Corpus, a collection of 100,000,000 words, was officially launched in autumn 1994, and many other more specialised corpora have been assembled for other lexicographic purposes. Lexicography already makes extensive use of basic text exploration techniques, and this is described in outline in section 3.1. Section 3.2 considers the implications of current uses of NLP techniques and possible future developments.

3.1. Basic text exploration techniques
3.1.1. Frequency lists
A frequency list for a corpus shows you the words that occur in it and the relative proportion that each contributes towards it. If your corpus is properly representative, this information can give you a reasonably accurate picture of the language as a whole. For the lexicographer this means that the words to be

included in the dictionary can be selected objectively with their frequency of occurrence giving a guide to their relative importance. Problems are likely to arise from the separation in the lists of word forms belonging to the same lemma (see Chapter 3, section 1.2.3) and from the existence of homographs (see Chapter 3, section 2.2.3 and Chapter 6, section 3.3). Software capable of lemmatising the lists has been developed, but homographs are normally disambiguated manually.

3.1.2. Concordance lines

Concordance lines form the main source of information in computer assisted lexicography. For each of the words selected from the frequency lists KWIC concordances can be produced. They help the lexicographer to:

- identify the main senses of the selected word (and disambiguate homographs if this has not already been done)
- assess their relative frequencies of occurrence
- identify recurrent phrasal structures that include the word
- produce definitions for each of the senses identified.

The vast numbers of occurrences of the more common words in a large reference corpus would make the use of concordance lines impractical without some basis for automatic organisation and selection. Extensive use of the sorting options described in section 2.4 of Chapter 4 combined with sophisticated collocation analysis allows the data to be made more manageable.

3.1.3. Collocation analysis

Part of the purpose of a dictionary definition should be to provide some information about the word's normal linguistic environment, especially where it exhibits any unusual features. Collocation analysis can provide this information directly so that the lexicographer can consider it for inclusion in the dictionary. The identification of individual senses of the words and the identification of those senses within the mass of concordance lines can also be made much more efficient by the proper use of collocation information. Sophisticated software has been developed which can display the results produced by alternative significance measures in a form which is easily usable by the lexicographers while they are using the concordance software to consult the corpora.

3.2. NLP implications
3.2.1. Tagging and parsing

The grammatical information presented in a dictionary should be based on the real behaviour of words in the language rather than on grammarians' intuition. The examination of the words in the context provided by the concordance lines is the ultimate source of this information, but the use of taggers and parsers, even if they are initially based on inaccurate models of word behaviour, may help in the extraction of the evidence from the concordance lines.

The restricted information produced by taggers, relating to individual words in the corpus, is often more useful to the lexicographer on the practical level than the more complex structural information produced by parsers. This may suggest that the language models used as the basis of parsing are not as appropriate for the analysis of meaning as they are generally thought to be. The whole nature of parsing may need to be rethought in the light of the evidence provided by large scale reference corpora of the kind now used in lexicography.

3.2.2. Future developments

The provision of NLP capability within the basic lexicographic tools could tackle the problem of semantic disambiguation and assist in the production of definitions and the selection of suitable example texts. Ultimately, perhaps corpora could become self-documenting, so that any changes in the behaviour of words could be automatically detected and assessed by the software, and reflected in the information extracted by the computer from the corpus and in the definitions produced from it.

4. DATA RETRIEVAL

Wherever data are stored, retrieving the items that are most needed is always a problem. The classic example is probably the library, which contains huge amounts of information in books, journals, and so on, often indexed by a combination of titles and a limited number of keywords. Library users can waste significant amounts of time trying to track down the most relevant works on a subject. The inadequate nature of current indexing systems means that they will often both fail to discover important sources of information and follow up irrelevant works. The first of these problems is obviously rather more serious, but both reduce the usefulness of an expensive and fundamentally important research resource.

The main problem with current indexing systems is the vast human effort that would be involved in making index entries more precisely descriptive of the contents, scope and emphasis of the works in the library. The only solution appears to be greater computer involvement in the processes of indexing and of searching the indexes. To understand how this might be achieved, it would probably be useful to consider the nature of databases and of their indexing methods.

4.1. Databases and indexes

The traditional database formats developed in the early days of computing were modelled very closely on the concept of the record card. Each record, the basic unit of the data file, had a number of fixed length spaces available for the storage of data in a predetermined sequence. Limitations on storage space meant that the records were designed to minimise record lengths rather than to optimise the usefulness of the data, and this imposed a very formal structure on the information stored in the database. More serious constraints were imposed by the medium of computer storage. In the earliest days the main medium was magnetic tape, which could only be read sequentially, in the order in which items of data appeared along its length. If you needed to read the data in a different sequence, which would be necessary, for example, if you wanted to search for a book using its author rather than its title, the file held on the tape would need to be sorted into the required sequence and copied to another physically separate reel.

Many of these limitations have now been removed by developments in processing power and massive increases in storage space and memory, and the complete text of the OED can now be stored on a single CD-ROM alongside a huge array of indexes. These allow the text to be searched by headword, by variant spelling forms, by quotation author, by languages in the etymology section of the entry and so on. The entire text has been converted into a database, indexed in all of the ways that its compilers consider to be potentially useful. The construction of these indexes would have been made much easier by the fact that, once the database had been created, the various sections of the text which had been marked as headword, pronunciation guide, spelling forms, and so on, could be automatically summarised by the computer and linked to the dictionary entries in which they were found. The process involved in this is similar to that described in outline in section 2.1 of Chapter 4, where indexing of individual words is considered as an option in concordancing software.

The main disadvantage of this approach lies in its relatively unsophisticated nature. It is essentially a pattern-matching operation, similar to the techniques already described for frequency list creation and concordancing. It can take no account of the meaning or implications of the text which is being processed unless the mark-up codes specifically provide the necessary information. The main result of this is that the user may need to work quite hard to find a search strategy that will provide the results that are needed. Because the computer has no understanding of the data it is handling the entire search depends on the user's selection of the patterns to be used in the matching process. Limited wild card facilities are generally available, and quite sophisticated combinations of patterns can be specified, but the user cannot ask directly for the type of data which would be of interest.

4.2. The intelligent database

If the computer became capable of processing the data in the database in such a way that it could analyse the meaning of its contents, you could specify the object of your search in terms of the meaning of the data rather than its appearance, and the computer could construct the original indexes so that they also reflected this rather more useful aspect of the stored data. Database query systems already exist which use a language similar to English as the basis for user search requests, but they still suffer from a fundamental limitation. The computer does not understand the motive behind the request or the data contained in the database. It can only process the request by converting it into a conventional search pattern and matching it against the indexes available.

If the computer were equipped with language understanding ability the full nature of the request could be analysed. The user would no longer need to formulate the details of the search to be carried out, since a specification of the objectives should allow the computer to generate the appropriate instructions for itself. If the computer could understand the contents of the database in a similar way, the search could be carried out intelligently, using strategies at least as good as those which would be used by a human browser, but at far greater speed and completely automatically.

4.3. The self-searching library

Applying the general principle of the intelligent database to the library could produce an even more useful facility. Because of the nature of text, if the computer could understand natural language it could appreciate the contents of any texts stored in computer-readable form. It could produce summaries of their contents and assessments of their scope or emphasis, making it possible for user requests, couched in general terms of information requirements, to be matched automatically to the most appropriate texts. The computer would read the text as it went into storage and generate all the information needed to convert it into an intelligent and self-searching database. The computer would effectively become the librarian, and would have access to more knowledge of the texts under its care than the most conscientious human librarian could ever manage.

This may seem a little Utopian, but some success has already been achieved with the automatic production of text summaries. This seems to be possible without the involvement of full NLP capability, and could be used as a first stage to reduce the volume and complexity of the texts to be dealt with.

5. COMPUTER-ASSISTED LANGUAGE LEARNING

The use of the computer in language learning is another fairly well established tradition, and early assessments of the possible impact of computers in this field were perhaps a little extravagant. Many people have seen a parallel with the excitement initially generated by language laboratories and the subsequent problems encountered with them and the widespread disillusionment of language teachers. The appropriate role for the computer in language teaching has since been defined rather more carefully, and they make a useful contribution to it. The contribution would undoubtedly be even more useful if they were equipped with a rather better appreciation of natural language. The main areas of potential improvement are outlined below. They are specifically considered here in the context of computer involvement in language learning, but many of the points would be equally valid for the use of computers in other subject areas.

5.1. The student/computer interface

The constraints imposed on student communication with the computer and the computer's ability to feed information back to the student mean that this is probably the weakest point in any language teaching system. However well designed the software may be in other respects, if the computer cannot make the same type and level of intelligent guesses about the nature of the student's input as would be made by a human teacher, the student is likely to become very frustrated very quickly. Similarly, if feedback cannot be pitched at a level appropriate to the individual user of the system, it is unlikely to produce optimum results.

Many language teaching programs are effectively quizzes. Student's answers to the questions thrown up by the quiz need to be carefully assessed. It is not enough for the computer simply to identify correct and incorrect answers. If an answer does not exactly match the one required, the software should be able to determine both the degree of correctness shown by it and the most appropriate guidance to be given to the student in response. Some of the simpler programs of this type were originally set up so badly that the most minimal misspelling, or even the use of upper case rather than lower case, would result in the same error response as an answer which was completely unlike the one expected.

If the interface to the software were equipped with appropriate NLP capabilities student's responses could be interpreted properly to allow the program to produce more appropriate feedback. Over a reasonable period of interaction the computer could also gauge an individual student's ability with the language and adjust its feedback to the student to match it.

5.2. Selection of data for use in the learning process

Whether the teaching software is a simple quiz or a more complex form of language exploration, its effectiveness will be greatly enhanced if the computer is able to select appropriate data for the learner to work with. For quiz format software this can be organised fairly easily without involving NLP. Banks of possible questions can be maintained, already coded with their difficulty levels, and appropriate selections can be made on the basis of the student's rate of correct responses so far. For more complex text-based software it might be more rewarding to allow passages to be selected from authentic texts on the basis of levels of complexity assessed directly by the computer.

Before the computer could exercise this level of discretion it would need the ability to assess the complexity of the texts in terms appropriate to the work being undertaken with the student. For some areas of language learning this could still involve a relatively simple approach. For example, if the lexical complexity of the text is the most important feature, the computer could use frequency list techniques to ensure that no words are introduced beyond the appropriate level. If, on the other hand, semantic complexity is the main aspect, word forms would not provide the computer with the necessary data: semantic disambiguation would also be needed. Any decision based on syntactic features would similarly involve the recognition of the appropriate structural aspects of the text by the computer, which would demand a reasonable level of parsing ability. More complex decisions, involving the knowledge content or discourse structure of the entire text, would demand a high level of machine understanding.

5.3. Using the computer to explore texts

The ability of the computer to manage quizzes and other student exercises is a relatively trivial aspect of computer assisted language learning. Much more powerful learning environments are being constructed through the use of data-driven techniques, where the student uses the computer as an aid to the examination of the language. Using this approach, students can derive the information they need directly from the language, as though the computer were a tireless native-speaker informant, with rather greater potential knowledge of the language than the average native speaker.

Concordances have been used as the main realisation of this technique, but the inherent limitations of all pattern-matching techniques tend to restrict their usefulness for the student. Ideally it should be possible for the user to call up concordance lists not only of specified keywords, but also of syntactic structures, sequences of word classes and so on. It would also be extremely useful to be able to perform reverse semantic concordancing, so that the list would include all instances of a particular meaning being conveyed within the text, regardless of the word or phrase used to generate it. Before these facilities could be added to the concordance repertoire the software would need to be enhanced with fairly complex NLP capabilities.

5.4. Specialised word processing facilities for language learners

The utilities for checking spelling and grammar, built into most word processing software, could easily be adapted to provide language learners with valuable guidance on the production of texts in the target language. They would need to be made rather more discriminating, in the ways suggested in sections 2.1 and 2.2 above, and the warning messages and suggestions would need to be geared to the specific requirements of the language learner. It would also be extremely useful if the word processor were equipped with a direct link to an appropriate learner's dictionary and thesaurus, navigable according to the user's needs through the computer's ability to process and understand the implications of definitions, semantic ranges, and so on.

6. EXPERT SYSTEMS

As a development from the intelligent database artificial intelligence researchers have developed knowledge bases which are capable of accepting questions on the subject areas for which they were constructed and of formulating answers based on the information held in their database. There are at least two advantages to this approach. Human experts are relatively few in number and can be difficult to contact in an emergency. Because of this the use of them tends to be expensive. If their specialised knowledge can be replicated in a computer system it can be consulted more readily, more continuously and by a significantly larger number of people.

The second advantage is rather more fundamental. Human experts eventually age and die, taking a great deal of their expertise with them. There are limits to the extent of the knowledge that any given human expert can accumulate during a lifetime, augmented though it will be by access to the literature. There are no real limits to the amount of information that could be stored in a database and made accessible to an expert system, and the system could be, at least theoretically, immortal. This means that its expertise could become greater than that of any human specialist. If the system is equipped with appropriate algorithms, its knowledge base can be modified by the results of its earlier suggestions, so that it can learn from its experiences in a similar way to the human specialist. Because it could be exposed to far more sources of new information than a human expert, the learning process could also be faster, and would not diminish with age.

For this to work properly, the expert system needs to have appropriate knowledge handling and learning algorithms which are the province of artificial intelligence developers. If it is intended to make it directly available to human users, it will also need a powerful natural language interface to allow it to communicate with them and to produce its answers in an understandable, unambiguous form. Prototype examples already exist, covering applications as different as the early stages of medical diagnosis and airport enquiry systems.

7. MACHINE TRANSLATION

The sentence below is taken from the instruction book for an Italian oven. It is the original Italian text from the section dealing with the controls:

> Sul frontalino sono riuniti tutti gli organi di comando e di controllo del forno.

In addition to the original Italian version of the text the instruction book contains translations into French, English, Spanish and Dutch. The English version of the same sentence reads:

>All the oven controls are on the front panel.

Even if you have no knowledge of Italian, it is obvious from the numbers of words in the two sentences that significant changes have been made during the translation process, and that the task of translation was not a simple matter of substituting individual English words for their Italian equivalents. The details of the translation of this particular sentence will be examined later, but it is important to emphasise the complexity of the translation process before considering the possibilities of computerisation.

The amount of translation needed in the world on a daily basis is prodigious. The demands of international trade, political negotiation and scholarship are fairly obvious and represent an enormous translation exercise in their own right. This instruction book alone involved four separate translation tasks, and most similar manuals, produced in some form or another for all but the simplest of products, contain more languages. It can also represent a huge domestic task for countries which have more than one official language, since all their public announcements and records need to be produced in each of them.

Given the scale of the effort involved in translation, it is hardly surprising that this was one of the first areas of language analysis earmarked for automation by computers. Given the complexity of the problem, it is perhaps also hardly surprising that machine translation proved much more difficult than was first expected, and is still not entirely successful. The sections below describe some of the main problem areas in detail, together with approaches that have been adopted in the attempt to overcome them.

7.1. Problems with word-for-word mapping between languages

The example sentence given in the previous section can provide a starting-point for considering the complexity of the translation task. The original Italian text is:

>Sul frontalino sono riuniti tutti gli organi di comando e di controllo del forno.

Taking this word by word, replacing each Italian word with its most likely English equivalent would produce the following translation. Phrases which translate single words in the original are joined by the underscore _.

>On_the front_piece are combined all the organs of command and of control of_the oven.

A comparison with the English version in the instruction book shows the extent of the rearrangement involved in the translation process:

>All the oven controls are on the front panel.

The following types of change can be seen:

- expansion of words from the source language to the target language (e.g. *sul* becomes *on the*, *frontalino* becomes *front panel*)

- contraction of phrases from the source language to the target language (e.g. *sono riuniti* becomes *are*, *organi di comando e di controllo del forno* becomes *oven controls*)

- changes in the sequence of units (e.g. *sul frontalino* is at the start of the Italian sentence, *on the front panel* is at the end of the English one).

The exact nature of these changes will vary from one pair of source and target languages to another. The French version of the sentence given above preserves some features of the original Italian, while incorporating some of the changes made in the English version:

Tous les organes de commande et de contrôle du   four sont
All   the organs of command   and   control of_the oven are

réunies   sur le bandeau frontal.
combined on the   panel   frontal.

The phrase *all the organs of command and of control of_the oven* exactly parallels the corresponding items in the Italian original, rather than the greatly condensed and reordered English version. As in the English version, however, it appears at the start of the sentence rather than at the end. Similarly, the phrase *are combined* remains intact in French, while it is collapsed to *are* in the English version. The single Italian word *frontalino* has now become *bandeau frontal*, echoing the English *front panel* but reversing the order of noun and adjective.

7.2. Ambiguities in the original text

The word-for-word translations given in the previous section have deliberately ignored a major potential problem in machine translation. The meanings selected for the words in the original Italian text were not the only potential interpretations of those words, but were chosen on the basis of the meaning which appeared to be appropriate from the English version. The degree of potential ambiguity, even in this one sentence, is quite extensive. The following analysis gives the potential meanings listed in an Italian–English dictionary for all of the words which could be ambiguous:

riuniti	reunited, united, brought together, reconciled, combined
tutti	all, everybody
organi	organs, newspapers
comando	command, order, headquarters, control
controllo	checking, verification, inspection, control, marking
forno	oven, bakery, furnace, kiln, incinerator

There are probably few difficulties involved in selecting the appropriate meaning for the human translator, although the combination of *comando* and *controllo* as two separate elements, both of which seem to mean 'control', has led to the translation of the entire phrase *organi di comando e di controllo* by the single English word *controls*. Similarly, the possible meanings of *riuniti* are completely suppressed in the translation. Both the selection of the appropriate meaning and the decision to omit certain elements altogether represent significant problems for any form of automatic translation. The selection of the appropriate semantic equivalent in the target language presupposes a successful exercise in semantic disambiguation within the source language.

7.3. Stylistic problems

Every instance of language use involves stylistic choices, often unconsciously made as an automatic adaptation to the surrounding circumstances. This creates a further problem for machine translation since the characteristics of a particular style in the source language may be completely different from the characteristics of the corresponding style in the target language. For the computer to automatically appreciate the stylistic qualities of the original text and translate them into a version which possesses similar stylistic qualities would involve NLP capabilities which extend beyond the structure of individual sentences and into a grasp of the structure of the overall discourse. This is a level of natural language understanding which has not yet been achieved.

7.4. Approaches to the problems

Although fully effective machine translation software has not yet been developed, there are packages which are capable of providing useful guidance on translation and which can significantly reduce the extent of the task. The reasons for the success that they have achieved lie in the ways in which they have reduced the complexity of the problems they are dealing with. These can be considered under two main headings: reducing the complexity of the source language, and limiting the computer's involvement in the task.

7.4.1. Reducing source language complexity

In many cases the texts to be translated in a particular situation will belong to a specific area of language use. If this is the case, the restrictions automatically imposed on the source language may be sufficient to allow it to be treated as a sublanguage. The normal characteristics of sublanguages, and the advantages which can arise from using them as the basis of language analysis, are described in section 4 of Chapter 6. This approach does not strictly affect the complexity of the source language, but because some of the difficulties that could arise with unrestricted texts can be ignored, the whole translation process may be significantly simplified. Section 3 of Chapter 8 provides an example of an application which uses the sublanguage approach.

If the source texts are not sufficiently restricted, a more direct way of reducing their complexity may need to be adopted. A simplified form of language can be specified for them. This approach can, obviously, only be used if the circumstances allow. The origination of the text must be under the control of those responsible for translating it, or it must be possible for them to simplify the text before they pass it to the automatic translation process. Specifications for acceptable levels of complexity can then be agreed for the source texts so that the worst translation problems are avoided. Another advantage may arise from this approach. Because the language to be used in the source text would be strictly controlled, the quality and clarity of the writing may actually be improved. Setting these boundaries may effectively create a sublanguage, so that the benefits of that approach may also be available.

7.4.2. Limiting the computer's involvement

If it is not possible to reduce the complexity of the texts in either of the ways described in the last section, it may be necessary to carry out part of the process manually. This is usually the case to some extent even in the most effective systems, simply because some checking and editing will always be needed to ensure that the final output is appropriate. In addition to this post-editing of computer output, it may also be useful to carry out pre-editing of the input to the system. The work carried out at this stage could range from the simplification of the constructions used, as suggested in the last section, to the manual tagging of problem items, idiomatic phrases, complex syntax, and so on. Although this may seem to attack the integrity of true machine translation, systems which allow an appropriate level of manual adjustment seem to operate more efficiently and more usefully.

8. SPEECH RECOGNITION

The applications considered so far all assume that the computer has machine readable text to work with. From the earliest days of artificial intelligence research, attempts have been made to provide computers with the ability to process human speech directly, but little real progress appears to have been made. It may be useful to examine the problems involved and the ways in which they have been tackled.

8.1. Problems in identifying linguistic units in speech

Perhaps the most obvious feature which distinguishes spoken language from the written form is its lack of real division into linguistic units. Whereas words in written texts are reasonably easy to identify because of the spaces and punctuation marks used between them, speech is produced in rather larger chunks, separated by fewer and less systematic pauses. The resulting sound units need to be analysed into appropriate linguistic units before any useful processing can take place. This in itself creates a level of complexity beyond any experienced in text analysis for the speech recognition process. Some difficulty exists in converting clearly separated spoken words into their written forms, and the difficulty involved in splitting the stream of sound produced during normal speech into words or corresponding units makes the whole process very much more difficult.

8.2. Ambiguity of sound units

To make an already complex situation worse, the amalgamation of several linguistic units into larger sound units may also increase the potential ambiguity of the sounds being recognised. As a very simple example, consider the sounds which would be produced by someone saying the following two phrases:

1.   the old display

2.   the oldest play

Purists may claim that there should be clear differences between these phrases if they were enunciated 'properly', but in normal speech few speakers would produce sounds which would allow them to be distinguished from each other. There would be no evidence in normal speech to allow the word boundaries to be identified, and in phonetic transcription they would both probably be represented as:

ðioldıspleɪ

Clearly, this phonological ambiguity would cause severe problems for the computer. If disambiguation is to be carried out successfully the system needs a good enough grasp of context to allow the correct interpretation to be selected. The capacity to understand natural language is needed even before the linguistic units can be properly identified.

8.3. Simplifying the input

As with all NLP applications, some of the complexity of speech recognition arises from the need to cope with the whole range of the spoken language. The strategies used to simplify the input for machine translation, described in section 7.4.1, can also be used here. In particular, the system can be designed to handle only a limited range of spoken language, perhaps spoken with artificial clarity, probably with words clearly separated by pauses. If the range of language is sufficiently restricted the word separation may not be necessary.

8.4. Restricting the recognition process

In some situations it may also be possible to apply the other strategy suggested for simplifying machine translation, described in section 7.4.2: limiting the computer's involvement. This approach has already been used where a transcript of the spoken language already existed, and the computer was needed to align the sound patterns with the appropriate parts of the transcript rather than to decode the sound patterns in from first principles. This may not sound a very useful process, but it would allow the soundtrack of a video, for example, to be searched for the occurrence of particular word forms, so that intelligent searches could be carried out on recorded sound rather than simply on the transcript. The frame numbers within the video could be indexed automatically to the transcript once the accompanying sound had been matched to it, and topics dealt with within the soundtrack could be found using keywords or more sophisticated search methods based on the textual contents.

9. SUMMARY

The range of practical applications which involve language analysis is extremely wide. Existing general purpose software, such as word processors, more specialised areas such as lexicography, and the development of new forms of automation in areas such as machine translation and speech recognition are all affected. Both the simple language analysis tools – frequency lists, concordances and collocation measures – and the more sophisticated techniques of NLP, can make a significant contribution to these applications. The problems involved in the development of full natural language processing capabilities have severely restricted the practical exploitation of these techniques, but progress is being made, especially where more limited objectives are being pursued.

FURTHER READING

Boguraev, B. and Briscoe, T. (1989) *Computational Lexicography for Natural Language Processing*, London and New York: Longman.

Brierly, W. and Kemble, I. R. (eds) (1991) *Computers as a Tool in Language Teaching*, Chichester, Ellis Horwood.

Leech, G. and Candlin, C. (eds.) (1986) *Computers in Engish Language Teaching and Research*, London: Longman.

Lehrberger, J. (1982) 'Automatic translation and the concept of sublanguage', in R. Kittredge and J. Lehrberger (eds), *Sublanguage: Studies of Language in Restricted Semantic Domains*, Berlin: Walter de Gruyter, Ch. 3 (pp. 81–106).

McEnery, T. (1992) *Computational Linguistics: A Handbook & Toolbook for Natural Language Processing*, Wilmslow: Sigma.

Case studies

1. THE USEFULNESS OF CASE STUDIES

In this book I have tried to show the potential advantages of using computers in language research, together with the problems that can arise and some ways of overcoming them. The descriptions of the basic techniques and the current applications have necessarily been rather general, and the examples used to illustrate them have been kept fairly simple to make them as clear as possible. The case studies in this chapter are not simplified examples. They are accurate accounts of real research projects, with the difficulties left in to show how they were dealt with. Because they are authentic projects their application is less general, but I hope that they will provide encouragement and useful examples of the type of approach that can be adopted in similar situations.

2. PUSHING THE FREQUENCY LIST TO ITS LIMITS: INVESTIGATING SPELLING VARIATION IN CHAUCER'S *CANTERBURY TALES*

The general background to this project is explained in the first chapter. Anyone who has ever tried to use a spelling checker or a concordance program on a Middle English text, or who has translated such texts using a glossary, will probably understand why I became interested in spelling variation in the first place. Whenever I used a computer to handle Middle English texts I became acutely aware of the problems caused for text exploration software by spelling variation, and of the difficulty involved in overcoming them. This project was an attempt to do something about it. The main decision, whether or not to use a computer, was effectively irrelevant, since the point of the project was to develop a software tool. The selection of the data for examination was also the result of a fairly limited choice, as explained in section 1.1 of Chapter 1. The first real stage of the project was the conversion of the text provided by Oxford into a form suitable for use

2.1. Data preparation

Although the text of *Canterbury Tales* was available from Oxford
Computing Services, it was not immediately usable in the project. The need
to transfer it from its initial storage medium to one that was appropriate for
the computer used for the project has already been described in section 1.2 of
Chapter 1. Even after conversion the text had some special features which
could have caused problems during processing. It was in upper case throughout, and each line was preceded by a complex reference number which
defined its position in the text as a whole. As an example, the first few lines
looked like this:

```
101010000010    WHAN THAT APRILL WITH HIS SHOURES SOOTE
201010000020    THE DROGHTE OF MARCH HATH PERCED TO THE ROOTE,
301010000030    AND BATHED EVERY VEYNE IN SWICH LICOUR
401010000040    OF WHICH VERTU ENGENDRED IS THE FLOUR;
501010000050    WHAN ZEPHIRUS EEK WITH HIS SWEETE BREETH
601010000060    INSPIRED HATH IN EVERY HOLT AND HEETH
701010000070    TENDRE CROPPES, AND THE YONGE SONNE
801010000080    HATH IN THE RAM HIS HALVE COURS YRONNE,
901010000090    AND SMALE FOWELES MAKEN MELODYE,
1001010000100   THAT SLEPEN AL THE NYGHT WITH OPEN YE
1101010000110   (SO PRIKETH HEM NATURE IN HIR CORAGES);
1201010000120   THANNE LONGEN FOLK TO GOON ON PILGRIMAGES,
```

The upper case letters caused no real problems since the software developed
for the project deals with lists of words extracted from the text files, and these
were all changed to lower case within the word frequency program. The reference number was a potential problem, since it would interfere with the concordancing used to check the spelling variations. The solution was provided almost
incidentally as part of an attempt to make concordancing more efficient.

The original word frequency lists were produced in standard ASCII text
format. To make concordancing work as quickly as possible I decided to index
the text files, and the indexing process was built into the word frequency software. The principles behind this approach are explained in section 2.1 of
Chapter 4. In this case, the final versions of the word lists incorporated references, through a separate file, to all the positions in the text in which the word
occurred. The text files themselves were transformed into databases so that
these line numbers could be used to gain rapid access to the text needed for
the concordance lists. The transformation process provided the opportunity to
strip out the unwanted information, but it soon became apparent that the last
few digits were extremely useful. They contained the original manuscript line
numbers associated with particular pieces of text in the printed edition.
Because these did not necessarily correspond to the physical line numbers in
the new text databases, they were incorporated into the new files to allow
them to be printed as part of the concordance list. This meant that when I
needed to check a line against the printed edition for possible data entry
errors or to get a wider context, the line number could be used as a reference.

As the project proceeded the word frequency lists revealed some problems with fragments VII and X of the text. Both contain substantial prose passages ('The tale of Melibee' in Fragment VII and 'The Parson's tale' in Fragment X). They had been entered into the text file exactly as they were printed in the original edition, often with hyphens marking word breaks at the end of each line. Because the line of text was the basic unit used for the production of the word lists, any parts of words occurring at the ends of lines had been treated as whole words and had produced incorrect entries. To overcome this problem a simple program was written, which examined the last character of every prose line. If it ended with a hyphen it then checked whether it was being used as a word break or as a dash by examining its immediate context. Every word break found was then adjusted automatically by moving the remaining letters from the beginning of the next line to complete the word. In this way the text of these two fragments was substantially corrected before final word lists were made. The program is described in Appendix 3.

2.2. Outline project description

The basic approach was selected from two main possibilities. I could have started with a set of spelling rules formulated from commentaries on Chaucer's language and used the computer to test them. I felt that this would be too dependent on existing theories and might not reveal enough about the underlying characteristics of the text. I decided instead to use the computer to identify the rules. This involved a four-stage process:

a)   produce a word frequency list for the entire text

b)   select pairs of words from the list which could be spelling variations of each other

c)   sort and summarise the resulting pairs to establish types of variation

d)   check selected word pairs from the main types for spelling variation

All the stages except (d) could be carried out automatically by the computer. I originally intended to use standard word frequency software for stage (a), and standard concordance software to help with stage (d), but it soon became obvious that specially written programs would make the task much easier. The frequency list software was unremarkable except that it produced an indexed version of the text file, capable of being used more easily with the software developed for stage (d).

2.2.2. Selection of word pairs

Because the computer was being used to identify the potential spelling variants the criteria for selection needed to be as simple as possible. In the end one criterion was adopted. Special software was written which compared the words in the frequency list with each other and listed all pairs of words which differed by only one letter. While the use of such an uncomplicated test simplified the selection process considerably, and made it possible to concentrate on one aspect of a word's variation at a time, it also meant that any word pairs which exhibited multiple variation were ignored. Because of the enormous number of comparisons needed to select the word pairs, even after an optimising short-cut had been developed, the program ran for over 30 hours. It eventually produced a list of 17,912 pairs. A sample of pairs from this list shows some of the differences between them:

blesseth	blisseth	prively	pryvely
broches	brooches	savacion	savacioun
gise	gyse	sort	short
heede	hende	sour	soure
houres	houses	spare	spared
lawes	clawes	speke	speeke

Specially written software sorted the word pairs so that all those that differed in a similar way were brought together, and produced a frequency list of differences. The main types of single letter difference were then arranged into seven categories:

- additional final letter (e.g. *sour* and *soure*)

- additional initial letter (e.g. *lawes* and *clawes*)

- doubled letter (e.g. *broches* and *brooches*)

- insertion of a letter inside the word (e.g. *sort* and *short*)

- substitution of one vowel for another (e.g. *prively* and *pryvely*)

- substitution of one consonant for another (e.g. *houres* and *houses*)

- substitution of a vowel for a consonant (e.g. *heede* and *hende*)

Random samples were selected from the most frequent differences in each category for detailed checking. These included final *e*, initial *s*, inserted *u*, doubled *e*, *i* substituted for *y*, *d* for *n* and *e* for *t*. Some of these seemed intuitively to be more promising than others, but the selection was made by the computer without my interference.

2.2.3. Detailed checking

The special concordance program used for the detailed checking allowed both words in each pair sample to be displayed on the screen in their context. It was then possible to check whether they were spelling variants of each other, and to record the decision. Once ten word pairs in any one sample had been examined the program checked to see if the results were consistent. If not, checking continued until a conclusive result was found or the sample was exhausted. By the end of the checking process each of the differences had accumulated figures representing the total number of spelling variations found and the total number of pairs checked. These totals were used to estimate the probability that the difference would result in a spelling variation. The rules derived from these probabilities represented the set of spelling variation rules identified by the computer.

The differences contained in the final rules were those which were most likely to cause spelling variations. They included:

> *i* substituted for *y*
> doubled *a*
> doubled *c*
> inserted *u*
> doubled *e*
> final *e*
> doubled *o*
> doubled *t*

These rules were tested by allowing them to operate on a sample of words from the original word frequency list. For each word, any rule which could be relevant to it was used to generate an alternative spelling, and the alternatives produced were checked against the entire word list to see if they existed in the original text. If they did, they were listed out for checking against the word from the sample. As an example, after manipulation according to the variation rules the word *brought* gave rise to three possible variants which existed in the original word list:

> broughte
> broghte
> broght

All three were spelling variants of *brought*, correctly predicted by the rules derived from the investigation. The overall success rate was around 80 per cent.

2.3. Summary

This project was based almost entirely on a word frequency list, which could have been produced using standard software. The detailed investigation was carried out using concordance lines, which again could have been produced using standard software. The specialised elements within the project were:

a)   identifying word pairs differing by one letter;

b)   summarising the types of difference found;

c)   collecting the results of the detailed checking;

d)   applying the results to the final word sample.

Stage (a) used the frequency list as its basis, stage (b) created frequency lists of types of difference to aid the selection of samples, stage (c) recorded the decisions made for each sample and stage (d) went back to the original word frequency list to find predicted variants. The use of the word frequency list as the basis for the research shows how useful it can be in its own right when you are investigating individual word forms rather than their relationships to each other.

3. EXPLORING A SUBLANGUAGE: FINDING A GRAMMAR FOR DICTIONARY DEFINITIONS

Natural language processing systems need large amounts of detailed information about the behaviour of words and phrases, and dictionaries contain at least some of it. For some time now researchers working in NLP have been using computer readable dictionaries as a source of this information. As part of a research project funded by the EC (described in detail in Sinclair, Hoelter and Peters 1995), I became involved in an investigation of the possibility of using a dictionary in this way. The dictionary was part of the Cobuild learners' dictionaries range, and followed the normal Cobuild policy of defining its words in complete English sentences. The project involved the construction of a grammar for the set of definition sentences which would allow usable linguistic information to be isolated and extracted.

At first sight, this may seem like a fairly complex NLP project in its own right. However, because the set of definition sentences had a fairly restricted number of basic structures, it was possible to treat them as a sublanguage in the way described in section 4 of Chapter 6. This approach greatly reduced the complexity of the investigation. The validity of the sublanguage approach used in the project is assessed briefly in section 3.1, and the main stages of the investigation are described in section 3.2. The results are examined in section 3.3.

3.1. Assessing the sublanguage approach

The approach adopted in this project relies on the treatment of the Cobuild definition sentences as a sublanguage of English. The six characteristic features of sublanguages, described in section 4.1 of Chapter 6, are considered individually in sections 3.1.1 to 3.1.6.

3.1.1. Limited subject matter

It is difficult to decide whether or not this restriction applies to the definitions. On the one hand, the subject matter is the meaning and usage of a subset of English vocabulary, but the range of subjects covered by the headwords included in even the smallest dictionary is not exactly restricted. The explanation of the meanings of a very small vocabulary can involve reference to information related to a wide range of areas of knowledge. As an example, forty definitions taken from one page of the *Collins Cobuild Student's Dictionary* dealt with at least eleven different subject areas. Such a wide range of subjects encountered in such a small sample of definitions does not imply restricted subject matter. However, although the range of subjects may appear to be wide, the level at which each is covered is quite superficial. The absolute minimum of information is provided to enable the meanings of the words to be understood, and the vocabulary associated with each subject area is restricted to the simplest terms.

3.1.2. Lexical, syntactic and semantic restrictions

The *Student's Dictionary* contains a list of words used ten or more times in the definitions, and it contains around 2,000 words. A sample taken from editions of *The Times*, containing exactly the same number of tokens as the set of definition sentences, had 4,456 word forms occurring ten or more times. The overall word frequency list for the definition sentences, excluding the headwords, shows 8,579 different types, a token to type ratio of 46.95. The *Times* sample had 27,814 types, or only 14.48 tokens per type. There are only 2,501 single frequency words in the definition texts, against 12,107 in the *Times* sample.

The *Times* text is probably a representative sample of the language of a particular kind of journalism, which is a fairly specialised form of language in its own right and may also be affected by some lexical restrictions. Bearing this in mind, the significantly lower numbers of types found in the definitions is probably quite significant. The requirement for lexical restriction within the sublanguage seems to be fulfilled.

The syntactic restrictions are perhaps not quite so obvious, but they do exist. In the first place, all the definitions consist of statements. Many of them are simple statements of equivalence between the word being defined and its counterpart in the definition, often using an appropriate part of the verb 'to be' or the word 'means' as the link between them. The definition sentences are also almost completely independent of each other. This means that the use of pronouns to replace repeated elements and the other normal features of text cohesion are only found on a very limited scale, and are contained within the single definition sentence.

There are clear semantic restrictions which limit the range of meanings of the already restricted vocabulary. There is a strong tendency for the most general meanings of words to be used in the definition sentences rather than any of their more specific senses. This was established by an examination of the uses of the most frequent lexical words in the word list described above.

3.1.3. 'Deviant' rules of grammar

Cobuild definitions are written in natural English sentences, constructed to give learners guidance on usage at the same time as explaining meaning. This means that the unusual linguistic features found in some sublanguages, for example the 'telegraphic style' found in weather bulletins, do not appear in the definitions. All the definition sentences conform to the grammatical norms of the English language as a whole, and they could be described using a general grammar of English. However, a special grammar of the definition sentences is far more useful as basis for retrieving the information that they contain about the words being defined. This would not be the case with all other English sentences, and the grammar of the definitions can, in this respect, be said to be deviant.

3.1.4. High frequency of certain constructions

The development of the definition structure categories, described in detail in section 3.2, depends on the high frequency of a relatively small number of structural patterns. Many of the patterns were evident from the initial words of the definition sentences, as described in section 3.2.1. The 'frequent constructions' criterion is not simply met by the definitions, it is almost their most striking feature.

3.1.5. Text structure

Even within the text of the definitions themselves there is a highly specialised text structure which affects the meanings and functions of individual words and constructions. The words to be defined are bounded in the dictionary by mark-up codes, realised in the printed edition as bold type. The positions of these codes in the definition text were used throughout the project to divide each definition sentence into its major structural components

3.1.6. Use of special symbols

Except for the bold type markers described in section 3.1.5 there are no special symbols within the text of the definition sentences, but there are grammar codes in another part of each dictionary entry. These special symbols are outside the definition sentence itself, but can be considered as an aspect of the definition sublanguage because in some cases they make it easier to differentiate between sentences which use apparently similar structures for different types of words. As an example, consider the following definitions, which are preceded by their grammar codes (all page references to the *Collins Cobuild Student's Dictionary*, 1990):

> ATTRIB ADJ
> A **charitable** organization or activity helps and supports people who are ill, handicapped, or poor. (p. 83, sense 2)
> SING N
> A **minority** of people or things in a group is less than half of the whole group. (p. 355, sense 1)

The basic structure of each of these sentences is very similar. Their grammar codes, which show that *charitable* is an adjective and *minority* a noun, were used to distinguish them and to make their analysis work properly.

3.2. Outline project description

Once the definitions had been established as a potential sublanguage it was possible to start exploring the details of their structure. The investigation began with a computer readable version of the entire dictionary text, the file supplied to the printers for typesetting. This contained significant amounts of information which were not needed in the investigation. Section 3.2.1 describes the extraction of the necessary data from the dictionary text and the pre-processing needed to make it suitable for investigation. The main stages of the investigation itself are described in sections 3.2.2 and 3.2.3.

3.2.1. The extraction of definition data from the dictionary text

Each entry in the dictionary text file was marked up using a detailed coding system for each of the elements of information. As an example, here is the first part of the entry for *drink*:

```
[EB]
[LB]
[HW]drink
[PR]/dr*!i!nk/,
[IF]drinks, drinking, drank
[PR]/dr!a!nk/,
[IF]drunk
[PR]/dr*%u!nk/.
[LE]
[MB]
[MM]1
[GR]VB [GS]with or without [GC]OBJ
[DT]When you [HH]drink [DC]a liquid, you take it into your mouth
    and swallow it.
[XB]
[XX]We sat drinking coffee.
[XX]He drank eagerly.
[XE]
[ME]
```

Each of the codes in square brackets signals the start of a different element of information. '[DT]', for example, marks the beginning of the definition sentence itself. Using these codes a file was extracted which contained the definition sentence for each sense of a word together with the other information needed for the project. Once the extraction was complete some simple text manipulation programs were written to make it easier to process. For example, the '[HH]' and '[DC]' codes in the definition sentence, which enclose the word being defined, were converted to a single separator which was used to divide all the elements of information. After pre-processing the first definition sentence together with the other relevant information looked like this:

```
When you |drink |a liquid, you take it into your mouth and swallow it.|1|VB
with or without OBJ|8116|drink+drinks+drinking+drank+drunk||
```

3.2.2. Initial word frequencies and sentence types

The first stage of the investigation was, almost inevitably, the use of a frequency list. Because there seemed to be some significant patterns associated with the first words of the definition sentences a frequency list was produced for them. This counted the number of definition sentences which began with each initial word. The results were fairly dramatic. The ten most common initial words, shown in the list below, accounted for over 97 per cent of all the definition sentences. The list below shows the initial words followed by the number of definition sentences they introduce. The third item in the list, marked *no first word*, represents the number of sentences which began with the word being defined, which was in itself a significant pattern.

if	10,206	the	1,472
a	6,805	an	1,106
no first word	5,174	something	1,026
you	1,908	to	670
when	1,487	someone	659

The first word of a sentence would seem a very inadequate basis for classifying sentences into groups with similar structural patterns if they were drawn from all the possible sentences in an entire language. Because these sentences belong to a restricted sublanguage the list proved a very useful starting-point for building a classification system for the definitions based on simple text patterns. The taxonomy which was eventually constructed for them is shown in section 3.3.1.

3.2.3. Identifying structural patterns

The groups of definitions with the same initial words formed the basis of the next stage of the investigation, the identification and analysis of the underlying structural patterns of the sentences to determine their grammar. Some significant patterns were obvious at first glance. For example, consider the general structure:

A *or* An *or* The **noun** is a *or* an *or* the ...

This is the main definition type used for nouns, and its relative simplicity and frequency in the dictionary (over 5,600 examples) made it one of the first candidates for analysis. As the project developed, it became obvious that other optional elements could be present without the structure changing sufficiently to need a different parsing strategy. Once the grammar had been amended to take account of these optional elements, this one definition type covered 10,494 sentences, over a third of the total number.

The process was not always so straightforward. Once the definitions with the most obvious structural patterns had been eliminated, particularly those most dependent on the initial words of the sentences, I needed to search more deeply to identify the remaining structures. As an example, the frequency list in section 3.2.2 shows that *you* is the fourth most common initial word, beginning 1,908 definition sentences. Whereas the words *a*, *an* and *the* introduce a fairly limited set of sentence types, those beginning with *you* are more various. A sample taken from them shows something of the range of possibilities:

You address a judge in court as **your honour**; (p. 268)

You can refer to a disorganized group of things of various kinds as **odds and ends**; (p. 384)

You also say '**There you are**' or '**There you go**' when you are giving something to someone. (p. 588, phrases)

You use **time** after numbers to say how often something happens. (p. 594, sense 5)

You can acknowledge someone's thanks by saying '**You're welcome**'. (p. 641, phrases)

These do not fit one obvious definition structure pattern, but there are some parallels between them and the subsequent words and phrases tend to recur both in these definitions and in those beginning with other words. As an example, the word *use* in the definition of *time* shown above occurs in a similar context in more than 1,200 of the definitions beginning with *you*. When I explored similar contexts for the other definitions, I found exactly parallel structures in sentences beginning with *people, some people, Americans* and *communists*, as in these examples:

Americans use **after** to tell the time. (p. 11, sense 5)

Communists use **bourgeois** when referring to the capitalist system and to the social class who own most of the wealth in that system. (p. 57, sense 2)

Some people use **love** as an affectionate way of addressing someone; (p. 334, sense 6)

People use **really** in questions when they want you to answer 'no'; (p. 462, sense 3)

The process of analysing these other aspects of the patterns, gradually extending them further into the definition text, brought out the less obvious patterns and made it easier to explore the sentences introduced by less frequent initial words. It is a cyclic process, in which the initial word frequency list provides clues to patterns which are more deeply embedded in the words, and the pattern-matching process allows the usefulness of the patterns to be assessed.

To investigate the text patterns in the sentences I used a technique similar to the concordance approach. The simplicity of the text structure made it easier and more effective to use a general text search utility rather than specialised concordance software. To understand why you may need to look back at section 3.3 of Chapter 4. Each definition sentence is of course a sepa-rate piece of text, and was contained in a single line of the text file. When the search utility extracted lines matching the pattern from the file of definitions each line corresponded to a sentence, the only meaningful text unit in the file. This meant that I could take full advantage of the speed and flexibility of the search utility, including its powerful regular expression capability.

3.3. Summary of results

The project outline given above describes the basic work carried out to iden-tify the structural patterns of the definition sublanguage. As a result of this work it proved possible to construct a taxonomy for the definition sentences, which in turn allowed the development of both a functional grammar for them, which described the ways in which they explained the meanings of the words, and parsing software which could take a definition from the dictionary and analyse it into the components specified by the grammar. The parser was used to generate information which could be used in NLP applications, and has many other potential uses within lexicography, language teaching and so on, all described in detail in Barnbrook (1995). The taxonomy   described in outline in section 3.3.1, and the grammar and parser in section 3.3.2.

3.3.1. The taxonomy

The classification system produced for the definition sentences from the investigation described above is summarised below. The type labels A to X used for the definition types were allocated during the development of the taxonomy and reflect the order in which the patterns were identified rather than any meaningful structural relationship between them. Because of this, they have been gathered into four major structural groups, and the individual types are listed in approximate order of similarity to each other. The frequency of occurrence is given for each type, followed by a typical example.

GROUP 1

A 10,494 An **issue** of a magazine or newspaper is a particular edition of it. (p. 301, sense 3)

I 689 The earth's **crust** is its outer layer. (p. 127, sense 3)

L 358   **Forgot** is the past tense of **forget**. (p. 218)

H 2,212 A **secluded** place is quiet, private, and undisturbed. (p. 504)

E 2,202 Something that is **hidden** is not easily noticed. (p. 263, sense 1)

M 172   New people who are introduced into an organization and whose fresh ideas are likely to improve it are referred to as **new blood, fresh blood,** or **young blood**. (p. 52, phrases)

C 1,441 To **commit** money or resources to something means to use them for a particular purpose. (p. 101, sense 2)

GROUP 2

B 7,528 When a country **liberalizes** its laws or its attitudes, it makes them less strict and allows more freedom. (p. 322)

F 1,813 If someone is **run-down**, they are tired or ill; (p. 491, sense 1)

G 1,714 If you do something **in class**, you do it during a lesson in school. (p. 89, phrases)

N 14   You ask what has **got into** someone when they are behaving in an unexpected way; (p. 233, sense 3)

GROUP 3

J 1,524 You can also say you **admire** something when you look with pleasure at it. (p. 8, sense 2)

D 561   If you say to someone that something is **their own affair**, you mean that you do not want to want to know about or become involved in their activities. (p. 10, sense 4)

K 224   You can refer to a change back to a former state as a **return** to that state. (p. 480, sense 10)

Q 76   When someone creates something that has never existed before, you can refer to this event as the **invention** of the thing. (p. 298, sense 3)

O 362   **Equatorial** is used to describe places and conditions near or at the equator. (p. 182)

GROUP 4

P 17   In **humid** places, the weather is hot and damp. (p. 272)

X 6   Roads, race courses, and swimming pools are sometimes divided into **lanes**. (p. 313, sense 2)

Each type has its own associated grammar and parsing software, with the exception of type X, which represents anomalous definitions. The grammar and parser are outlined in the next section.

3.3.2. The grammar and parser

The grammar developed for each of the types describes their components in terms which are appropriate for the extraction of the required information. Because the formal statement of the entire grammar is rather complex and repetitive, here is the specification for the type A definition as an example of its main characteristics:

$$(A)_1 \quad (M^r) \quad H^d \quad (Q^r) \quad H^i \quad (A_m)_1 \quad (D^{r1}) \quad S \quad (D^{r2})$$

The notation used in the grammar is highly abbreviated. Here is the key:

Symbol	Meaning
A	Article
M^r	Modifier, preceding a noun
H^d	Headword
Q^r	Qualifier, following a noun
H^i	Hinge
D^{r1}	Preceding discriminator
S	Superordinate
D^{r2}	Following discriminator

Optional elements are shown in normal brackets, with a subscript 1 if they can only appear once in a definition. Matching elements have a subscript m.

The meaning of the symbols used in the grammar may become clearer if you see how the parser allocates the components within an actual definition sentence. The definition of sense 2 of *architecture* in the *Student's Dictionary* is:

The **architecture** of a building is the style in which it is constructed.

The parser analyses this into:

```
A       The
Hd      architecture
Qr      of a building
Hi      is
Am      the
S       style
Dr2     in which
Qrm     it
Dr2     is constructed.
```

The analysis clearly separates the elements which make up the thing being defined – 'the architecture of a building' – from the elements used to define it – 'the style in which it is constructed'. It also identifies the individual components of these two main units and the items in the second part which repeat elements in the first part, such as A_m and Q^r_m. Each of the components identified in the parsed output is now available for use in an NLP application.

4. BETWEEN WORD PROCESSING AND THE DATABASE: MANIPULATING THE OUTPUT FROM A QUERY PROGRAM

Many of the texts which are available on CD-ROM are held in a special format. The text may be compressed because of its size, or encrypted to prevent it from being downloaded *en masse*. Whatever the reason, the special format will probably make it impossible to use standard text handling software such as word frequency or concordance programs, and you will need to use the suppliers' software provided with the text.

This is true of the CD-ROM version of the *Oxford English Dictionary*, which contains the complete text of the dictionary comprehensively indexed for rapid access to entries through a wide variety of features. The software provided with the CD-ROM includes a fairly sophisticated query language. It allows you to specify complex search criteria, to output the results into the file of your choice, and to use files produced by one query as the basis for other queries. The detailed operation of the query language is fully specified in the user manual provided with the CD-ROM. As part of an investigation of Shakespeare's use of new words I needed a list of words from the OED whose first quotation came from Shakespeare, together with the date of the first quotation and the quotation itself.

The query language made it easy enough to find the words, and other facilities in the software allowed selected elements of the entry for each word to be output to a text file. The only problem was that the software did not allow me to be quite as selective as I might have wished. The first three entries in the text file looked like this:

OED2 on CD-ROM (c) Copyright Oxford University Press 1994

\abode, v.\1593 Shakes. 3 Hen. VI, v. vi. 45 The Owle shriek'd at thy birth, an euill signe, The Night-Crow cry'de, aboding lucklesse time.\1603 – Henry VIII, i. i. 93 This tempest Dashing the Garment of this Peace, aboaded The sodaine breach o't.\1603 Greenwey Tacitus, Ann. (1622) iii. ii. 67 The which when Piso perceiued, to aboade his vtter destruction.\1665 J. Spencer Prodigies 83 Lest it should abode the running of that Vessel upon rocks.\1659 Hammond On Psalm lix. 5 This abodes most sadly to Saul at this time.\1673 Lady's Calling ii. §4. 16. 30 No night raven or screech-owl can abode half so dismally as these domestic birds of prey.

\abodement1\1593 Shakes. 3 Hen. VI, iv. vii. 13 Tush man, aboadments must not now affright vs.\1651 Reliquiæ Wottonianæ 119 The Lord Bishop<dd>took the freedom to ask whether he had never any secret abodement in his minde.\1665 J. Spencer Prodigies 179 But where matters ungrateful fall before us, we usually serve our little hatreds, by deriving upon them the Opinion of being ill abodements.

\Abraham, Abram, a.\1599 Solim. & Pers. (Hazlitt's Dodsley V. 363) Where is the eldest son of Priam, That Abraham-colour'd Trojan? Dead.\1607 Shakes. Coriol. ii. iii. 21 Our heads are some browne, some blacke, some Abram, some bald fol. of 1685 alters to auburn.\1627 Peacham Compl. Gent. 155 (1661) I shall passe to the exposition of certain colours.–Abram-colour, i.e. brown. Auburne or Abborne, i.e. brown or brown-black.

The first and second of these, *abode* and *abodement*, meet the criteria: both have Shakespeare as the author of their first quotation. The third has Shakespeare as an author, but only of the second quotation. The other problem is that too much information has been output for each word, since only the first quotation was needed.

It was possible to manipulate the output from the standard software using a very simple pattern-matching program, described in Appendix 3. The program selects data from the original output so that only the first quotations are output for each word, and then only for words with Shakespeare noted as the author of their first quotation. After using it, the beginning of the new file looked like this:

OED2 on CD-ROM (c) Copyright Oxford University Press 1994

abode, v.
1593 Shakes. 3 Hen.VI, v. vi. 45 The Owle shriek'd at thy birth, an euill signe, The Night-Crow cry'de, aboding lucklesse time.

abodement1
1593 Shakes. 3 Hen.VI, iv. vii. 13 Tush man, aboadments must not now affright vs.

a'brook, v.
1592 Shakes. 2 Hen.VI, ii. iv. 10 Sweet Nell, ill can thy Noble Minde abrooke The abiect People, gazing on thy face.

abutting , ppl. a.
1599 Shakes. Hen. V, 1 Prol. 21 Whose high, vp-reared, and abutting Fronts, The perillous narrow Ocean parts asunder.

accoutred, ppl. a.
1596 Shakes. Merch.Ven. iii. iv. 63 When we are both accoutered like yong men.

a'ccuse, n.
1593 Shakes. 2 Hen.VI, iii. i. 160 And dogged Yorke<dd>By false accuse doth leuell at my life.

The extraction of the relevant data from the rest of the text file has effectively customised the standard software so that it meets the user's requirements more closely.

The development of this program was in itself a trivial process, and the manipulation that it is carrying out on the data file is extremely simple, but in many research projects simple tools like this could make a difference between the use of standard software which just fails to meet all of your requirements, and the development of complex, expensive, customised programs.

5. SUMMARY

The case studies described above hopefully give a more practical illustration of the range of language research projects and tasks that can be tackled using a computer, and of the approaches needed to make them work properly. The most important qualities needed by anyone who wants to use a computer to explore and analyse language are imagination, flexibility and, of course, patience.

FURTHER READING

Barnbrook, G. (1992) 'Computer analysis of spelling variants in Chaucer's *Canterbury Tales*', in G. Leitner (ed.), *New Direction in English Language Corpora*, Berlin: Mouton de Gruyter, pp. 277–87.

Barnbrook, G. (1993) 'The automatic analysis of dictionaries – parsing Cobuild explanations' in M. Baker, G. Francis and E. Tognini-Bonelli (eds), *Text and Technology*, Amsterdam: John Benjamins, pp. 313–31.

Barnbrook, G. and Sinclair, J. (1995) 'Parsing Cobuild entries', in J. Sinclair, M. Hoelter and C. Peters (eds), *The Languages of Definition: The Formalisation of Dictionary Definitions for Natural Language Processing*, Luxemburg: Office for Official Publications of the European Communities, pp. 277–370.

Berg, D. L. (1993) *A Guide to the Oxford English Dictionary*, Oxford, Oxford University Press.

Glossary

These explanations are intended to be informative rather than authoritative. The word being explained is highlighted within the explanation using **bold** type, and any words used in the explanation which have their own entry are in *italics*.

algorithm   a way of performing a particular task, often incorporated into a computer *program*

ANSI (American National Standards Institute)   sometimes used as a substitute for *ASCII* to describe standard computer text

application   an area of work that the computer is used for; *word processing* is an application

array   a structured *variable* in which individual pieces of information can be separately specified by attaching a *subscript* to the variable name

ASCII (American Standard Code for Information Interchange)   character set; the standard set of *characters* used in computer text *files*

assembler language   a *programming* language which allows you to write programs that are very close to the computer's *machine code*

assign   *to assign* a value to a *variable* in a computer program, is to set the variable equal to that value

back up   *to back up* computer *files*, is to copy them on to another storage *medium* in case the originals get damaged

byte   an individual *character* in a computer *file*

CD-ROM   a *storage medium* which uses a CD to store computer *data*; one CD can typically hold about 650 *megabytes*

character   a single unit of *data*, corresponding to an individual letter, number, punctuation mark or other symbol; the word 'character' consists of nine individual characters

colligation   *collocation* patterns based on syntactic groups rather than individual words

collocation   the patterns of combination of words in a text

compiled   if a programming language is *compiled*, it is translated into *machine code* in a one-off operation, and the translated version is used whenever it is run

compiler   a special piece of *software* which converts instructions written in a *programming language* into *machine code*; the conversion produces a new file, which is then used to run a *program*

computer-readable   *computer-readable* text is held in a suitable form for processing by computer; it may need to be manipulated to make it readable by a particular type of computer

corpus/corpora   a collection of texts, selected to represent a particular type of language and held in *computer-readable* form

data   information, whether in *computer-readable* form or not; it is often used in a more restricted way to describe the information gathered for a particular project

data capture   a technique which allows you to obtain *data* directly from another *computer-readable* form rather than using some form of *data entry*; it often involves the conversion of *files* held in another *format*

data compression   is a technique used to allow more *data* to be fitted on to a particular *storage medium*; when *data* has been compressed it usually needs to be uncompressed before it can be used

data entry   the process of making *data* available to the computer, either by *keying* it in or *scanning* it, rather than by some form of *data capture*

debug   to debug a *program*, is to correct the errors in it that are stopping it from working properly

desktop publishing (DTP)   involves the use of computer *software* and *hardware* to produce editions of books and other publications

development environment   a *program* for a *programming language* which allows programs to be written, tested and *debugged* in that programming language

electronic text/e-text   text in *computer-readable* form; many different e-texts are available from *text archives* held at various sites around the world

e-mail   a communication system which sends messages and computer *files* very quickly to computer sites around the world

field   unit of information within a·*record*

field separator   a symbol used to mark the boundaries between individual *fields* in a *record*

file   in a computer system, a collection of *data*, held on an appropriate *storage medium*

floppy disk   a magnetic *storage medium*, used to store fairly small amounts of *data* for *back-up* or to transfer it between computers

format   (a) to *format* a *storage medium* like a *floppy disk*, is to prepare it to receive *data*; (b) The *format* in which *data* is held is the way it is stored on a particular *storage medium*

frequency list   a list of linguistic units of a text (often words) which also shows their frequency of occurrence within the text

hard disk   a large-scale magnetic *storage medium*, usually fixed in the computer and capable of storing up to several thousand *megabytes*

hardware   the physical equipment which makes up a computer installation

high level programming language   has instructions which are more closely linked to the user and the problems it will be used to tackle than to the computer's own *machine code*; BASIc, Pascal, C and awk are all fairly high level languages

IBM-compatible PCs   computers which operate in the same way as the IBM-PC series and similar models; they can generally use the same *operating systems* and run the same *software*

indexing   a technique for making it easier to search *files*; a small index file is searched, and this gives the position of the *data* in the main file

input   the *data* that is fed into a computer from the keyboard or a *file*

internet   the set of all the computer sites world-wide which are connected together through the academic and commercial communication *networks*

interpreted   if a *programming language* is *interpreted*, the translation into *machine code* is carried out by an interpreter *program* every time a program is run

interpreter   a special piece of software which converts instructions written in *programming language* into *machine code*; the conversion is carried out every time a program is run

keying   *to key data* into a computer *file* involves entering it directly through the keyboard

keyword   the word input to a concordance program to obtain the required lines of text

lemma   the set of different forms of a word, such as the singular and plural of a noun or the various parts of a verb

low-level programming language   a *programming language* more closely linked to the computer's own *machine code* than to the user; *assembler* and machine code are both low-level languages

machine code   the language that the computer operates in; *programs* produced directly in machine code can be very fast, but they tend to be difficult to write

macro language   in an *application* allows some of its procedures to be automated; *word processing* macros can sometimes be used as simple language analysis tools

magnetic tape   a *storage medium* generally used nowadays for large-scale *back up* storage

mainframe   a large, powerful computer, normally housed in its own special computer room and capable of dealing with large numbers of users at the same time

mark-up codes   added to *computer-readable* texts to provide extra information or to assist text processing

megabyte   approximately one million *bytes*

metacharacter   in a *regular expression*, a character which is used as part of the regular expression syntax rather than as part of the *string* to be matched

modem   a piece of computer hardware which converts *data* into a suitable form for transmission on telephone systems

monitor   a special form of television unit used as the display for a computer

MS-DOS   the *operating system* used in *IBM-compatible* PCs

multimedia   involves the combination of text, sound, visual images and animation in a computer's *output*

mutual information   a statistical significance measure based on the ratio between observed and expected results

network   a set of computers joined in some way so that they can communicate with each other and share *files* and *software*

node   in collocation analysis, the word whose collocates are being investigated

operating system   the *program* allowing a computer to work, controlling *input*, *output* and *processing*

Optical Character Recognition (OCR)   the technique of converting the graphical image of scanned text into its constitutent characters so that it becomes *computer-readable text*, and the software used in the process

output   the *data* that a computer sends to a *monitor*, a *printer*, a *file* or some other similar device

parsing   the analysis of text according to a grammar

PC (personal computer)   a personal computer, rather than a multi-user computer such as a *mainframe*; PCs are sometimes called desktop or laptop computers

printer   in a computer set-up, the device used to produce *output* on paper

processing   the general term used to describe all the actions carried out by the computer

program   the set of instructions that makes the computer carry out the *processing* required; a program is a form of *software*

programming language   a special language used to write computer *programs*; a special program, called a *compiler* or an *interpreter*, translates the instructions written in the language into the computer's *machine code*

record   a set of pieces of information relating to the same basic unit of *data* within a *file*

reference corpus   a very large *corpus* which is used to establish the general characteristics of a language

scanning   a process which allows text to be read directly into a computer, using a scanner to *input* a picture of the text and Optical Character Recognition (OCR) *software* to convert the shapes into *characters*

search-word   the word input to a concordance program to obtain the required lines of text

shareware   *software* which is available for free trial through specialist suppliers and *software archives*; if you find it useful you are expected to pay the appropriate registration fee to the producers

software   the set of *programs*, including the *operating system*, the general *utilities* and the specific *applications*

sorting   a process which allows data to be rearranged into a different sequence

specification   for a *program* or project, the list of tasks to be performed and an outline of the method to be adopted; it is very useful to produce a detailed specification as part of the decision on the computerisation of a project

spell-checker   in *word processing*, a tool which checks that words have been spelt correctly

Standard Generalised Mark-up Language (SGML)   a set of conventions and procedures which allows consistent approaches to be adopted in adding structural and other information to *computer-readable texts*

storage medium   a means of storing *data* in a computer system; the most common media in modern computer systems are: *floppy disks, hard disks, tape cartridges,* CD-ROMs

string   in computer *processing*, a sequence of *characters*; e.g. the word 'string' is a string, and so is this entire explanation

subscript   a marker used to specify individual elements of information within an *array*

tagging   marking items in a text with additional information, often relating to their linguistic properties

***t*-score**   a statistical significance measure based on the difference between observed and expected results

tape cartridge   a form of magnetic tape used as *back up* storage; it is capable of holding very large amounts of *data*, but can only be read in the sequence in which it was written

text archives   large collections of *computer-readable* texts held at computer sites; unlike *corpora* they are not normally selected to represent a particular type of language

text editor   a *program* which allows you to create and alter text *files*; it has some of the features of a *word processor*, but normally handles only plain text files (usually in *ASCII format*)

text formatting   the way the appearance of text is controlled; it includes special features of *characters*, such as bold type and italics, as well as paragraph and page layout; *word processors* normally give you full control over text formatting

tokens   in a word frequency list, individual occurrences of words; the number of tokens in a text *file* is the same as the total number of words

types   the number of *types* in a word frequency list is the number of unique *word forms*, rather than the total number of words in the text

Unix   a powerful operating system often used on large computer *networks*

utilities   *programs*, often supplied with an *operating system*, which allow you to carry out the routine tasks needed on a computer; they perform operations such as *sorting*, *file* copying, etc.

variables   in computer programming, *variables* hold *input data* or the results of *processing*

viruses   harmful *programs* deliberately written and distributed to damage, and sometimes destroy, *data* and *software*; it is important to be aware of the potential danger of viruses, especially when obtaining *data* or *software* from other sites

word form   in a text, a unique sequence of *characters* which makes up a word; e.g. 'word' is one word form, 'words' is another

word processing   a computer application which allows you to create, modify and save text *files*, often with complex *text formatting* instructions included

z-score   a measure of statistical significance based on the difference between observed and expected results

Appendix 1
Programming languages for language programming

The variety of programming languages available can be bewildering to anyone whose main interest is in carrying out practical language research using a computer rather than studying the programming languages for their own sake. This appendix describes the main characteristics of a range of currently available languages and discusses their suitability for developing programs for language analysis. Each language description includes an assessment of:

- the difficulty involved in learning and using it
- its availability for different operating systems
- the level of discipline inherent in its overall approach
- the development environments available for it and their facilities for development and debugging
- the speed of processing
- its general suitability for language work.

The generic name is given for each of the languages rather than a specific commercial brand name, and the assessment has been made for the language as a whole rather than for any individual implementation. This is intended as a rough guide rather than a definitive account of any of the languages and it is greatly influenced by my personal experiences and prejudices. You should consult standard introductions to the languages if you want to consider them in more detail.

1. awk

awk may seem rather strange and abbreviated at first sight, but it is fairly easy to learn. It is available for both Unix and MS-DOS, but is much more robust on Unix systems, probably because it relies on the operating system to do so much of its work. There is little inherent discipline in the language, and as with C you can write totally chaotic programs, but it also allows you to produce very disciplined and effective ones. There are no development environments as such, but all you really need is a good text editor. Debugging help is very primitive, and it is a good idea to keep programs as short as possible. It is very slow-running, but this shows up less on Unix systems than on MS-DOS because of the power of the operating system.

Despite its limitations and eccentricities, awk is an excellent all-round tool for developing language analysis programs. It is particularly useful for analysis at word level, though it is rather less easy to use for handling substrings. In this it is no worse than most other languages.

2. BASIC

BASIC is relatively easy to learn, partly because it originally developed as a teaching language. It is widely available within MS-DOS and the older operating systems, but never really made it to Unix. It allows a very unstructured approach, and some versions seem rather to encourage this by making it difficult to develop genuine subroutines which can be updated and modified without affecting the rest of the program. A wide range of development environments exist, some with sophisticated editing and debugging tools, and there are even some compiled versions around, though most implementations are interpreted. Programs written in BASIC tend to be fairly slow running, unless you do use a compiled version.

It can be reasonably useful for language analysis, but it is limited in its string-handling capabilities and sometimes rather cumbersome when dealing with lines of text and breaking them down into words.

3. C

C is a rather low level language, slightly closer to the computer than to the user or the problem, and so is a little more difficult to learn than BASIC and Pascal. It is probably the most widely available and easily portable language, and is equally at home under MS-DOS or Unix. In terms of discipline, it allows you to produce extremely well structured programs, but with a little effort you can also produce ones that are at least as chaotic as anything written in BASIC. Some of the development environments are very sophisticated and user-friendly, others are extremely primitive and more oriented towards the professional programmer. C is always compiled, and is usually very fast, partly because of its low level origins. It is also very versatile, but you often need to build up your text-handling routines from very low level procedures.

Overall, there is almost nothing that you could not do with C in terms of writing a language analysis program – much of the commercial software is written in it – but it is probably not an entry-level language for casual use because of the time needed to develop sufficient expertise.

4. PASCAL

Pascal also developed as a teaching language, though at a rather different end of the user range to BASIC. It is reasonably easy to learn, though some find its rigorous insistence on discipline and housekeeping irritatingly fussy after BASIC. It is available in several different versions for MS-DOS and some other operating systems, though not as widely implemented as C. It encourages a very disciplined and structured approach which is easier to debug, modify and extend. Some very sophisticated environments are available for it, with excellent development and debugging facilities. It is normally a compiled language, and so is reasonably fast.

Overall, it is quite useful for language work, but it has similar text-handling problems to those described for BASIC, and programs tend to be rather long and elaborate even when they are only dealing with simple tasks.

5. PROLOG

Prolog is not an easy language to learn, and if you have already learnt another language you may find it even more difficult, since it uses a completely different approach to most others. It is declarative rather than procedural, and this means that you supply it with facts, relationships and goals rather than a sequential set of instructions. It is based on formal logic, and the name originates from 'PROgramming in LOGic'. To some extent, the details of the program's operations once you have asked it to do something are under the control of the language rather than the programmer. It is fairly widely available for MS-DOS, but it is more at home on Unix-based machines and on powerful mainframes. Its development environments are generally fairly primitive, and it is rather slow-running, partly because it is interpreted and partly because of its processing method, which needs enormous computing power.

Prolog has been fairly widely used in parser development and in AI work on expert systems and the like. It is not easily usable for simple language analysis.

Overall, I have found awk the most useful programming language for developing analysis tools. It originated from an attempt to generalise some simple Unix text search and manipulation tools,[1] and has developed into a versatile programming language capable of handling complex tasks in a very simple way. A brief introduction to awk is given in Appendix 2, and programs written in it are used to illustrate some of the examples in Appendix 3.

NOTE

1. See Aho, Kernighan and Weinberger 1988: v for a detailed description of its evolution.

Appendix 2
awk: a very brief introduction

1. INTRODUCTION

You should not need any specific knowledge or experience of computer programming to understand this brief guide to the awk programming language. On the other hand, it is not a complete guide to programming in awk. After you have worked through it you should be able to appreciate the workings of the examples shown in Appendix 3 and to modify them to meet your requirements more exactly. You may even be able to write your own programs in awk to perform simple text manipulation and analysis tasks, though you will need to consult one of the handbooks on awk if you want to develop more complex programs, or explore the language in more detail.

2. THE NATURE OF awk

To get awk to do things for you, you simply give it instructions in the sequence in which you want them performed. In some cases you need to give the program information about the data that it is going to handle, and this needs to be done before it processes it. awk shares these characteristics with all of the languages listed in Appendix 1 except Prolog, which works in a rather different way. The main difference between awk and other languages that you may have come across is that it is partly set up to handle text already, although it can easily be adjusted to handle data held in other forms.

It is almost impossible to learn a practical technique like programming as an abstract concept, so it is probably best to start with an example of an awk program and see how it works. Here is the word frequency list program used to generate some of the examples used in Chapter 3. Line numbers have been added to make references easier.

```
BEGIN {FS="[^a-z]"}
      {
      for (i=1;i<=NF;i++)
          {
          if ($i != "") count[$i]++                    5
          }
      }
END   {
```

```
for (i in count)
    {                                                                  10
    print "\t" count[i]
    tokens+=count[i]
    types++
    }
print "Tokens\t" tokens                                                15
print "Types\t" types
}
```

This probably looks quite daunting. I have deliberately chosen a program which illustrates several aspects of the awk language and which actually performs a useful analytical technique rather than an artificially simplified example. Once the program is broken down into its main processing stages and examined in detail, it will become much easier to understand. One apparently trivial point of detail needs to be dealt with before we begin the detailed examination. You need to remember that awk is case-sensitive, so that any distinctions between upper and lower case in the words of the language or the names of its variables must be preserved in your programming.

2.1. The main processing stages

In the frequency list program shown above several sets of instructions are enclosed within pairs of braces, '{' and '}'. The instructions which follow the word 'BEGIN' on the top line are enclosed within one pair, while the instructions following the word 'END' are set within a more complicated arrangement of braces. If you look at the indentation in the program text, there are three sets of instructions altogether which begin and end with braces set at the first level of indentation. In the first place there is:

```
BEGIN {FS="[^a-z]"}
```

This is followed by a further set of instructions, this time not preceded by anything:

```
{
for (i=1;i<=NF;i++)
    {
    if ($i != "") count[$i]++
    }
}
```

The last set is:

```
END   {
for (i in count)
    {
    print i "\t" count[i]
    tokens+=count[i]
    types++
    }
print "Tokens\t" tokens
print "Types\t" types
}
```

These are the three main processing stages. The set of operations headed BEGIN is performed before the input is read, the middle set is performed for every item in the input, and the set headed END is carried out after the input has been read.

2.1.1. Before reading the input

The instructions preceded by BEGIN in the program represent processing which needs to be performed before the main program can start. To understand what is being done in the word frequency program, you need to know something about the way awk handles the data input to it.

The input for the word frequency program would be a text file of some sort. This would be divided into individual lines of text, and the program needs to split each line into words and then count identical word forms. awk treats its input file as a collection of 'records', generally corresponding to the lines in a text file. Within each record, it treats each separate unit of information as a **field**, and it can access any of the individual fields. The division of the records into fields is under the control of a variable built into the awk language, and given the label 'FS' for **field separator**.

Unless you change the value of FS it will recognise blank spaces or tab characters as field separators and divide up the record accordingly. This is almost what we need to be able to access individual words in a line of text, but it would leave any punctuation marks as part of the word. Because of this, the first instruction has been used to set FS to a new value. This needs to be done before processing begins so that it will allow the first line of the file to be read and dealt with properly. The details of the new value are explained in section 3.1.

2.1.2. General processing

The middle set of instructions is carried out, in this program, for all of the input records. The details of the counting process are explained in section 3.4. For now, I want to establish the fact that each line of the input file will be subjected to each of the instructions in this set. Once they have been completed for a particular line, the next line will be read in and dealt with, and so on until the end of the file is reached.

2.1.3. After reading the input

The set of instructions headed END is not performed until after the last line has been read and fully dealt with. It handles the tasks needed to produce the frequency list when the counting is finished. The details of the processing in this program are covered in section 3 of Appendix 3.

2.2. What awk already knows

The explanation of FS in section 2.1.1 shows that awk is already prepared, to some extent, for text handling, and that its approach can be altered if its predetermined values are not what you want. FS is not the only variable built into awk, and one of the others is used in this program. Look again at the beginning of the middle set of instructions:

```
for (i=1;i<=NF;i++)
```

The built-in variable is 'NF', which stands for 'number of fields'. Because awk sees each record as a set of individual fields, it can also count the fields and use the count to control processing. In this case, we want to ensure that every word, each one of which is an individual field to awk, is counted. This instruction sets a counter ('i') to 1 and then increases it by one each time the processing is run through, making sure that it never goes above NF, the number of words in the line. The details of the 'for' structure are explained in section 3.2.

For each value that i is set to, the program is able to access the 'i'th word in the line through the preset field names $1 to $NF. The '$' symbol in this context is simply a way of labelling the field number. The name $0 is reserved for the entire record, so that the whole line can be processed as one field if necessary. In this program, as i increases by one each time, the next word in the line is counted.

Before you can write programs successfully in awk you need to know the names of all the built-in variables and understand their contents and implications. Apart from the fact that you may need to use the information they contain, you also need to avoid using their reserved names for your own variables since this will make awk report an error and stop it working. The books on awk include complete lists of the built-in variables and explanations of their contents and use.[1]

2.3. Patterns and actions

The three sets of instructions in this program were allocated to the appropriate processing stages using a fundamental principle of awk. Every 'action' in the program is carried out only on records which meet the 'pattern' specified for it. In this case BEGIN and END are built-in patterns which correspond to the stages before and after reading the input, and the general processing is to be carried out on all the input records, and so uses the 'empty' pattern which does not restrict it to any specific type of record. In the program used to manipulate the OED output, shown in section 16 of Appendix 3, a more specific pattern is used:

```
BEGIN {FS = "\\"}
$0 ~ /^ OED2/    {print $0 "\n"}
$3 ~ /Shakes./   {
     print $2
     print $3 "\n"
     }
```

For various reasons the line detailing copyright, which began with two spaces followed by 'OED2', was to be printed out intact. The other general processing instructions were to be performed only if field 3 contained the string 'Shakes.'. The patterns:

```
$0 ~ /^ OED2/
```

and

```
$3 ~ /Shakes./
```

allow the appropriate differentiation to be made.

3. PROGRAMMING DETAILS

Now that the basic nature of awk has been explained, we can look at the details of the frequency list program. There are many ways in which this could be organised, but I suspect that it may be easiest to go through the instructions in the program one by one, in the order in which they appear, explaining both the background to them and any important alternative possibilities on the way.

3.1. Variable assignment

The first instruction in the example program is:

```
FS="[^a-z]"
```

As already explained in section 2.1.1 this sets the field separator to something more useful for processing words. The texts that will be input to the frequency list program have already been converted to lower case letters throughout, so that words can be considered as consisting of strings of lower case letters and nothing else. This assumes that you will want to treat hyphens, apostrophes and any other punctuation as word boundaries. The value which is being assigned to FS is enclosed in double quote marks ("...") so that it is treated as a literal string of characters rather than a variable name, and is also enclosed in a pair of square brackets ([...]). These operate as metacharacters in awk regular expressions: they are a way of specifying a pattern to be matched rather than an exact string of characters. The metacharacter '^' immediately after the opening bracket specifies that the pattern to be matched is anything other than the characters specified immediately after it. The expression 'a-z' which follows it specifies a range of letters, all the lower case letters from a to z, so that the field separator – the word boundary – becomes anything other than a lower case letter.

This is the result that I wanted, but you may decide that you want to include hyphens in words, in which case you could add them after the excluded range. The assignment instruction would then become:

```
FS="[^a-z-]"
```

Dealing with apostrophes properly is rather more difficult. The syntax of regular expressions in awk is fairly complex, and you will need to consult one of the handbooks if you want to construct your own.

A similar variable assignment is being performed in line 3, within the 'for' instruction:

```
for (i=1;i<=NF;i++)
```

In this case the value being assigned is numeric, rather than a character string, and is a single item rather than a regular expression.

3.2. Comparisons

The for instruction in line 3 of the program is in three parts, set in brackets and separated by semi-colons. The first element has already been explained in the previous section: it assigns the value '1' to the variable i. The second element carries out a comparison between two variables:

```
i<=NF
```

In a comparison in awk you can specify whether one variable should be greater than (>), equal to (==), not equal to (!=) or less than (<) another, plus the combinations exemplified here. This comparison will be true if i is less than or equal to NF. In the for instruction it sets the limit for the processing cycle that it creates, so that it only goes on until the number of words in the line has been reached.

There is a similar comparison in line 5, used as the basis for an `if` instruction:

```
if ($i != "")
```

This checks that the word being examined,$i, is not equal to the empty string `""`. Without this check, bogus words would be created wherever one word boundary comes immediately after another, and would be counted as valid words.

The comparison in line 3 is performed between two numeric values. In line 5 it is between two character strings. There is a further type of comparison which is restricted to character strings. It is a very powerful technique, because it allows the use of regular expressions in place of character strings, but it is not used in this program. The basic form of it is shown in the program used to exemplify patterns in section 2.3. Lines 2 and 3 of this program contain the patterns:

```
$0 ~ /^ OED2/
$3 ~ /Shakes./
```

The basic operator in this form of comparison is '~' (or its inverse '!~'), and this stands for 'matches'. The comparisons in the program will be true if the string specified on the left of the ~ matches the regular expression specified on the right. Regular expressions are enclosed in a pair of '/' characters to distinguish them from character strings. The first of these two uses the metacharacter '^' again, but it has a different meaning in this context to the one that it has in specifying a range (see section 3.1). Here, it denotes the beginning of the string specified on the left of the ~, so that this comparison will only be true if $0, the entire line of text, begins with two spaces followed by 'OED2'. The second comparison will be true if the third field contains the string 'Shakes.' somewhere within it.

3.3. Arithmetic operations

The frequency list program counts word forms, and to do this it needs to increase the appropriate variable by 1 every time a particular word form is encountered. This is done in line 5:

```
count[$i]++
```

The variable, `count[$i]`, is incremented by 1 by the '++' appended to it. This is a shorthand form of the alternative expression:

```
count[$i]=count[$i]+1
```

Both ways of expressing the instruction have the same effect.

The instruction in line 12 is similar, but this time another variable is being added to the first:

```
tokens+=count[i]
```

This is a shorthand form of:

```
tokens=tokens+count[i]
```

The full range of arithmetic operations is available in awk, including subtraction (–), multiplication (*) and division (/), together with a wide range of mathematical functions. Full details are given in the handbooks.

3.4. Arrays

The variables used to collect the word-counts are not straightforward single items like i or tokens. Here is line 5 again:

```
if ($i != "") count[$i]++
```

There is not a single variable called count, but one for each word form in the text. The full set of individual values is held in a structure called an **array**, and the appropriate element in the array is accessed using the information in square brackets, called the **subscript**. The value of the subscript in this case is $i, which is the label for the word being counted. To put it another way, the counts are held in an array which is referenced by the words themselves. The ability to do this is an unusual and very powerful feature of awk, and one of the many characteristics that make it so useful for language processing.

When the entire text file has been read, the instructions in the END section go through the whole array to extract the counts accumulated for each of the word forms. A special form of the 'for' instruction is used:

```
for (i in count)
```

This sets the variable i, previously used to count through the words in each line of the text, to each of the array subscripts (or word forms) in turn. For each of them the instructions in the next set of braces are carried out.

3.5. OUTPUT

Once counts have been accumulated for all of the word forms in the text, when all the input records have been read, they need to be output in some way. Lines 11, 15 and 16 contain the instructions to do this:

```
print i "\t" count[i]
...
print "Tokens\t" tokens
print "Types\t" types
```

The print instructions output the items specified on the same line. The elements enclosed in double quotes are literal strings, and within these "\t" stands for the 'tab' character. In line 11 the word form corresponding to the variable i, the one currently being dealt with as the array reading process makes its way though all of the counts, is printed, followed by a tab, followed by the count accumulated for the word. In lines 15 and 16 the totals accumulated for tokens and types are output preceded by appropriate labels. In all three cases the information is completed with a 'new line' character so that the counts and totals are all output as separate lines. There is a more complex output instruction, 'printf', which allows detailed formatting instructions to be given. Details of this will be found in the handbooks.

Despite the word print in these instructions they send the specified data to the output channel that has been selected by the user or by the operating systems. More details are given in section 4.1.

4. WHAT'S NOT IN awk?

This brief examination of the frequency list program has obviously not covered every aspect of programming in awk. It has only explained the features found in one fairly simple program at a level of detail sufficient to enable you to get a reasonable idea of what is going on in this and other similar programs. There are some features of awk which you need to know about which are not covered in this program, for the simple reason that they are not features of the language. Because these missing elements might confuse you if you are already familiar with any other programming languages, and because they seem to me to be important for a full appreciation of the benefits of using awk, they are explained in this section

4.1. Control of input and output

You may have noticed that the frequency list program does not seem to mention input at all. It seems to be assumed in the main processing section that records are being read in from somewhere, and that the program can tell when they come to an end. No details of file structures are given, beyond setting the field separator before processing begins, and no test is carried out to see if the end of the file has been reached. Similarly, there seems to be little real specification of output. If the print instructions described in the previous section can pass the data to a range of possible output channels, why is there no mention here of file structures, printer controls or any other specific needs?

The simple answer to both of these questions is that, in general terms, awk does not care where its data comes from or where it is going to, because it does not need to know. Both aspects of processing are under the control of the operating system, and awk is set up to assume, most of the time, that everything is being dealt with properly, although you can adjust this if you need to. Unless it is told to do anything else, awk uses 'standard' input and output in its processing. Both UNIX and MS-DOS are normally set up to regard the keyboard as standard input and the monitor screen as standard output, unless otherwise instructed. If you leave things as they are, the program will expect to get its input records from the keyboard, a line at a time (in other words, separated by carriage returns), and will send its output to the screen for you to read.

This is often not the way you will want to work. It would be rather tedious, having obtained a computer readable text, to have to type it all in through the keyboard for awk to process it, and it would be almost as bad to have to copy the results of processing from the screen. Because of this, awk and the operating system between them provide the means to 'redirect' input and output. The easiest way to do it is through an alteration to the command used to start awk running. The exact details may vary from one operating system and installation to another, but a typical command to run an awk program would look like this:

```
awk -f freqlist.awk frank10.txt > frank10.lst
```

The command does several things. It:

● starts the awk interpreter program going
● directs the interpreter (through the -f option) to get the program listing from a file named 'freqlist.awk'
● specifies a file, named 'frank10.txt', in place of standard input, and
● redirects the frequency list output (using the redirection symbol '>') to a file named 'frank10.lst'.

This is the normal way of using awk for large scale text processing, but there may be times when you would want to use it more casually with standard input and output. To do this you simply leave out the redirection options.

4.2. Initialisation of variables

In the frequency list program, variables like count, tokens and types were **initialised** (or set up) simply by assigning values to them. The variable i is even used for two completely different types of data at different stages in the program: numeric values in the general processing, character strings at the end. Even the array count, set up to accumulate all the word form counts, is simply incremented by 1 every time a word form is encountered, whether this is its first appearance or not.

awk is rather unusual among programming languages. Not only can variables be initialised simply by being named in assignment instructions, which is a feature it shares with BASIC, you do not even have to tell the program what type of variable you are dealing with. If you assign a numeric value to a variable, it can behave both as a number and as a character string. Arrays can have numeric values, referenced by string subscripts and so on. This degree of freedom might be dangerous in some contexts, but so long as you exercise appropriate care in writing your programs it makes the development of simple language analysis tools extremely easy and efficient.

5. VARIETIES OF awk

Several versions of awk are available, generally in the public domain as free software. The program that you get is actually the awk interpreter, the program that translates your awk instructions into the correct variety of machine code for your computer. Most Unix-based computers have awk available as a standard tool, and several versions are available for MS-DOS. In my experience, the Unix versions are generally far superior to the MS-DOS ones, but this probably has more to do with the differences between Unix and MS-DOS than anything else. Within the Unix environment, again in my experience, the version provided by the Free Software Foundation, 'GNU-awk', seems to be the best.

Whichever version of the language you use, make sure that you have a version-specific manual and one of the detailed handbooks on awk available if you want to get the most out of it. This account has covered only a very small part of the description of awk and its potential for language analysis work.

NOTE
1. For example, see Aho, Kernighan and Weinberger, 1988: 36.

Appendix 3
Detailed programming examples

1. GENERAL POINTS AND AN IMPORTANT WARNING

The programs given below are fairly simple exams of practical language analysis and text manipulation tools. The commentaries explain the main processing steps. To make the commentaries easier to follow I have added line numbers to the program listings. *These are not part of the listing and should not be typed in if you are typing the programs into a computer to use them.* Feel free to use and modify the programs in any way you want. You will need access to one of the awk handbooks if you want to carry out more than very minor modifications.

I cannot guarantee the successful operation of these programs on your own data. Some line breaks are caused by page size limits. Check the line if in doubt.

2. RHYMING SCHEME FREQUENCY LIST PROGRAM (CHAPTER 1, SECTION 4.3)

```
BEGIN {FS="\t"}
       {count[$2]++}
END    {
       for (i in count)
           {                                            5
            print i "\t" count[i]"
            total+=count[i]
            }
       print "Total\t" total
       }                                                10
```

This is a form of frequency list, a slightly simpler version of the one described in Appendix 2. The first field in each line of the input file is the number of the nursery rhyme in the book, followed by a tab, followed by the scheme as a series of letters, such as 'ABAB'. Line 1 sets the field separator to the tab character. As each line is read the appropriate part of the count array is increased by 1 in line 2. The END processing in lines 3–6 outputs the entire contents of count. Line 7 accumulates an overall total, which is output in line 9.

3. THE FREQUENCY LIST PROGRAM (CHAPTER 3, SECTION 1)

```
BEGIN {FS="[^a-z]"}
        {
        for (i=1;i<=NF;i++)
            {
            if ($i != "") count[$i]++                        5
            }
        }
END     {
        for (i in count)
            {                                                10
            print i "\t" count[i]
            tokens+=count[i]
            types++
            }
        print "Tokens\t" tokens                              15
        print "Types\t" types
        }
```

This program has already been examined in some detail in Appendix 2. The counting method uses both the field structure inherent in awk and the special properties of its arrays. If you are using another programming language these concepts may not be portable. Section 2.1 of Chapter 3 outlines the general approach.

For the counting process to work properly, the text should all be in the same case, since otherwise *For* and *for* would be counted as separate types. Some versions of awk have a built-in function which allows text to be converted to lower case within the program. If yours does not, the program below will convert the entire text file to lower case so that it can then be fed into the frequency list program.

4. LOWER CASE CONVERTER (CHAPTER 3, SECTION 1)

```
BEGIN {
        upper="ABCDEFGHIJKLMNOPQRSTUVWXYZ"
        lower="abcdefghijklmnopqrstuvwxyz"
        for (i=1;i<=26;i++)
            {                                                5
            letter[substr(upper,i,1)] = substr(lower,i,1)
            }
        }
        {
        for (i=1;i<=length($0);i++)                          10
            {
            upletter = substr($0,i,1)
            if (upletter in letter )
                {
            $0 = substr($0,1,i-1) letter[upletter]
```

```
    substr($0,i+1)                                              15
                    }
                }
        print $0
    }
```

Lines 1–9, the initial stage of the program before the text is read, set up an arrays which contains all the lower case letters indexed by their upper case equivalents. The main processing reads through each line of text one character at a time (line 10 sets this up, incrementing i from 1 to the length in characters of the line of text), and if a character is upper case (line 13) it is replaced by its lower case equivalent (line 15). Once the whole line has been read, it is output (line 18). This is not a very efficient program, but it works. Again, it may not work in other programming languages, but most have case conversion functions built in. It may even be possible to carry out the conversion using your text editor or word processor.

5. STRING REVERSER (CHAPTER 3, SECTION 1.2.1)

```
BEGIN {FS= OFS="\t"}
    {
    reverse=""
    for (i=length($1);i>=1;i--)
            reverse = reverse substr($1,i,1)               5
    print reverse, $2
    }
```

The initial stage (line 1) sets the field separator and the output field separator to the 'tab' character, because this is the separator used in the frequency list. the variable reverse is initialised to a blank string (line 3) because it is used to collect the reversed string by having it added to it character by character (line 5) rather than being assigned a value in the normal way. The program simply reads the line backwards, using an index (i) which is originally set to the length of the word, and then decreased by 1 each time until it reaches 1 (line 4). Each character is added to reverse as it is read in reverse order (line 5). When the word has been read, reverse is output together with its original frequency (line 6). The comma in the print instruction means that fields 1 and 2 are output with an output field separator (set to 'tab' in line 1) between them.

You use this program to produce a frequency list which has the word reversed. Use a standard sort utility to sort the new file into alphabetical order, then put the new file through the reverser, and you have a reverse alphabetical order frequency list with readable words. The same technique should work in other languages, although the details will obviously change. The main stages are:

1.   Find the end of the word section of the data, immediately before the first tab: this may involve reading it character by character until you get there.

2.   Read the word backwards, probably still using an index set initially to the length of the word, and accumulate the results in a variable.

3.   Output the reversed string when you reach the beginning of the word.

6. CREATING A LIST IN WORD LENGTH ORDER (CHAPTER 3, SECTION 1.2.4(B))

```
BEGIN {FS=OFS="\t"}
      {
      print length($1), $1, $2
      }
```

Apart from the field separator initialisation this is a one-liner. All the program does is to add the length of the word as the first field of the new file, followed by the original line of the file, still separated by tabs. Sort the new file, and strip off the word length using this one-liner:

```
BEGIN {FS=OFS="\t"}
      {
      print $2, $3
      }
```

This should be almost as easy in other languages, but you may need to split the input line at the first tab (to isolate the word), and be more explicit in your specification of the output.

7. CUMULATIVE FREQUENCIES (CHAPTER 3, SECTION 1.4)

```
BEGIN             {FS=OFS="\t"}
$0 ~ /^Tokens/    {tokens = $2}
$0 !~ /^T/        {
                  total+=$2
                  print $0, total, sprintf("%3.2f",
(total/tokens) * 100)
                  }
```

The field separator and output field separator are set to tabs in line 1 to conform to the frequency list. The version of the list sorted into frequency order has two lines at the start containing the total tokens and total types. line 2 uses the pattern specifying that the line starts with 'Tokens' to set the value of tokens equal to the total in field 2 of the first line of the file. Line 3 uses the same principle to ensure that the field containing the types total is not processed with the others. Line 4 calculates the cumulative total so far, and line 5 outputs the word, its frequency, the total so far and the percentage of the total number of tokens so far. The last figure is formatted by the sprintf function so that it has three places before the decimal point and 2 after it.

Once the data had been split up, any programming language would allow you to carry out similar manipulations.

8. LINKING PHRASES (CHAPTER 3, SECTION 2.4)

```
BEGIN {phrase=" (tak(e(s|n)?|ing)|took) place"}
      {
      x = 0
      RLENGTH = 0
      sofar = 0
```

5

```
        newstring = ""
        rest = substr($0,x+RLENGTH+1)
        while((sofar+RLENGTH) <= length($0))              10
             {
             x=match(rest,phrase)
             if (x > 0)
                  {
                  sofar=sofar+RSTART+RLENGTH               15
                  mphrase=substr(rest,RSTART,RLENGTH)
                  gsub(" ","_",mphrase)
                  newstring=newstring
    substr(rest,1,RSTART-1) mphrase
                  rest = substr(rest,RSTART+RLENGTH)
                  }                                        20
             else
                  {
                  sofar = length($0)
                  }
             }                                             25
        print newstring rest
        }
```

The idea behind the phrase linker is that any occurrences of the specified phrase will have their spaces replaced by an underscore, so that they behave like single words for the frequency list and concordance program. It becomes slightly complex because of the need to allow for more than one occurrence of in any line. Line 1 sets up the regular expression, phrase, for the phrase to be matched. This particular example will match any of:

take place
takes place
taking place
taken place
took place

Lines 3–9 initialise the variables that need to be cleared at the start of each new line, and assign the text line to the string rest. The while instruction in line 10 allows processing to end when the end of the line is reached. Inside the while loop, the match function in line 12 is used to find the next occurrence of phrase. The match function provides enough information to allocate the form of the phrase found to mphrase in line 16, and this has its space replaced by "_" in the gsub function in line 17. In line 15, sofar keeps track of the position of the processing relative to the end of the line of text, and in line 18 newstring accumulates the amended version of the text line. Once no more matches are found, sofar is set to the length of the text line so that processing can finish, and then newstring and the remaining text left in rest is output.

The program relies quite heavily on awk's regular expression and pattern matching capabilities. These would exist in some form in other languages, but they would probably need extensive development work.

9. SPAN TRUNCATION (CHAPTER 5, SECTION 3.1)

```
BEGIN {FS= "[ +-*| *-+]"}
    {
    halfway = int((length($0))/2)
    $0 = substr($0,1,halfway) "@" substr($0,halfway+1)
    for (i=1;i<=NF;i++)                                          5
        {
        if ($i ~ /@/)
                nodenum = i
        }
    i = nodenum                                                 10
    print $(i-5), $(i-4), $(i-3), $(i-2), $(i-1),
$(i+1), $(i+2), $(i+3), $(i+4), $(i+5)
    }
```

Some of the features of this program are conditioned by the form of the concordance program output, but it should be possible to adjust it to suit any program which produces output in ASCII format. Line 1 sets the field separator to either one or more spaces followed by zero or more hyphens or one or more hyphens followed by zero or more spaces. This allows spaces, dashes and hyphens to act as word boundaries. It leaves other punctuation marks on the words, but this makes no difference to the frequency list used to count the words in the span text.

Line 3 finds a point within the occurrence of the node word in the middle of the output by finding the mid-point of the line, line 4 marks the node word by putting the symbol '@' in it at the mid-point, and lines 5–9 check through all the fields in the line until the one containing the '@' is found. This slightly cumbersome procedure allows the program to identify the field number of the node word within the whole line, and nodenum is set to this number in line 10. Line 11 outputs the words within the five-a-side span (this can easily be adjusted to suit your needs), but not the node word. If you want this as well, simply include $i between $(i-1) and $(i+1).

10. Z-SCORE CALCULATION (CHAPTER 5, SECTION 3.4.1)

```
BEGIN {
    FS=OFS="\t"
    tokens=75214
    spansize=640
    }                                                           5
    {
    fo=$2
    fe=($3/tokens)*spansize
    v=spansize*($3/tokens)*(1-($3/tokens))
    sd=sqrt(v)                                                  10
    z=(fo-fe)/sd
    printf "%s\t%.2f\n", $1,z
    }
```

The input to all three collocation calculation programs is a file which contains the span frequency and the total text frequency for each word that occurs 3 or more times in the in the span. It was produced by bringing together data from the span frequency list and the frequency list for the text. Field 1 in the file is the word, field 2 the span frequency, field 3 the frequency in the whole text or corpus, and they are all separated by tabs.

Line 1 sets the field separators to the tab character, and lines 2 and 3 set the total tokens and the size of the span sample in words. These figures need to be supplied from your own data. Line 7 sets fo to the actual span frequency. Line 8 calculates the expected frequency (from the total frequency divided by the total tokens multiplied by the span sample size) and puts it in fe. Line 9 calculates the variance (v) according to the z-score formula and line 10 takes the square root as the standard deviation (sd). The z-score (z) is calculated as the difference between fo and fe expressed as a number of standard deviations in line 11, and is output to two decimal places, following the collocate word, in line 12.

11. *T*-SCORE CALCULATION (CHAPTER 5, SECTION 3.4.2)

```
BEGIN {
      FS=OFS="\t"
      tokens=75214
      spansize=640
      }                                                          5
      {
      fo=$2
      fe=($3/tokens)*spansize
      t=(fo-fe)/sqrt(fo)
      printf "%s\t%.2f\n", $1,t                                 10
      }
```

Lines 1–8 are the same as the z-score program. Line 9 calculates *t* according to the formula given in section 3.4.2 and line 10 outputs it.

12. MUTUAL INFORMATION CALCULATION (CHAPTER 5, SECTION 3.4.3)

```
BEGIN {
      FS=OFS="\t"
      tokens=75214
      spansize=640
      }                                                          5
      {
      fo=$2
      x=($2*tokens)/(spansize*$3)
      mi=log(x)/log(2)
      printf "%s\t%.2f\n", $1,mi                                10
      }
```

Lines 1–7 are identical to the z-score program. Line 8 takes a little shortcut. The expected frequency would be given by:

$$\frac{\$3 \times spansize}{tokens}$$

The ratio of observed to expected would then be:

$$\frac{\$2}{(\$3 \times spansize)/tokens}$$

This simplifies to:

$$\frac{(\$2 \times tokens)}{(\$3 \times spansize)}$$

as in the calculation of x in line 8. Line 9 calculates mi as the logarithm of x to the base 2, and line 10 outputs it.

13. PARTIAL PARSING (CHAPTER 6, SECTION 3.2)
13.1. Group collector

```
BEGIN {FS=OFS="\t"}
$1 ~ /clause|group/ && group != "" {
                if (tags ~ /^;/)
                        tags = substr(tags,2)
                print tags, group                                    5
                group=tags=""
                if ($1 ~ /clause/)
                        print "*"
                          }
        {                                                            10
        if (group=="") space=""
        else space = " "
        group = group space $3
        tags = tags ";" $2
        }                                                            15
END     {
        if (tags ~ /^;/)
                tags = substr(tags,2)
        if (tags ~ /;$/)                                             19
                tags = substr(tags,1,length(tags)-1)
        print tags, group
        }
```

This is the first of the partial parsing programs described in section 3.2 of Chapter 6. It takes the list shown at the start of the section and uses the 'clause' or 'group' boundary markers in field 1 to identify the end of the group it is working on.

Line 1 sets the field separators to tab. Lines 2–9 only operate if field 1 begins with 'clause' or 'group'. If it does, and there is something in the variable group, the string of tags and the group contents built up in tags and group are output in line 5. Lines 3 and 4 ensure that any leading semicolons in tags are stripped off first. Line 6 clears the contents of tags and group ready for the next item, and lines 7 and 8 output a line containing an asterisk if it is a clause boundary.

Lines 10–15 build up tags and group. Lines 11 and 12 set the variable space to the empty string if group is empty, otherwise it is set to a single space. This avoids leading spaces in group. Line 13 accumulates the words in group, separated by spaces, and line 14 accumulates the tags in tags, separated by semicolons.

The END routine simply outputs the last group data in the file.

13.2. Group identifier

```
BEGIN {FS=OFS="\t"}
{group = ""}
$1 ~ /pron|noun/ {group = "NOMINAL"}
$1 ~ /_verb|finite/              {group = "VERBAL"}
$1 ~ /preposition|adverb/     {group = "PREPOSITIONAL"}
$0 ~ /^\*/          {printf "%s\n*\n", $2}                          6
!($1 ~ /\*/)              {printf "%s\t%s|", $2,group}
```

The second program takes the accumulated groups and tags from the first and uses them to identify the type of group.

Line 1 sets the field separators as usual. Line 2 clears group ready for the next item. Lines 3–5 use patterns to check for the main types of group and set the label group accordingly. This is not a completely exhaustive or totally rigorous exercise in its present form! If the input line begins with an asterisk, line 6 outputs its second field, a new-line character, an asterisk, and another new-line character to mark the end of a clause. If not, it outputs the words in the group and its label separated by a tab, followed by a new field separator, '|'. Any further groups in the same clause will be output on the same line separated by this symbol.

13.3. Component allocator

```
BEGIN {
        FS="|"
        OFS="\t"
        }
$0 !~ /^\*/ {                                                        5
        for (i=1;i<=(NF-1);i++)
            {
            x=gsub(/VERBAL/,"PREDICATOR",$i)
            if (x > 0)
                {                                                   10
                prednum =i
                }
            x=gsub(/PREPOSITIONAL/,"ADJUNCT")
            }
        for (i=1;i<prednum;i++)                                     15
            {
            x=gsub(/NOMINAL/,"SUBJECT",$i)
            }
        for (i=prednum+1;i<=(NF-1);i++)
```

```
        x=gsub(/NOMINAL/,"COMPLEMENT",$i)                 20
    for (i=1;i<=NF-1;i++)
        printf "%s\n",$i
    }
$0 ~ /^\*/ {
        count++                                           25
        print "\tEND OF CLAUSE " count
        }
```

The last program in the set takes the output from the previous program and allocates clause component labels. This is not intended to be a serious contribution to parsing software. It is a starting-point for exploring the possibilities of the information provided by the tag and boundary information.

Line 2 sets the input field separator to '|', and line 3 sets the output field separator to tab. The 'one clause per line' layout was only for the previous program's output.

The processing in lines 5–23 is only carried out if the input line does not begin with an asterisk, the marker between clauses. Lines 6–14 go through the fields from $1 to $(NF-1). If the group label for a field is 'VERBAL' the gsub function in line 8 will replace it with 'PREDICATOR' and set x to 1. If that happens, lines 9–12 set prednum to the value currently reached by the field index i, in other words the number of the field containing the predicator. Line 13 replaces 'PREPOSITIONAL' with 'ADJUNCT' in any field which has it as its group label.

Lines 15–18 replace the group label 'NOMINAL' with 'SUBJECT' in any field before the predicator, and lines 19 and 20 replace it with 'COMPLEMENT' for any field after the predicator. This is the most embarrassing part, linguistically, since it relies on a very crude sense of word order and allows for no sentence complexity.

Once the replacements are complete, lines 21 and 22 output the groups with their new labels. Lines 24–27 only operate for clause boundary markers. count keeps count of the number of clauses, and line 26 outputs 'END OF CLAUSE' and the number.

14. TAGS-ONLY TEXT (CHAPTER 6, SECTION 5.1.)

```
    {
    for (i=1;i<=NF;i++)
        {
        x=index($i,"_")
        if (x != 0)                                       5
            tag = substr($i,x+1)
        else tag = ""
        if (tag != "")
            printf "%s ",tag
        }
    printf "\n"                                           10
        }
```

This is a very simple program. The tags are attached to their words by the underscore '_'. Lines 2–9 set up a routine for every field in the text line, using the default field separator. Line 4 uses the index function to find the '_' in each field, and if it is found (line 5), line 6 sets tag equal to the substring of the field starting immediately after the '_'. This is the tag part of each word in the text. If there is no underscore, lines 7 and 8 ensure that the field is ignored. Otherwise, line 8 outputs the tag followed by a space, and line 10 puts a new-line character at the end of each original text line.

15. HYPHEN CORRECTION (CHAPTER 8, SECTION 2.1)

The original program was developed in Pascal and is rather long-winded and cumbersome to describe. Instead, here is an account of the main processing stages followed by a new version of the same program in awk.

The main processing stages are:

a)   read in a line of text (line 1)
b)   check the end for a hyphen
c)   if there is one, check that it is actually a hyphen and not a dash (dashes in this text had spaces either side)
d)   if it is a hyphen, read the next line (line 2)
e)   find the first word boundary in the line 2
f)   add the string up to the word boundary to the end of the line 1 (omitting the hyphen)
g)   remove the string added to the line 1 from the beginning of the line 2
h)   output line 1
i)   repeat the process for line 2 etc.

This description of the stages can be used as 'pseudo-code', a non-specific program description which can be converted fairly easily into any programming language.

In awk, the program could look like this:

```
NR == 1     {old = $0}
NR > 1      {
            if (old ~ /-$/ && old !~ / -$/)
                {
                old = substr(old,1,length(old)-1) $1      5
                print old
                x = match($0,$1 " ")
                old = substr($0,RSTART+RLENGTH)
                }
            else                                          10
                {
                print old
                old = $0
                }
            }                                             15
END    {
        print old
        }
```

Line 1 uses the built-in variable NR, which counts the number of lines read from the input file, to do something special with the first input text line. It is read into old, and nothing else is done. Lines 2–15 deal with the subsequent lines. If old ends in a hyphen which is not a dash (line 3), old is trimmed to remove it and the first field of the next text line is added (line 5) before it is output in line 6. The first field added to old is removed from the current text line in lines 7 and 8, using the match function. The space is added to $1 for the matching process to remove the leading space that would otherwise be left. The trimmed version of $0 goes into old ready for the next time round. If there is no non-dash hyphen (line 10), old is output as it is and replaced by $0. At the end, the last line of the file is output.

16. FINDING SHAKESPEARE FIRST QUOTATIONS (CHAPTER 8, SECTION 4)

```
BEGIN          {FS = "\\"}
$0 ~ /^ OED2/              {print $0 "\n"}
$3 ~ /Shakes./   {
    print $2
    print $3 "\n"                                          5
    }
```

The field separator is set to the backslash used in the OED output in line 1. This is a metacharacter in awk, and so needs to be protected by a backslash, since its 'meta-function' is to protect metacharacters. Line 2 outputs the copyright notice in the file unchanged. Lines 3–6 only operate on lines containing 'Shakes.' in their third field, the point where the first quotation author comes. The word (held in field 2) is output on a line by itself in line 4, and the first quotation is printed intact in line 5, followed by a blank line to separate it from the next word.

17. SUMMARY

Once you have got a general idea of the awk approach from reading through these programs and the commentaries, you will probably feel the need to develop similar tools of your own. Suitable books on awk are listed in the References. The potential is limitless!

Appendix 4
Suggestions for the exercises

CHAPTER 1
1. Chaucer project questionnaire

Possible answers to the questionnaire are given below. Finding out how much the computer could do was an essential feature of the project, and no feasibility study like this was undertaken. Some of the comments on software reflect the assumptions that I would have made if I had filled in the questionnaire before starting.

A) THE SCALE OF THE INVESTIGATION
How much data needs to be processed?

> About 20,000 lines of verse and prose, amounting to about 180,000 words.

How long would manual analysis take?

> Difficult to estimate. The stages needed in the analysis are:
> 1. Reading the text word by word and producing a card for each word form, checking each time that a potential variant does not already exist and noting it if it does
> 2. Sorting and summarising spelling variations to establish any patterns
>
> Stage 1 would be a lengthy process, but could be done manually, although the need to check for existing variants of each new word encountered would become more wearisome as you progressed through the text. Stage 2 would be rather more difficult, and would involve extensive rewriting of the notes made during stage 1.

B) AVAILABILITY OF COMPUTER-READABLE DATA
Is the data already available in computer-readable form?

> A version of *Canterbury Tales* is easily available. Smaller works in a variety of other Middle English dialects can also be obtained fairly easily, cost about £25.

If not, how will it be made readable, and what costs will be involved?

> Not applicable.

If it is, how much preparation will be needed before processing can take place?

> Only available on magnetic tape, and needs to be transferred via a mainframe computer (with expert help) to IBM-compatible PC format. Estimated time, one week, no other extra costs.

C) SUITABILITY OF EXISTING SOFTWARE
Can existing software be used for all or part of the processing?

Yes, standard frequency list and concordance software. The following stages are involved:

1. identifying the word forms in the text: frequency list program;
2. establishing possible variants: specially written software;
3. examining the context of potential variants to see whether they are spelling variants: concordance software;
4. sorting and summarising the results: special software.

How much adaptation of the software or the data will be needed to make them compatible?

Possible problems with size and contents of text. Either the text or the software will need some adjustment. Allow one week to cover research and processing time.

D) SOFTWARE DEVELOPMENT NEEDS
What new software will need to be developed?

Special programs for:

establishing possible variants;

sorting and summarising.

What programming language will be used, and how much time and other costs will be involved in acquiring the necessary expertise?

Pascal – basics already grasped. Allow two weeks for development and testing.

What other costs will be involved?

Acquisition of compiler and development environment (Turbo Pascal) about £75.

E) OTHER FACTORS
What other factors need to be taken into account in making the decision (including any differences in the nature of processing which depend on the selection of the method)?

Manual processing gives a better chance of identifying spelling variants correctly, since they are being examined in their original context.

Computer processing should make selection more objective.

2. Finding passives
It would be a good idea first of all to decide what is meant by 'investigating the use of the passive'. The suggestions below assume that you want to be able to identify each clause in the text which uses a passive construction, and perhaps be able to count them or list them afterwards.

A) MANUALLY
1. Read the next clause.
2. Check whether it contains a passive construction (using your inherent knowledge of language etc.).
3. *Either* mark the text with a highlighter pen (photocopies only, please!);
   or copy the text on to a list of passive clauses (perhaps using a word processor, unless you want to be a real purist).

B. USING A COMPUTER

Ideally this should go something like:

1. Read the next clause.
2. Check the clause for passive verb forms.
3. Tag the clause or output it to a file of passive clauses.

Unfortunately, there are one or two elements of the procedure not fully specified. Stage 1 involves a method of identifying clause boundaries, which you may not have, and the successful identification of passive verb forms by a computer would be a rather complex procedure. You could supply the program with a list of potential passive constructions, but it would need to be a fairly long list and could easily be confused with other syntactic structures. It might be more realistic to allow some operator intervention. This might be a useful compromise:

1. Computer reads the next sentence (easier to identify) and presents it to the operator for checking.
2. Operator checks each clause in the sentence for passive verb forms.
3. Operator marks clause boundaries and inputs passive decision.
4. Computer tags the clause or outputs it to a file of passive clauses.

3. Identifying rhyming schemes

This would be a challenge, especially if the verse is in English and even more so if it is older than the nineteenth century. Even ignoring spelling variations, pronunciation has changed considerably. As a starting-point you would need to convert at least the later part of each line into its phonetic equivalent. A computer-readable dictionary with a pronunciation code for each word would be very useful, but some words would inevitably be omitted and would need manual conversion. A comparison could then be carried out between the phonetic equivalents of the ends of the last words, possibly reversing the strings to make the process easier. Initial consonants would need to be ignored in this process, which would attempt to match the vowel and final consonant sounds of end syllables. Matching items could then be turned into sequences of encoded rhyming schemes.

CHAPTER 2

1. British schoolchildren

There is obviously a very wide variety of written text which could be read by British schoolchildren, and the age-range that you are interested in would be one of the main factors to be considered. In terms of sources, you would need to include a selection of:

comics
school reading books
school textbooks
newspapers
magazines
books read outside school (fiction and non-fiction).

Determining the proportion that each category should contribute to the corpus and selecting the representative items might involve complex research. Library borrowing records and discussions with teachers would help.

2. Casual spoken English

The design of the corpus would depend on the types and aspects of casual conversation that you were pursuing. The choice of sites for collecting casual conversation ranges from private homes to public or semi-public locations such as shops, public houses, clubs, and so on. Different types of conversation are likely to be found at each.

The collection of spoken language usually involves two stages, recording and transcription. Before you can do the recording, of course, you have to find somewhere to put the recorder, and this can cause difficulties. If the speakers know that they are being recorded it can affect the casualness of their speech, if they do not, you could be invading their privacy. You may be able to overcome the first problem by carrying out regular recording sessions in semi-public places with appropriate permission, in a way that allows the speakers to become used to the presence of the recorder or to forget that it is there. Appropriate safeguards would need to be instituted to preserve confidentiality. This is likely to restrict the design choices that you could make, and might invalidate your research in extreme cases.

Transcription is less fraught with legal and moral problems, but it is still a complex business, and decisions would need to be made once the data had been collected about the conventions to be used and the amount of information to be encoded.

3. Medieval texts

SCANNING

Advantages:

>   reasonably fast and reliable with well-printed text;
>
>   can be carried out by relatively unskilled staff.

Disadvantages:

>   extremely slow and unreliable with old and badly printed texts (and impossible on manuscripts);
>
>   does not deal with special characters very well (such as thorns and yoghs in medieval texts);
>
>   error correction can involve almost as much work as direct keyboard entry.

KEYBOARD ENTRY

Advantages

>   allows some editorial decisions to be taken during input;
>
>   allows mark-up codes to be entered;
>
>   no problems with special characters (once a coding system has been agreed).

Disadvantages:

>   slow, and expensive;
>
>   needs to be carried out by skilled staff;
>
>   some errors will still need correcting, even with double-keying.

The question says that the texts are not available elsewhere, but if any word processing files of recent editions were available, they would obviously be the best choice.

CHAPTER 3
1. Word boundaries
At first sight the list is fairly obvious. Apart from the space you would need the full stop, exclamation mark, question mark, comma, hyphen, single and double opening and closing quotes, and perhaps the colon and semicolon. But it is never quite that simple. The full stop is used in the abbreviation 'B.B.C.', and if it becomes a word boundary this will be separated into three meaningless single-letter words. Similarly, the single closing quote is also the apostrophe, used in words like *can't*, *they're* and so on. If you want to preserve these words, you will need to do something more complex. Lastly, the hyphen is used as a dash, but it is also in *dining-room*, and this will be split if it becomes a word boundary. Compromises will need to be made, decisions will need to be taken.

2. Lemmatising the frequency list
The first problem is that the lemmatising process would also involve sorting out some spelling variations, including:

abhominable	1
abhomynable	6

This is fairly straightforward, but in some cases you might need to consult a concordance (see Chapter 4) to be sure that differences are simply caused by spelling variations.

The second major problem is the decision as to what should be included in the lemma. As an example,

abiden	1
abideth	2
abidyng	2
abidynge	1

fairly clearly belong together. On the other hand, *abood* is not such an obvious part of the same lemma, but may need to be included. Again, a concordance will help the decision. In the same way, *abowndone* probably belongs with other forms of *abandon* found earlier in the list.

3. Rhyming schemes revisited
The first obvious subject for further investigation is the pair of dominant schemes, 'ABCB' and 'AABB'. The original input to the frequency list program preserves the numbers of the rhymes in the collection, and they could now be compared to each other to see if any other patterns can be found, in terms of the types of nursery rhyme, their age, their contents and so on. Similar work could be done on the less common schemes 'ABAB' and 'AABCCB'.

The exact nature of the 'X' scheme items needs to be elucidated. There may be common features in these nursery rhymes, or the schemes may need to be differentiated in more detail.

The less popular schemes should also be looked at to see whether there are any particular reasons for their general avoidance.

Overall, the frequency list has allowed the researcher to focus attention on the areas of particular interest for further investigation, in just the same way as a word frequency list.

CHAPTER 4
1. *go* keywords
You would need to enter:

go
goes
going
gone
went

Even if your software has a wild card facility, you would be ill-advised to enter *go** or its equivalent (to get any word beginning with *go*). This would retrieve *go, goes, going* and *gone*, along with rather a lot of occurrences of *god, gold, good* and so on. Entering just the keywords shown above will still produce the noun senses of *go*, but these will probably not be too overwhelming.

2. Senses of *good*
I managed to find four main categories, and ten separate senses. The phrases have been treated as separate because the sense of *good* is lost in each in a different way.

NOUNS
    benefit (3, 4, 5, 7, 8, 22)
    moral virtue (17, 20)

ADJECTIVES
    valid, effective (1, 18, 27)
    pleasing, appropriate (2, 6, 19, 26, 29)
    morally virtuous (15, 30)

INTENSIFIER
    very (16, 25, 28)

PHRASES
    good afternoon (9, 10, 11, 12, 13, 14)
    good-bye (24)
    good heaven (21)
    for good and all (23)

3. *Frankenstein* concordances
The concordance lines for *being* include several cases where the word refers to the organism created by Frankenstein, for example lines 1, 6, 7, 8 and 10. In many other cases it forms part of the phrase *human being* with more or less general reference (for example 2, 5, 9 and 11). In most cases the adjectives used in association with the word are either morally neutral (like *tremendous* in line 45) or positive (like *sensitive, divine* and *admirable* in lines 19, 22 and 42). These are not necessarily references to Frankenstein's creation, but they are uses of a word which is used for him.

    The word *creation*, on the other hand, is less positively accompanied. It is used for the process of creation rather than the being himself, and its associations are generally either neutral (as in lines 3, 4, 5 and 6, all from the point before the being is created) or negative (as in lines 2 and 7). The only adjectives used in association with it are *deformed and abortive* (line 2) and *filthy* (line 7).

References

Aho, A.V., Kernighan, B.W. and Weinberger, P.J. (1988), *The AWK Programming Language*, Reading, Mass.: Addison-Wesley.

Barnbrook, G. (1992), 'Computer analysis of spelling variants in Chaucer's *Canterbury Tales*', in G. Leitner, (ed.), *New Directions in English Language Corpora*, Berlin: Mouton de Gruyter, pp. 277–87.

Barnbrook, G. (1993), 'The automatic analysis of dictionaries – parsing Cobuild explanations' in M. Baker, G. Francis, and E. Tognini-Bonelli (eds.), *Text and Technology*, Amsterdam: John Benjamins, pp. 313–31.

Barnbrook, G. (1995) 'The language of definition: A Cobuild sublanguage parser', unpublished Ph.D. thesis, School of English, University of Birmingham.

Barnbrook, G. and Sinclair, J. (1995), 'Parsing Cobuild entries', in J. Sinclair, M. Hoelter and C. Peters (eds), *The Languages of Definition: The Formalisation of Dictionary Definitions for Natural Language Processing*, Luxemburg: Office of Official Publications of the European Communities, pp. 13–58.

Berg. D.L. (1993), *A Guide to the Oxford English Dictionary*, Oxford: Oxford University Press.

Boguraev, B. and Briscoe, T. (1989), *Computational Lexicography for Natural Language Processing*, London and New York: Longman.

Brierley, W. and Kemble, I.R. (eds) (1991), *Computers as a Tool in Language Teaching*, Chichester: Ellis Horwood.

Church, K., Gale, W., Hanks, P.W. and Hindle, D. (1991), 'Using statistics in lexical analysis', in U. Zernik (ed.), *Lexical Acquisition: Using On-line Resources to Build a Lexicon*, Englewood Cliff, nj: Lawrence Erlbaum, pp. 115–64..

Clear, J. (1987), 'Computing', in J. Sinclair (ed.), *Looking Up*, London: Collins ELT, pp. 41–61.

Clear, J. (1993), 'From Firth principles: computational tools for the study of collocation', in M. Baker, G. Francis and E. Tognini-Bonelli (eds.), *Text and Technology*, Amsterdam: John Benjamins, pp. 271–292.

Collins Cobuild English Dictionary (1995) ed. J. Sinclair, London and Glasgow: Collins.

Collins Cobuild English Language Dictionary (1987) ed. J. Sinclair, London and Glasgow: Collins.

Collins Cobuild Student's Dictionary (1990) ed. J. Sinclair, London and Glasgow: Collins.

Coniam, D.J. (1995), 'Boundary Marker: a partial parser', unpublished Ph.D. thesis, School of English, University of Birmingham.

Dougherty, D. (1990), *Sed & awk*, Sebastopol, Calif.: O'Reilly.

Drabble, M. (1977), *The Realms of Gold*, Harmondsworth: Penguin.

Garside, R., Leech, G. and Sampson, G. (eds) (1987), *The Computational Analysis of English*, London: Longman.

Grishman, R. and Kittredge, R. (eds) (1986), *Analyzing Language in Restricted Domains: Sublanguage Description and Processing*, Hillsdale: Lawrence Erlbaum Associates.

Grune, D. and Jacobs, C.J.H. (1990), *Parsing Techniques: A Practical Guide*, Chichester: Ellis Horwood.

Halliday, M.A.K. (1961), 'Categories of the theory of grammar', *Word*, 17: 241–92.

Halliday, M.A.K. (1985), *An Introduction to Functional Grammar*, London: New York, Melbourne and Auckland: Edward Arnold.

King, P. and Johns, T. (eds) (1991), *Classroom Concordancing: English Language Research Journal* Vol. 4, Birmingham Centre for English Language Studies, University of Birmingham.

Krishnamurthy, R. (1987), 'The process of compilation', in J. Sinclair (ed.), *Looking Up*, London: Collins ELT, pp. 62–85.

Kytö, M., Ihalainen, O. and Rissanen, M. (eds) (1988), *Corpus linguistics, Hard and Soft*, Amsterdam: Rodopi.

Leech, G. and Candlin, C. (eds) (1986), *Computers in English Language Teaching and Research*, London: Longman.

Leech, G., Myers, G. and Thomas, J. (eds) (1995) *Spoken English on Computer*, London: Longman.

Lehrberger, J. (1982), 'Automatic translation and the concept of sublanguage', in R. Kittredge and J. Lehrberger (eds), *Sublanguage: Studies of Language in Restricted Semantic Domains*, Berlin: Walter de Gruyter, ch. 3.

Leitner, G. (ed.) (1992), *New Directions in Corpus Linguisitcs*, Berlin: Mouton de Gruyter.

McEnery, T. (1992), *Computational Linguistics: A Handbook and Toolbox for Natural Language Processing*, Wilmslow: Sigma.

Malmkjær, K. (1991), *The Linguistics Encyclopedia*, London: Routledge.

Oostdijk, N. and de Haan, P. (eds) (1994), *Corpus-Based Research into Language: In Honour of Jan Aarts*, Amsterdam: Rodopi.

Opie, I. and Opie, P., (1951), *The Oxford Dictionary of Nursery Rhymes*, Oxford: Oxford University Press.

Renouf, A. (1987) 'Corpus development', in J. Sinclair (ed.), *Looking Up*, London: Collins ELT, pp. 1–40.

Renouf, A. (1992), 'What do you think of that? A pilot study of the phraseology of the core words in English', in G. Leitner (ed.), *New Directions in English Language Coprora*, Berlin: Mouton de Gruyter, pp. 301–17.

Sinclair, J. (1991), *Corpus, Concordance, Collocation*, Oxford: Oxford University Press.

Sinclair, J. Hoelter, M. and Peters, C. (eds) (1995), *The Languages of Definition: The Formalisation of Dictionary Definitions for Natural Language Processing*, Luxemburg: Office for Official Publications of the European Committees.

Stubbs, M. (1995), 'Collocations and semantic profiles: on the cause of the trouble with quantitative studies' in *Functions of Language*, 2 (1): 23–55.

Svartvik, J. (ed.) (1992), *Directions of Corpus Linguistics: Proceedings of the Nobel Symposium 82*, Berlin: Mouton de Gruyter.

Index

Some terms are dealt with throughout general sections. These are listed in this index with a cross-reference to the appropriate general section.